An Argentine in my Kitchen

An Argentine in my Kitchen

How I followed my heart to Buenos Aires

CAROLYN KERR

A note about the author: Carolyn Kerr is Australian. She is a business communicator and writer who began her career as a scientist. She has travelled widely in Argentina and Latin America and has written two non-fiction books and a collection of short stories. This is her first novel.

ISBN 978-0-6485776-0-7

FOR CLAUDIO

A BOOK WITH THREE DIMENSIONS

An Argentine in my Kitchen contains three dimensions – the main story, Argentine sayings and expressions, and recipes.

The main story stands alone. It can be read without reference to the Argentine expressions and sayings, and without reference to the recipes.

The Argentine expressions and sayings complement the story and are indented, in a slightly smaller font. The first line is the Spanish expression or saying. The second line is the literal English translation. The third line, if necessary, clarifies the meaning, or displays an English saying with a similar meaning. In some cases, the possible origin of the expression or saying is also provided.

At the end of each chapter, in italics, a recipe is introduced by a description that also complements the story.

CONTENTS

ONCE UPON A TIME

José frowned at Santiago.

'You can't be serious,' he said. 'The wall has to stay.'

Santiago didn't respond. He stood in the middle of the kitchen, leaning back so that he could examine the wall in question from end to end. He mused as he ran his pencil through his thinning hair.

> *Se le estaban volando las chapas.*
> The metal sheeting on his roof was flying off.
> Meaning: He was going bald.

Inspired, Santiago straightened up and pointed to the corner on the left. With a flourish he swept his arm to the right.

'We'll put a bar counter along there,' he declared.

Looking upward, he said, 'And a wine rack above it, against the beam. It'll look fabulous!'

He grabbed his tape measure and approached the wall. José had to step aside.

I hovered in the doorway, observing the interaction.

It was plain that José didn't like to be ignored. As the head contractor, he was at least as important as Santiago, the carpenter.

'If we get rid of the wall, the kitchen will be open to the living room. The whole place will smell of cooking,' José cried.

This fact was indisputable, and José assumed it would stop Santiago in his tracks. Folding his arms, he waited for Santiago's retaliation.

Santiago moved to the breakfast table and hummed to himself. Engrossed in his measurements, he traced lines across graph paper. It was as though José didn't exist.

A mí me importa un pepino tu idea.
I don't give a cucumber about your idea.

'The counter will be just over one metre high,' Santiago said, turning to my husband Pedro to gauge his reaction.

Pedro had the currently difficult task of project managing our kitchen renovation in Buenos Aires.

José pretended not to hear. His smile radiating confidence, he uncrossed his arms, moved back to the wall, and inspected it more closely. He wiped his finger across one of the tiles, his moustache shifting with a grimace.

'It's filthy!' And only now realizing the garishness of the wall, he said, 'And the tiles are hideous.'

I couldn't disagree. The tiles featured apricots emerging through a latticework of leaves.

José glanced at Pedro, clearly expecting him to put a 'preservation order' on the wall that separated the kitchen and the living room. After all, though José was younger than Santiago, his ideas were surely more practical. His every posture suggested that he was convinced the old adage that 'wisdom comes with age' did not apply here.

El diablo sabe por diablo, pero más sabe por viejo.
The devil is wise because he is the devil, but he is even wiser because he is old.
Meaning: Wisdom comes with age.

Both Santiago and José waited for direction.

I was interested to see how Pedro would engineer his way through the disagreement.

I couldn't help wondering how on earth we had ended up in this 'renovator's delight' on the other side of the world, with Pedro needing to persuade José to our way of thinking without upsetting him.

Scrutinizing the kitchen, I was disheartened by its miserable appearance. I compared it to the one in Sydney, and a pang of homesickness shot through me. Even though the Sydney one would fit into this one twice over, it had more bench space. And even though its oven was fifteen years old, it wasn't a rust bucket like this one. And even though it wasn't the most modern kitchen in the world, the cupboards were not scratched and stained as these were.

Had this all been a terrible mistake? Moving to Buenos Aires for six months at the age of forty-eight, landing in a massive city of thirteen million people whose language I did not speak fluently, all while providing moral support to my husband whilst he bought and renovated a decrepit apartment?

If I had said 'no' to Pedro that first day, would I simply have postponed the inevitable? I thought back to the moment when it had all started . . .

*

It was autumn in Sydney, the sky a dome of blue, the leaves of the eucalypts motionless, the sun's warmth radiating through the crisp air. We soaked up the warmth on our balcony as we gazed at the harbour. Spinnakers flashed by like rainbows against the blue water.

Pedro offered me a glass of Malbec. The wine was from Mendoza, a region in Argentina, and was designed to impress. He proposed a toast, and surprised me by reminding me that we'd been married for three years.

'Those yacht races always remind me of how we met,' he said, 'at the dinghy sailing lessons in Rushcutters Bay.'

I nodded, smiling, remembering. I'd impulsively joined the sailing class as an antidote to the stress at work. I loved the motion of the waves, the cawing of the gulls, the sea air in my lungs, the wind in my hair.

During the third lesson, I sailed a dinghy on my own. The other four students watched from the beach. The instructor shadowed my moves from another dinghy.

I had hardly set off across the waves when the wind direction changed unexpectedly. I forgot to loosen the sheet, the sail filled, and the dinghy capsized. I swallowed a mouthful of salt water before I surfaced, coughing and sputtering.

I held on to the hull of the boat, and took a few deep breaths to calm myself. The instructor appeared alongside to check I was okay, and I told him I'd swim to shore, whereupon he nodded and secured the boat.

Turning toward the beach, I now saw only three students by the water's edge. The other one was swimming toward me – it was the cute Argentine guy with the Antonio Banderas accent. My heart skipped a beat.

'No broken bones?' he asked, grinning as he approached. He knew I could swim – it was a pre-requisite for the lessons – but had thrown himself into the water regardless.

'No – still alive and kicking.' We both laughed, even though I felt myself shaking from the cold and the shock.

He stayed by me as we swam to shore, and as we dripped our way across the sand to the clubhouse. I stole glances at him, guessing he was in his early fifties, with his grey hair and the smile wrinkles at the edges of his eyes. He told me that he was the first aid officer at his work, and that the sooner I got into dry clothes and drank something hot and sweet, the better. And because he'd been so courteous to all of the students, I didn't think it unusual that he suggested we meet at the bar after changing.

'This will help,' he said, when I returned from the change room. He was holding out a cup of sweet black tea. His blue eyes were looking unswervingly into mine.

'Your dinghy went over gracefully,' he said. 'I didn't realize you were in trouble. Then the mast hit the water and you disappeared.'

I wasn't sure what to say, he sounded so concerned, and that look he'd given me had been so unsettling. I babbled something inane like, 'It was all so sudden – thanks for swimming out.'

The other students gathered round to listen to my story. I recounted the adventure, laughing and calmer as I drank the tea. From time to time Pedro looked across at me as another student spoke.

The others gradually drifted off and Pedro and I were left at the bar. At last I realized that he was interested in *me*, and not merely in 'the first aid treatment for shock after capsize.' My heart skipped a few more beats.

We chatted for ages. I found that Pedro had been married but that they'd split up a long time ago, and that his three kids were grown up and lived in other cities in Australia. I also found that we were both going to the same concert that evening.

We seemed to 'click' somehow, and over the next few weeks we found that we had more and more in common. Of course we also found that we had many differences – he was passionate about politics and I was cynical, he was practical and I was all thumbs, he was garrulous and I was quiet. But we never argued, and if we upset each other, we realized immediately, and made up.

I was single when I met him, and my previous relationships had not worked out as I thought they would. But within a short time of meeting Pedro I knew that I wanted to spend the rest of my life with him. Falling in love was the most natural thing in the world. Soon we were inseparable, and he proposed on the six-month anniversary of the capsize event.

Actually, we sort of proposed to each other. We were standing on the promenade at Balmoral Beach, holding hands, and watching two kids building a sand castle. Near the water's edge, a bride and groom posed for a photographer.

I glanced at them and said, 'My aunt doesn't believe in marriage, but I do. For some reason I like the idea.'

And Pedro said, 'Me too. I like the idea of marriage.'

Trying to hide my nerves, and laughing, ready to play it off as a joke, I asked, 'Are you proposing?'

Whereupon Pedro moved to take hold of my other hand with his free hand, and stared directly at me.

He said, 'Yes.'

My heart was beating hard, but not enough to stop me from saying, 'Yes, I will marry you.'

And that was that.

I was amazed at how quickly I settled into a conjugal state, so sedate and routine compared with my frenetic single life. Captivated by Pedro and his world, I allowed myself, at the age of forty-five, to become immersed in a state of domestic bliss.

Meeting him had been like finding a home after a long journey. I felt a wonderful sense of belonging when he called me 'his better half.'

> *Mi media naranja. Mi peor es nada.*
> My half-orange. My 'better than nothing.'
> Meaning: My better half.

*

So here we were, on the balcony of the apartment we shared, unwinding with a glass of wine.

I was soon to discover that the wine was part of a plan to lull me into a state of calm. Because, suddenly, with no prior warning, Pedro said, 'How about we go to live in Argentina for a few years?'

I know that I appeared outwardly calm. Having a straight face in surprising situations was essential in my work as a communications professional, and this tactic had permeated my private life.

Perhaps my eyes flickered, but otherwise I was sure there was no physical reaction. The fact was, though, that I was simply unable to process what I'd heard.

I felt a flutter of panic inside. I managed to hide my consternation, murmuring, 'Uh uh,' as the flutter took wing and choked any further response.

I waited for his usual cheeky smile and big laugh. I expected, 'I didn't mean it,' or, 'Just kidding.' He often joked about serious issues to provoke me. For example, he thought it funny to pretend he'd been electrocuted whilst he fooled around with wires as he changed a wall socket. No, he kept looking at me, his eyebrows raised, his face animated and expectant.

I sensed disaster. I couldn't process Pedro's suggestion.

He waited for a more intelligent response than a mumble.

Then something strange happened. As my thoughts clarified, my imagination fired up and ran riot.

I pictured a flat world. At its furthest point, on the other side of a massive black ocean, was the western side of South America. The eastern half, including most of Argentina, hung in space. South America was slipping off the edge of the known world. I saw the two of us, a tiny couple of miniature dolls. We were standing at the end of the earth where the map folded over into nothingness. In slow motion, as Argentina continued its slide, we fell, arms and legs flailing. We plummeted into the void of outer space.

5

I reached out my hand for the balcony railing, steadying myself. The cool solidity of the metal made me recall the important fact that my other hand held a glass of excellent wine. I took a gulp to see whether I could impose a state of numbness on my brain.

This test failed.

It wasn't that I didn't like travel, or Argentina, or Latin America. I'd visited Argentina three times, briefly, with Pedro – and Mexico and Peru before we'd met. I'd loved the Latin friendliness of the region.

Visit, yes, but *live* there? For a few *years*? My knees had gone weak. A couple of our former Argentine friends had returned to Buenos Aires two years previously – and we had never heard from them again. It was easy to imagine that *they* had indeed fallen off the map.

'Uh, uh,' I repeated in a mumble, and glanced across at Pedro. His shoulders drooped. He was crestfallen.

*

Only a week later, Pedro and I loitered over a light lunch on that same balcony. There was a slight breeze coming off the harbour. Salt air mingled with the scent of frangipani.

Pedro must have thought I'd recovered from the 'Let's live in Argentina for a few years' shock, because he mentioned it again. This time his approach was oblique.

'Lambrusco?' he asked, pouring the wine into my glass.

He paused for a moment before continuing.

'You know, when I first met you, I was surprised that you worked in the corporate world. You never mentioned the office. I loved the way your eyes sparkled when you told me about a piece of classical music, or explained a technique in an oil painting, or admired the architecture of an old building. Do you *really* like looking at numbers all day?'

I laughed. 'It's okay. It gives me security.'

'But you don't *love* it, do you?' he said, as I reached for an olive.

I gave him a sidelong glance. 'What are you getting at?'

'Well, if you *do* mention your work, your voice falls flat – unless it's a funny story.'

As usual, Pedro had read me correctly. I'd been miserable at work for a while, but I thought I'd succeeded in switching off after leaving the office.

The long meetings, late nights, and politics in my job – as an internal communications manager in a large corporation – had been wearing me down. I'd only recently grasped how serious it was. It was a Monday afternoon. After a two-hour meeting, I returned to my office to stare listlessly at sales results. Columns of numbers marched across my computer screen as they did each month, waiting to be transformed into staff

6

messages. It dawned on me that the numbers meant nothing to me. That they would continue to appear on my screen each month, armies of them grouped beneath their banners, rearing up phoenix-like from the vestiges of last month's figures. Echoing previous messages, my covering notes would hardly change. The bureaucracy of the organization would soldier on, political factions would rise and fall, and kingmakers would come and go. I felt like a robot. I had lost energy. I had lost my way.

Andaba como bola sin manija.
I went around like a ball without a handle.
Meaning: I was aimless. The expression probably referred to the *boleadora*, a weapon used by indigenous groups in Patagonian to catch game. It consisted of two or three round stones attached to a leather rope.

Pedro said, 'You love music, but your Granny's piano is sitting in the living room unplayed.'

'I used to play it. Before we met. *Way* before we met.'

'And you told me you used to paint, but your easel never leaves the cupboard.'

'I get tired easily. I don't know why.'

Actually, I *did* know why, but I didn't want to tell him. I didn't want to talk about myself at all.

I'd found out in the most mundane sort of way what was wrong with me, so mundane that I couldn't remember where I was at the time. Maybe in the dentist's waiting room reading a magazine, or at the hairdresser's, or at home with the weekend newspaper. I'd seen an article on executive stress and scored ten out of ten in the section entitled, 'Are you burnt out? Try our questionnaire.'

¡Ahí estaba la madre del borrego!
There was the mother of the lamb!
Meaning: *That* was the issue.

I attempted to change the focus of our conversation.

'What about *your* work? You've been stressed for ages,' I said.

'Yes, and my stress is similar to yours – we each have an internal conflict.'

I didn't understand how that could be. He was a scientist, and ran a number of university teaching laboratories. Visiting his workplace was, for me, comparable to landing on another planet. How could his stress be similar to mine?

'That's why I suggested we move to Argentina for a while. Not only because I think you'd love it, or because my kids have all grown up and left home,' he said.

7

I became more and more confused. I tried my usual 'staying calm' approach.

Tranquila como agua de pozo.
As calm as well water.

To gap the silence I asked a polite question.
'I beg your pardon?' I said.
He said, 'Well, my problem is the public education system – it's failing. My work feels meaningless.'
'So does *my* work. But it gives me an income.'
'Exactly,' he said. 'But you work so hard that you can't enjoy the things you love – classical music, art, and literature.'
'Maybe,' I said. 'But I'm sure things will get better, eventually. I don't know what I'd do in Argentina.'
'You don't know until you try,' he said. 'As for me, I want to work for myself. I'm sure I could make a living from renovating properties. In Buenos Aires, I could earn enough for us to live on – you could do something you loved. And I never lived in Argentina as an adult – I'd like to do that for a while.'
'Or I could quit next time the company reduces staff numbers, and find a new job. They've asked for volunteers twice already, and the payouts are good,' I said cynically.
Then I realized how harsh that sounded.
'I'm sorry,' I said. 'I know you had to leave Argentina when you were seventeen. And I love that you want me to find something different. It's such a . . . I don't know . . .'
I felt so ungrateful. I was too used to making decisions for myself alone.
Pedro shrugged. 'Changing jobs is one option. But being in Buenos Aires would give us a whole new outlook on our lives – in one of the most cultural and vibrant cites in the world.'
I reflected on what Pedro had said as I dozed off that night. Did he genuinely think that we could rethink our careers by spending a few years in another country? With each of us undertaking *radically different* activities? Was Buenos Aires *really* as cultural and vibrant as he'd said?
When at last I slept, I dreamed that I was in an art gallery. A spreadsheet wafted past. Musical notes fell from the cells on the spreadsheet, producing a melody as, one by one, they hit the floor. The notes jumped up and danced along behind the spreadsheet, trying to catch up.

*

A couple of months passed. Winter arrived with its cool sunny days. Pedro didn't raise the 'Argentina' issue again. We continued our everyday lives. We went to work, we came home, and we read the paper at the local café on Sunday mornings.

I worked at home on weekends, but found myself distracted by articles on Argentina or South America. I sought out Spanish-language movies, and, one weekend, I helped a work colleague with her Argentine travel plans, despite my limited knowledge of the country.

I found myself wondering what Buenos Aires was actually like – to *live* in. We'd spent our visits catching up with relatives, most of the time in their *barrios* or 'neighbourhoods'. My impressions of the city were jumbled – Latin vivacity, traffic chaos, a café society, graceful old buildings overshadowed by modern apartment blocks, wide avenues, the sensual rhythm and dance of the tango, succulent steaks, excellent wine, city parks and statues, late nights. My knowledge of Argentina was based on those brief visits, or from movies, or from occasional articles. Or, of course, from conversations with Pedro.

More specifically I wondered about our income, should we decide to move to Argentina. Would it be easy for Pedro to find renovation work? He *did* have experience in the area. He'd renovated one house after another over the years, and had helped many colleagues and friends, becoming their 'go to' person for home building or design. If he *did* find work, would the income allow us to do more than just 'get by'? It was unlikely we'd make a fortune, but would we, at least, be able to explore Argentina? Or South America?

No íbamos a hacernos la América.
We weren't going 'to make ourselves the America.'
Meaning: We weren't going to become rich.

I contemplated my own work situation. Pedro was right in saying that my job and my more consuming passions were unrelated. But I couldn't see how a continental drift to South America would change that. And if we lived in Argentina for a few years it would be difficult to find another job when we returned to Australia. My business contacts would be rusty, and age would not be in my favour. I may as well kiss my career goodbye. Why not stay in Sydney with predictable incomes and *visit* Buenos Aires?

It wasn't only our financial future and my employment that concerned me. I had no friends in South America. I imagined being lonely, missing loved ones in Sydney, despite the fact that Pedro and I would be together. Friends were important to me. They inspired me, they were a source of laughter and fun, they bolstered me when I needed help, and I liked to think that I offered them the same support and encouragement in return.

In contrast to my friendless situation in Argentina, Pedro would be returning to a city he'd left as a teenager. He was still in touch with his old friends from kindergarten, from primary school, from secondary school, from his old *barrio*, from the YMCA where he had spent all his time outside school hours, and from the times he'd skipped school and gone fishing.

As for relatives, he had his mother, stepfather, father, stepmother, brother and a gaggle of at least seventy cousins. Would I cope? Did I want to be enveloped by his family?

As I pondered the pros and cons of a move, the seed of an idea sprouted in my mind. I raised it tentatively with Pedro.

'How about a trial period in Buenos Aires? We could rent a place for a few months. It would help us to know if we, or at least I, would like to spend a few years there.'

No iba a tirarme a la pileta.
I was not going to throw myself in the pool.
Meaning: I wasn't going to jump in at the deep end.

Pedro's eyes lit up.

'Let's *buy* a place,' he said excitedly. 'My savings would cover the cost of an apartment – prices there are a fraction of Sydney prices – way less than ten per cent.'

The ground swayed beneath me. *Buy a place?* I thought. *He's mad.* But I managed to hold my composure and say, 'Ten per cent?'

'Well, they *are* pretty small compared to Sydney apartments, and the economy over there hasn't been going too well. Besides, we'd always have a place to stay when we visit.'

My face must have shown my hesitation because he looked at me, frowning. 'It's okay,' he said. 'I'll buy it myself.' He sounded adamant.

A wave of relief flooded over me. It was a big enough step to go off on a trial run to another country, let alone to have my little nest egg tied up there as well.

Even so, I felt nervous. *He's deadly serious about the move,* I thought. *It's as though he's been planning the whole thing for a long time.* I recalled his excited look on the balcony the day he'd proposed the move, and his disappointment when I hadn't jumped at the idea.

It was all starting to sink in. For him, the only thing that hindered his Argentine future was . . . *me.*

And in fairness, I couldn't hinder him any more. All I had to do was to take a break from work and agree that he would buy us a place in Buenos Aires for future visits.

I agreed.

How lovely to see a smile on his face again. And what a relief that I hadn't needed to make 'the big decision.' It was too much of a life and career change for me to 'up and go,' just like that.

> *Mejor no poner todas las manzanas en la misma canasta.*
> Better not to put all the apples in the same basket.

Not that I was a person who found it hard to make up my mind. After all, I made the biggest decision of my life in that split second when Pedro admitted he was proposing to me. But this prospective Argentina move had shaken me to the core.

*

We agreed that a six-month trial period would be sufficient to experience life in Buenos Aires. Pedro immediately applied for six months 'leave without pay.' Like the outstanding bureaucrat that he was, he presented a comprehensive plan to his boss, allocating his responsibilities to other team members. His boss was trapped by the logic and simplicity of the approach, and could not refuse the request.

> *Pisó el palito.*
> He stepped on the little stick.
> Meaning: He fell into the trap. This referred to a trap for birds, using a cage with a lid that could be propped open. If a bird landed on a perch inside the cage, the lid snapped down.

Pedro would be free in two months.

As for me, I dragged my feet for a couple of weeks, not sure how to approach my manager. Pedro and I had taken three annual holidays of five to six weeks each, mainly to Europe, with short stops in Buenos Aires. Those holidays had been easy to negotiate because they coincided with 'down' times at work – but six months was a big ask.

Luck came my way when the company announced another reduction in staffing levels, and offered a payment for those who volunteered to quit. I volunteered and was accepted – I was ecstatic. The payout would help to tide us over when we returned from Argentina.

When I broke the news to my younger sister Annie, she said we'd lost our senses. She couldn't hold back her shock and disappointment.

'What about your job? You're leaving your *job?* It's not like you to act so impulsively.'

> *Pan para hoy, hambre para mañana.*
> Bread for today, hunger for tomorrow.
> Meaning: A temporary solution, making things worse later.

11

'Pedro as well? Oh, only you – *not* Pedro? He's taking leave from his job? At least *he* has his two feet on the ground.' Annie must have temporarily forgotten that it was *his* idea to go, not mine.

Annie and I were close. She'd been upset when my company moved me to London for three years. Soon after, our brother had moved to Europe, further splintering the family. Now I was off *again*.

She had more to say. 'Why would you move to a country that's such an economic mess? I mean, even for a 'trial run'? And you *must* think that there's a possibility you'll end up there for longer? Why don't you just live here and *visit* Argentina – you could easily persuade Pedro to stay.'

'As I said, it's only for six months. *Six months.*'

She didn't believe me.

'I know it's hard for you to see it, but to me it's pretty clear,' she said. 'Six months will become seven, then eight, then a year. Soon you'll be gone for ever.'

When I didn't budge from my 'only six months' statement, she said, 'Okay, okay, six months. If you insist! You always *were* stubborn, once you made up your mind.'

> *Siempre fuiste dura de pelar.*
> You were always hard to peel.
> Meaning: You were always stubborn; a hard nut to crack.

Then she softened her approach. She said, 'We'll miss you. Six months is a long time.'

'I'll miss you too,' I said, relieved at her change of tone.

But then she tried another tack, appealing to my own uncertainties.

'You'll miss Australia and you'll wish you'd never gone. And didn't you say once that your Spanish was quite basic?'

> *Lo hablás medio a lo Tarzán.*
> You speak it a bit like Tarzan.
> Meaning: You speak it in a rudimentary way.

I *would* miss Australia. And I *had* told her that my Spanish was basic, but that was a few years back when I gave up my Spanish lessons due to work pressures. As with the sailing classes where I met Pedro, I'd taken up the Spanish lessons in an attempt to reduce my stress levels. I'd progressed to a basic conversational level.

My Spanish had improved since meeting Pedro, who encouraged me to speak the language. But I found his Argentine pronunciation challenging, because it was so different to the mainland Spanish I'd learned. And many words were different. For example, why would you call a 'pea' an *arveja* in Argentina and a *guisante* in Spain? Why would *paro* mean a 'workers' strike'

12

in Argentina and 'unemployment' in Spain? And why did *retar* mean 'to challenge' in Spain, whilst in Argentina, it also meant 'to scold'?

Now that we'd decided on the 'trial', I was making even more of an effort with the language. Having been given two Argentine novellas by Pedro's aunt on our last visit to Buenos Aires – *El encierro de Ojeda* or 'The Confinement of Ojeda' by Martín Murphy, and *Pájaros en la boca* or 'Birds in the Mouth' by Samanta Schweblin – I read in Spanish to Pedro as he drove me to work. It was a good way to test my Argentine pronunciation and vocabulary, and for us both to experience the unusual fringe literature of the country. My vocabulary was improving, and the only drawback was that I found *written* Spanish much easier to understand than spoken Spanish.

Even so, I was confident that I could get by. Hopefully.

My uncle made a series of emphatic declarations. 'Wow, that's a big step. I'm guessing Pedro is the driving force and that you're going along with it. You'll probably end up there permanently.'

But I disagreed. 'You know me better than that. We'll be back and settled in Sydney before you even know we've gone.'

We prompted a wide range of reactions from friends . . .

One provided time-warp assistance. 'I'll give you the contact details for someone I knew at the Australian Embassy in Buenos Aires. Mind you, I hope she's still there. It's been twenty years.'

Another friend, also trying to help, said, 'My second cousin lives in Argentina, perhaps you could have a coffee with her from time to time – here's her address.'

I glanced at the last line in the scribbled note – Salta. I'd recently read a travel article regarding a Salta museum that specialized in high-altitude archaeology – and knew that the city was over a thousand kilometres from Buenos Aires. I thanked her, not brave enough to say it was unlikely we would ever meet.

> *Inútil como cenicero de moto.*
> As useless as an ashtray on a motorbike.

And there was a chilling reminder of the past from a casual acquaintance. 'My father left Argentina during the military regime in the seventies. He never mentions the past, and he can't understand why anyone would want to go back.'

Pedro also left the country during that time, to avoid compulsory military training in an army that ultimately caused over thirty thousand people to disappear. It was an ethical choice forced upon him. He settled happily in Australia, but remained curious about his own country.

I found these reactions unhelpful until one of our Argentine friends looked at us with longing in his eyes. 'We wish we could organize ourselves to move back, but you know, kids. The family's growing up here. We don't want to destabilize the children. Phone us, Skype us, email us, send us photos, don't forget us. We miss our extended family. We miss all the cafés. And all the theatre, all those concerts! And dining out at one o'clock in the morning.'

There it was again – Buenos Aires and its cultural offerings. How cultural could it *be*? Tango, yes. Steak and red wine, yes. But theatre? *Lots* of concerts? I wasn't so sure.

Our neighbour downstairs became despondent. 'You *can't* leave us. We love those mouth-watering aromas that waft through the stairwell in the evenings.' Pedro was a fantastic cook, and luckily for me, he could create delicious meals anywhere.

One of Pedro's friends had retired in Argentina after many years of work in Australia. He phoned Pedro when he heard the news. 'You've seen the light. You're coming home at last. After ten minutes in Buenos Aires you'll feel as though you never left.'

My friend Sarah was supportive. 'I've heard it's one of the most exciting and sophisticated cities in the world. Why *wouldn't* you move there? *I'll* visit you. I can't believe my luck. You can be my tour guide.'

And it wasn't only Sarah – other friends told us they'd change their travel plans to include Buenos Aires.

I secretly welcomed those prospective visits. It would not feel like such a drastic displacement if friends spent time with us 'in situ.' I would feel more grounded, less like a fish out of water in my husband's country, surrounded by his family and friends and speaking another language.

My mother said, 'That's nice, dear.'

*

So there I stood in that kitchen in Buenos Aires, on a sunny day in 2016, asking myself how on earth I'd ended up in Argentina. Had it been the stupor induced by the wine on that perfect day? The fact that Pedro had not pushed me into it? A yearning deep inside, to experience more from life? I would never know. All I knew was that we had resolved to 'do it.'

> *Tomamos el toro por las astas.*
> We took the bull by the horns.

Pedro thought I'd love Buenos Aires and that we'd stay for at least the few years he'd proposed. I was convinced we'd be going home to Sydney after six months.

I glanced at my husband. His eyes shone. His dream to spend time in Buenos Aires had become a reality. He'd won me around, at least temporarily, and now he was immersed in his favourite pastime — renovation.

Al pie del cañón.
At the foot of the canon.
Meaning: At the ready.

Pedro offered Santiago and José a coffee. And as he ground the beans and frothed the milk, he worked his magic and José eventually came around. Demolishing the wall, after all, would mean more work and more income, and that did the trick.

Corderito patagónico en cocción lenta — Slow-cooked Patagonian Lamb

José and Santiago left. The kitchen, as we knew it, was about to disappear. Pedro, the executive chef of our household, had planned a special 'last supper' — a slow-cooked leg of Patagonian lamb.

He told me it was a safe dish to cook in the 'reliable rust-bucket,' as I called the oven. I'd developed an odd sort of fondness for the rust-bucket, and I'd made it usable after a mammoth cleaning afternoon, emptying three cans of oven cleaner and wiping away endless black streaks. I'd even made a delicious Jamie Oliver loaf of bread in it, hence the 'reliable' descriptor.

The butcher recommended by Pedro's mother specialized in beef, but the word 'beef' had not deterred Pedro. The previous week, he had asked the butcher if he could procure a leg of Patagonian lamb. Patagonia, a region to the south of Argentina and Chile, was famous for its sheep farming, and we'd recently spent a few weeks there. Patagonian lambs were known for their succulent gamey flavour.

The butcher suggested Pedro try Buenos-Aires-Province lamb instead, because Patagonian lamb usually arrived frozen. The local lamb would be fresh, and the butcher was confident that other clients would buy the rest of the animal. When Pedro agreed, the butcher phoned a farmer friend in the countryside. The farmer was standing in the middle of a field and said he'd call back. Pedro checked the next day, and was told the lamb would arrive in two days.

So now the leg of lamb sat in the fridge. A cast-iron pan, borrowed from Pedro's Mum, rested on the counter.

It was midday. Plenty of time for slow cooking.

Before dinner, I decanted a bottle of Malbec to remind ourselves of that day on the balcony in Sydney when Pedro first proposed a move to Argentina.

This was the first of Pedro's recipes that I recorded for our story. Pedro varied each of these popular recipes every time he prepared them, so it was no use asking him to list his ingredients or to describe his methods. To record a recipe, I had to decide in advance that I would stand beside him as he cooked, and note the ingredients and methods he used <u>that evening</u>. For all the recipes, he told me that the cooking times given depended on the temperature of the oven and the size of the pans. And that all the documented recipes could be found in so many different forms, that it was hard to credit any particular source as his inspiration.

Ingredients
1 leg of lamb — fresh Patagonian if possible
10 garlic cloves, each cut into 3 slivers
15 anchovy fillets, preferably salted, but fine if in oil
Fresh rosemary sprigs cut into 2-3cm pieces
1 large carrot cut into chunks
1 large brown onion cut into large pieces

1 cup white wine
1 cup beef stock
A generous bunch of herbs including fresh oregano and thyme
Salt and pepper

Method

Make about 30 small slits in the meat. Into each slit place a sliver of garlic, half an anchovy and a rosemary sprig. Ensure that you have an even distribution over the entire leg.

Seal the meat by searing it all over on the barbecue or in a flat pan on the stovetop.

In a cast iron pan with a well-fitting lid, place the seared leg of lamb.

Add the chopped carrots and onion.

Add the white wine, meat stock and bunch of herbs. The wine and stock will half-cover the leg of lamb.

Season.

Cover and place in the oven at 120°C (degrees Celsius) for 5 hours. Turn it over each hour or so, to make sure the meat is evenly cooked in the liquid.

When it's cooked the meat will be falling off the bone. Serve it over a bed of mashed potato or creamy polenta (as described in the Asian-Style Salmon recipe in Chapter 13), with French beans.

Hints

Add other vegetables to the stock if you want. For example, Pedro might add two sticks of celery cut into 2-3cm lengths, and/or a small fennel cut into quarters.

2

PEELING THE ONION

One of the conditions of quitting my job was to finalize all outstanding tasks within three weeks. With no new projects, I worked shorter hours, and could visit Pedro at the university for lunch. Possibly because these lunches were on campus, he told me more about his job than he ever had before.

When I first met Pedro, I was impressed with his passion for excellence in public education, and the energy he brought to his work. It was so refreshing to meet someone who was guided by his beliefs, and who had chosen a career in a subject – biology – that he'd loved since primary school. Pedro was initially a scientist in the private sector, taking on jobs with increasing responsibility, searching – unsuccessfully – for personal satisfaction.

At last he found that satisfaction in a university role. Within a short time, he was managing the laboratory experiments for thousands of students, liaising with academics as to the suitability of their experiments, and dealing with logistics and procurement.

But gradually things changed. By the time we met, Pedro's area had experienced a number of budget constraints, shrinking the money available per student and affecting the practical aspects of science teaching. At first it meant that students could no longer carry out experiments individually, losing some of that familiarity and closeness with the equipment and specimens that was so important for scientists in training. They had to share equipment in groups of three, and then as funds became tighter, in groups of five. Then laboratory experiments were scheduled once every two weeks instead of once a week, with tutorials replacing the intervening sessions.

Budget cuts also meant that Pedro was raced off his feet begging for essential equipment for key experiments from other departments. The job became an enormous physical and mental drain.

Era como remar en dulce de leche.
It was like rowing in caramel.

'Business-speak' invaded the university. Employees were told that they were 'customer service providers' rather than 'educators.' This annoyed Pedro and some of his senior colleagues, who were now called 'business managers.' They had to attend on-campus business seminars to learn how to manage the faculty staff who reported to them.

One lunchtime he was already at the café when I arrived.

'I thought you were busy,' I said.

'I am. But I can't go back to work yet. I'm too upset. I had to go to a business seminar and I walked out. I've heard some stupid things but this was the last straw.'

> *Por una sardina reventó el burro.*
> Because of one sardine, the donkey burst.
> Meaning: It was the last straw. From the practice in Galician fishing villages, where sardines were carried up from the harbour in a basket on the back of a donkey.

'What did they say?'

'We were told how to treat the faculty staff members who report to us. Whenever one of them makes a mistake we should 'soften the blow' by using the 'kiss-kick-kiss' principle. First we complement them, then we tell them off, and then we finish on a positive note. I can't believe that people take this stuff seriously. As though we're all machines, and the same approach works in all situations. It's crazy. I don't know how you can put up with that management babble.'

I made light of the whole thing.

'Oh, it's just brainwashing,' I said. 'I'm going to a compulsory management course right now – even though I'm leaving the company. To stay sane I think about a Bernini sculpture, or an aria from one of my favourite operas. I pay enough attention to the subject to be able to answer a random question.'

'I can't do that. They're talking nonsense. It's a waste of time – a waste of resources. They should use the money to improve the student experience. Or to stop the decline in the level of high school education.'

The changes Pedro described were an affront to his deep-seated belief in the importance of a high standard of public education.

He was disillusioned. His world was falling apart.

What kept him going were his hobbies outside work such as cooking, fixing up old cars, and making our home more livable. As soon as we moved into our apartment, Pedro fixed the creaking hinges so that all the doors opened and closed smoothly. Gradually the kitchen took on an entirely different appearance. A new stovetop made for more efficient cooking. Rails, hooks, and shelves made saucepans easy to access. Better lighting made bench work easier. And the following summer, new ceiling fans whirred above us and balcony awnings protected us from harsh sunlight.

I wasn't the only beneficiary. Our landlord was overjoyed, and he willingly paid for the improvements, leaving our rent unchanged.

As for cooking, Pedro said that he could relax and switch off from the laboratory by chopping the dinner ingredients and by finding ever more creative ways to prepare meals. He was always calm when I arrived home. The meals were delicious. Whenever I asked Pedro how he'd thought up a dish, he'd say something like, 'Oh, it's just that I can't remember how I did it last time – so I'm guessing a few ingredients.'

From time to time, Pedro would do his own 'take' on an Argentine or Spanish dish, but usually he created a new dish entirely. I never saw him looking at a written recipe before preparing a meal. And when he watched television cooking competitions he'd give the contestants advice, as though he were there in the kitchen alongside them.

His Spanish tuna fish pie became lighter with puff pastry instead of the thick heavy pastry typical of the dish, and it became tastier with more onion, capsicum – the American red bell pepper – and herbs than traditionally required. His lentil stews – of Spanish and Arab origin – had more complexity of flavour than any I had tried elsewhere, probably because of the quantities of herbs he used. He once saw a recipe for salmon fillets in pastry boats, and this inspired him to create a similar dish by adding crumbled bocconcini, home-made pesto with walnuts, slices of capsicum, and basil leaves.

But things with Pedro were not as calm as I thought. I should have taken his reaction to the management course more seriously.

*

One evening after work, a few days after Pedro walked out of his business course, I finally recognized the extent of his stress. He was chopping ingredients in the kitchen. I was setting the dining table in the living area.

'Catherine!' he cried out.

I was in the kitchen in a flash.

En un santiamén.
In a 'holy amen.'
Meaning: In a flash. Derived from *'En un Santu Amen,'* from *'En el nombre del Padre, y del Hijo y del Espíritu Santu. Amen.'* 'In the name of the Father, the Son and the Holy Spirit. Amen.' Possibly related to the compulsory and often very rapid finishing line to a prayer.

There was blood all over the chopping board, and it dripped down a half-sliced onion. Pedro held his hand over the sink. Blood streamed from a fingertip and pooled into the palm of his hand.

I stared at the scene, immobile, feeling faint and dizzy. Then I pulled myself together just enough to say, 'I'll call the doctor.'

'No – get me the first aid kit.'

Pedro's calm voice snapped me into action.

'Of course,' I said, and rushed to the bathroom. I rummaged in the cupboard and found the kit.

Pedro's first-aid-officer persona took over, and he talked me through the bandaging process. At last the bleeding stopped.

'I was chopping the onion and remembered what happened today,' he said. 'Stupid move. The knife slipped, and I sliced off the very tip of my finger. It's probably in here with the chopped onion.'

I looked at the mass of small white squares. I saw nothing that looked like the tip of a finger. 'Was it big enough for microsurgery?' I asked. 'If it was, we could find it and they could sew it back on. We'd have to keep it on ice.'

He laughed. 'Nope, but it was big enough to hurt like hell.'

I tried to laugh too, but only got as far as a smile.

He turned to me and his face became serious. 'Catherine, I can't do this much longer. Work was crazy today, and I was asked to take on more responsibilities.'

'You need to go to a doctor.'

'I'm not going anywhere. Did you hear what I said? I can't do it any more, even with six months off.'

'Yes I did hear. What about a different job?'

'I'm through with education – with science too.'

The next day he *did* go to the doctor, but afterwards, Pedro had me re-bandage the finger, giving me one of his typical technical explanations.

'This dressing from the Medical Centre's hopeless. The finger will only scar and stop the growth. The nurse should have used this one,' he said, handing it to me.

'It's impregnated with a gel. It's seaweed based. The wound stays moist and the tissue can regenerate. Going to the doctor wasn't any use.'

I was only half listening. I was thinking how important it was for him to leave his job – to be motivated. I wanted him to be happy. I wanted us to be happy together. But his idea of spending a few years in Argentina was a rather drastic solution to resolving our respective 'internal clashes.' I was glad he'd agreed on a short six months.

*

21

The day after the fingertip incident, I booked our flights to Buenos Aires. We'd already agreed on the first half of October – a week after Pedro finished work – and we'd also agreed that I'd make the arrangements. But unlike my usual organized self, I'd been employing delaying tactics. I was probably scared and reticent to accept that this was real. It hadn't 'sunk in' that we were leaving Australia with the outside possibility that it could be the first step in a long-term 'exile.'

Once we had the tickets, there was little to do except pack, and to establish what sort of apartment we'd look for in Buenos Aries.

It was at our local café in Sydney, a week before leaving, that Pedro and I debated our criteria for this 'home away from home' on the other side of the world.

I gazed at our laid-back neighbourhood and thought how different it was to Buenos Aires. I felt so 'at home' here. It was quiet and peaceful. I doubted I could ever feel 'at home' in Buenos Aires, a concrete jungle with three times the population of Sydney.

'Let's look in *Palermo*,' Pedro said. 'It's a fun area, full of shops and restaurants. There are plenty of tourists – if you want to speak English, you'll be fine.'

'But that's exactly the point,' I countered. 'I don't want to *be* in a tourist area. If we're staying there for more than a couple of weeks, I want to live like the locals. I want to be part of things.'

Pedro looked surprised, so I added, 'Six months is a long time. And longer than six months is a *very* long time.'

'Oh,' he said. 'Wouldn't you miss hearing English?'

'No, I need to become fluent in Spanish, and to be treated as a local – or at least, not as a tourist. Otherwise I'll feel utterly out of place.'

> *Como sapo de otro pozo.*
> Like a toad from another hole.
> Meaning: Like a fish out of water.

I hoped this initial disagreement did not presage a bottleneck. I tried to explain. 'Before we met, I always did the safe thing and stayed in tourist areas on my travels. But if I visited France, I soon found that I could only practice my French if I *left* those areas. Otherwise, everyone just talked to me in English. I imagine it'll be the same in Buenos Aires.'

I added, 'I'll never know whether I want to spend a long time in Argentina if I don't interact in Spanish and see how Argentines live . . .'

Pedro still looked confused. I felt I had to offer him an alternative.

'How about a place near your mother? You said once that it was only ten minutes into town on the subway.'

I hadn't seen any tourists when we visited the in-laws in *Villa Crespo*. It was a middle-class family *barrio,* and it possessed an unexpected villagey atmosphere amidst the high-rise buildings. Children tumbled out of the many schools into the arms of waiting parents or grandparents, and many of the smaller shops closed from midday to four in the afternoon. One shopkeeper struck up a conversation with us after a second visit, and another allowed us to owe her money when we couldn't find change. She waved to us every time we passed by.

Pedro was lost in thought for a few moments, stirring sugar into his coffee. 'Actually I don't mind where we live,' he said. 'I only thought of *Palermo* because of you.'

I sighed with relief.

Then he said, 'What *I'd* love is a decent-sized kitchen.'

'Oh,' I said. I was taken aback. I hadn't understood how important the kitchen was to Pedro. But I should have known. He had coped with our minuscule galley kitchen for over three years. Because he loved cooking so much, and because he cooked so often in order to de-stress, he'd rapidly become the executive chef in our household. I was the sous-chef, table setter, and of course, the voracious devourer of his meals.

Pedro spent more time in the kitchen than anyone I'd ever known. It was normal for him to make a mouth-watering dish such as pan-cooked chicken in orange and chardonnay, and then on an impulse, to turn the cooking liquid into a reduction with honey while I served the vegetables. Or he'd whip up a dessert such as caramelized figs cooked in butter with some sugar and a dash of cognac or brandy, served with a dollop of mascarpone and crushed pistachio nuts, while I cleared the main course.

I learned early on that it was no use trying to help with the cooking itself, because that hindered the creative process.

> *Muchas manos en un plato hacen mucho garabato.*
> Many hands in a dish make a big scribble.
> Meaning: Too many cooks spoil the broth.

He said, 'A *little* more kitchen space would be ideal. A *lot* more space would be fantastic.'

He waited for a response.

'Of course – a big kitchen – a *huge* kitchen,' I said, and we both laughed.

And he added, 'Oh, and the building needs to be solid. We can look for an unrenovated place – to spot any building defects. A renovated place is nice – but new paint could be hiding serious flaws. Like wide cracks in the walls.'

'Okay,' I agreed, without thinking, and imagining a new coat of paint and a few new door handles. I had no way of knowing that the simple word 'okay' was to launch me into a totally new life experience that would strongly test my fortitude.

Cheerful in my ignorance, I blithely said, 'Two bedrooms. We want to have friends to stay.'

'If I can afford it,' he said.

The sun shone unimpeded from a big blue sky. Joggers ran past us and around the huge sports field across the road. The field was green from recent rain.

I imagined the streetscape that Pedro's mother saw each day. Seven-storey buildings walled in the narrow tree-lined streets, forming chasms that blotted out large sections of sky. Cars raced along the one-way thoroughfares, rumbling across the occasional stretch of cobblestones. A few one- and two-storey houses remained, elegant reminders of a time when Buenos Aires was one of the richest cities in the world.

*

We walked up one of those Buenos Aires chasms ten days later, and straight into a real estate office. It was the second week of October, and the morning was crisp and cool. Perfect for house hunting.

Clara glanced up from her desk and smiled. She looked puzzled. It was plainly unusual for foreigners to stroll into her office. Not that Pedro looked foreign, but with his blue eyes, he became 'foreign by association' alongside tall, English-looking 'me.'

'Good afternoon,' she said, nodding for us to take a seat.

Pedro made a few general inquiries and Clara relaxed. Perhaps she was relieved to hear him speak in Spanish.

As Clara relaxed, so did I. *Soon*, I thought, *we'll be inspecting potential home-away-from-homes*. It was our third day in Buenos Aires, and we'd given ourselves three weeks to find a place to call our own. According to Pedro, the standard settlement period when buying a property was five weeks. Assuming all went to plan, that would leave us with four months to experience life in an apartment in this massive city of thirteen million.

But then Pedro asked about a house, not an apartment. I could hardly believe what I was hearing. On the way to Clara's office we'd seen a 'for sale' sign on the wall of a beautiful two-storey house. The date above the door was 1904, and the sign told us that there was an internal courtyard and fountain. It looked as though it would cost a fortune.

> *Valía un Perú.*
> It was worth a Peru.
> Meaning: It was very expensive.

It was this very house that Pedro described to Clara.

'But —' I said to Pedro, and, *'Discúlpeme, quiero decir algo en inglés'* 'Excuse me, I want to say something in English,' to Clara. I turned to face Pedro and spoke in English.

'A house? We want an *apartment*. Wouldn't a house break the bank? What about security when we're away? What about our criteria?'

Pedro shrugged and looked sheepish.

'I know, I know. But let's have a look anyway. How many people do we know with lovely houses like that? None.'

Clara found the property on her computer and moved the screen to show us. Up flashed photos of high-ceilinged rooms, the marble fountain with an Italian statue, and the beautiful tiled courtyard.

Seeing us both turn toward her, she launched into a description of the renovated bathroom.

I was getting anxious. All I could think of was our three-week plan and our criteria. The criteria for an apartment. Not a house.

I stepped over the precipice and launched into my first real-estate conversation in Spanish.

'Do you have a two-bedroom apartment?'

Clara looked at me. I could see that she was confused. She eyeballed Pedro and said, 'Apartment or house? Isn't it a *house* that you want? What exactly are you looking for?'

'An apartment,' I said, faltering, wishing my Spanish were better, or that Pedro hadn't mentioned a house in the first place.

Pedro was amused – pleasantly so – at the fact that I was practicing my Spanish *and* simultaneously trying to steer a conversation in another direction. It shocked him out of his house fixation.

He came to the rescue and explained that we loved the house, but actually we were there to buy an apartment.

'Ah, an apartment,' said poor Clara, the lines of her forehead creasing. But professionalism won out, and she started again.

'Right. You want it at the front of the building, of course?'

'Er, at the back,' I mumbled, unsure of the words. Pedro nodded encouragement.

She looked surprised. 'It will be dark.'

'We *do* want light, but . . .' I trailed off, fishing in my bag for our wish list.

> *No tiene ni pies ni cabeza.*
> It has neither feet nor a head.
> Meaning: It doesn't quite fit; it doesn't make sense.

Again, Pedro helped out.

'We want to be at the back – it needs to be quiet. But we don't want to

25

compromise on light.'

Pedro had explained to me that apartments at the back were often dark, because of the proximity of the buildings behind them, especially if the city block was narrow. People who lived at the front of the building paid more because of the light, but they endured the noise of non-stop traffic in a city that never slept.

'Umm, oh yes, and with a big kitchen,' I said. 'We enjoy cooking.'

More surprise from Clara. I knew from Pedro's Mum that many families in the area had domestic staff to help with cleaning and with meal preparation.

'The bigger the better,' I said.

'Unrenovated,' declared Pedro.

I could imagine Clara thinking to herself, 'What's all this about? They're only here for a holiday. They want everything.'

> *Quieren la chancha, los veinte y la máquina de hacer chorizos.*
> They want the sow, the twenty, and the sausage-making machine.
> Meaning: They want everything. 'The twenty' referred to twenty suckling pigs, or *lechones*.

Even though she was taken aback, Clara, we were finding, was resourceful. She turned to the computer screen. 'Balcony? Number of bathrooms?'

And so it went on.

'It's just as well that you want an unrenovated place,' she said as she searched. 'A two-bedroom apartment in a new building is way over your price range.'

Soon we'd chosen a number of apartments to inspect. Clara asked Pedro a question and he answered so quickly that I couldn't follow. Satisfied, she grabbed the phone and rattled away in a high-speed Argentine Spanish that I was getting used to not understanding. Pedro whispered to me, 'I said we could inspect them any day – we don't have other plans right now.'

Finally Clara finished.

'I've made all the appointments. I need one more confirmation if you can wait, and we're done.'

We agreed to wait, and she asked where we were from. Pedro surprised her by saying he was Argentine. His Spanish accent had been influenced during his years in Sydney, where many friends – from Spain, Colombia, Chile and Mexico – spoke with different accents and intonations.

He launched into a description of our life in Australia, and explained why we were spending a few months in Buenos Aires.

Pedro was animated as he talked, but I found myself becoming apprehensive. It was all too easy. Much too easy. Only a moment ago I had been impatient to see properties, and now I wasn't so sure. The decision we'd taken months ago on another continent was translating too rapidly into reality.

> *A todo vapor.*
> At full steam.
> Meaning: Full steam ahead.

The real estate office with its posters of properties proclaiming, '*Se vende*' or 'For Sale', Clara with her list of apartments to inspect, and the loud, unfamiliar greetings as customers entered the office, were all concrete reminders that I was hurtling toward an uncertain future in an unfamiliar metropolis, surrounded by the words and expressions of another language, another culture.

And Buenos Aires was nothing like my memories of it. The city was a maze. Every major intersection looked identical, with its corner cafés and multi-storey buildings. We'd spent two days travelling on public transport, visiting relatives. Whenever I assumed we were nearly 'home' – in other words, at the in-laws – Pedro told me that we were many blocks away. We always stepped off at a different bus stop, or surfaced from the subway at a different exit. I simply couldn't get my bearings.

> *Más perdida que turco en la neblina.*
> More lost than an Arab in the fog.
> Meaning: Disoriented. *Tuco* meant 'firefly' in *Quechua*, the indigenous language of the north. Over time, *tuco* became *turco*, or 'Arab.'

And I could hardly understand what people were saying. Clara's Spanish was clear when she talked to me directly, but when she spoke on the phone, it was indecipherable. All the Spanish-language films I'd watched, and the Argentine novellas I'd attempted more recently, lost their utility.

I drifted into a daydream, wishing I could magically improve my Spanish. I didn't want to slow down conversations, or risk being disregarded entirely, by constantly referring to a translation device or a dictionary.

> *Un mataburros.*
> A donkey killer. In other words, an ignorance killer.
> Meaning: A dictionary.

It wasn't only Clara. Last night at dinner, Pedro's mother had turned to me and said, '*Mi xxx xxx y xxx xxx fuimos xxxx xxxx xxx después xxx xxxxxx xxx xxxx casa xx xxxxxx hijos xxxx Australia xxx xxx xxx pero xxx xxx veintiuno?*'

I'd smiled, she'd smiled, and the conversation had sped on without me.

Later, unraveling the sentence in my head, and guessing the meaning of some words, I figured out how I should have answered.

It was easier to listen rather than to speak, because the in-laws carried on conversations at the speed of a bullet train. Pedro and his mother tended to talk to each other simultaneously, with barely any pauses. This appeared to be effective and to save time.

Whenever I asked for the meaning of an expression, Pedro's stepfather stopped, looked at me kindly, and explained it to me in one-syllable words. After that he jumped back into the conversation.

During one dinner, I heard Pedro's mother ask her husband, 'Can you understand what Catherine is saying?'

His stepfather answered, 'No, only a couple of words.'

Because they couldn't understand *me*, they assumed I couldn't understand *them*, and they talked about me as though I were absent. Pedro tried to correct the situation, saying, 'You *do* know that Catherine understood what you said, don't you?'

But they saw nothing wrong with it, and I knew they didn't mean to offend. It was an odd sort of loneliness, in a warm and welcoming house surrounded by well-meaning people.

> *Más sola que la una.*
> More alone than one o'clock.
> Meaning: Very lonely.

I caught myself feeling melancholy. I needed to snap out of it. After all, Pedro had arrived in Australia at the age of seventeen without speaking a word of English. If *he* could become fluent in another language, so could I. When I met Pedro, his English was perfect and he loved to use obscure words such as 'oligophrenic' or 'prestidigitator.' *Magic would not go astray right now*, I mused.

But musing would not help. The problems were clear. I lacked familiarity with the city, and I needed to improve my Spanish. I resolved to consciously take in my surroundings more, and to try harder with the language.

> *El que quiere pescado que se moje.*
> He who wants fish has to get wet.

I should also stop daydreaming when other people were speaking Spanish.

I looked across at Clara. She said, 'We have appointments for you to see five apartments. I didn't think we'd find more than two or three.'

As we left her office she added in a soft murmur, 'But no houses.'

Sopa de espárragos — Asparagus Soup

The asparagus season had recently started, and with the days still fresh and cool, Pedro prepared a soup to complement his Mum's main course. The in-laws loved it.

Many different foods shaped Pedro's memory, but soup did so in a negative way. His 'soup trauma' stemmed from a holiday long ago.

Pedro was six years old. His aunt and uncle, with their children Tamara and Guillermo, joined Pedro's family for a few days at the seaside. The holiday package included breakfast and dinner. The first course for dinner every night was soup. It was a brown, watery, tasteless potion with 'stuff' floating in it. Pedro could hardly bear to look at it, and could only consume it, eyes half closed, by adding heaps of Parmesan cheese.

The children spent their days on the beach. One afternoon, Pedro and Tamara worked side by side at the water's edge, each peacefully building a superb sand castle. Tamara used her new metal shovel, a present she'd been given for Reyes or 'Kings' — Epiphany — the day on which Argentine children traditionally used to receive presents. Pedro was happily depositing the sand he didn't need into Tamara's castle's moat, not realizing that Tamara was becoming increasingly upset with his 'trespassing' behaviour. Suddenly she whacked him on the head with her metal shovel. Blood gushed from a large cut and coursed down his forehead.

Pedro was rushed to the first aid station. His head was shaved and he was given five stitches. The wound needed to be kept dry, so he couldn't swim. His holiday was ruined.

The soup and the whack gave Pedro an indelible memory of the holiday, and for a long, long time he couldn't bear to look at a soup bowl, let alone make a soup. Eventually he made soups from packets, but never from scratch, and this astonished me when I first met him. Why would such a great cook make packet soup?

About a year after we met, one dreary winter's day when he was sick, I made him a soup using fresh vegetables and chicken broth. Admittedly the broth was packaged, but it was a good one. Pedro loved it. Years of built-up trauma evaporated, and the soup-maker in Pedro emerged.

I never got to make a vegetable soup the same way again, in fact when I tried to repeat it, he was horrified that I didn't take the time to prepare a brunoise. So I let him take over while I poured the wine.

The only soup that he ever prepared without a brunoise was this asparagus soup.

Ingredients
One bunch of asparagus — young and tender sticks
1 medium-sized brown onion
1 clove of garlic
2-3 tbsp olive oil
20-25g butter
1 tbsp sifted flour
1 litre vegetable stock, heated
Salt and pepper

Pinch of cumin
Pinch of dry thyme
A few leaves of parsley, optional – see Method
200ml fresh cream

Method

Chop off the woody end of the asparagus sticks and discard. Cut off the tips 3cm from the end and set aside. The asparagus tips will be cooked later and added to the soup for garnish, but if you prefer to leave this step out, slice them up with the rest of the asparagus. Slice the remainder into 1cm pieces.

Chop the onion and garlic finely.

In a saucepan, add the olive oil and butter. Don't allow this to get too hot. Add the onion and garlic and cook in the oil and butter, allowing them to sweat until translucent. Do not let them brown. If they dry up, add a dash of oil.

Add the flour to the onion mix and stir thoroughly to make a roux – as if you were making a béchamel sauce. Allow the flour to cook for a couple of minutes. After it has thickened, add the vegetable stock and stir continuously to avoid lumps from forming.

Add the asparagus slices, and salt and pepper to taste. Add the cumin and thyme.

Turn up the heat until it reaches almost boiling point and simmer for half an hour until the asparagus is thoroughly cooked.

Allow to cool. Blend the soup in a blender or food processor or use a hand mixer directly in the saucepan.

To enhance the green colour you could add a small amount of chopped parsley before blending – this will also add flavour. The parsley can be especially helpful if you have used a lot of the white stalk of the asparagus.

Cook the asparagus tips by steaming, boiling or microwaving, as preferred.

Add the cream and mix thoroughly as you heat up the potage, and add the asparagus tips so that they become warm.

Serves 4

Hint

If you add too much vegetable stock or water, the soup can taste watery and 'ungenerous.' Keep it thicker rather than watered down.

3

THE QUEST

The next day at Clara's office we met Elena, our 'inspection guide.' Elena kissed each of us on the cheek, said, '*Un minuto,*' and disappeared behind a desk. I was baffled as to why Elena had given us a kiss, whereas Clara, yesterday, had not. Perhaps it was because we were now 'known.' Or perhaps it was for some other reason entirely. I knew that it was mandatory to greet Pedro's relatives and close friends with a kiss on the cheek, even when first introduced. But now I sensed that a whole new realm of 'introduction etiquette' lay in wait, to confuse me. I decided that, until I fully understood Argentina's meeting-and-kissing behaviour, I'd be wise to take any cues from Pedro.

Elena took notes from her computer screen, presumably listing the inspection addresses. Next she made a phone call, and one minute became three. I decided it could easily become ten, and I sat on a visitors' seat.

Pedro sat beside me, but when he saw an elderly man pushing the glass entrance door from outside, he jumped up to help.

> *Estaba más cerca del arpa que de la guitarra.*
> He was closer to the harp than to the guitar.
> Meaning: He had one foot in the grave.

Pedro spoke to the man as he held the door, and the man answered. Pedro loved to initiate conversations with strangers, in the hope of finding like-minded people to discuss politics, the cultural scene, or the infrastructure and shortcomings of a city. The two of them were soon immersed in a discussion of how federal and city politics influenced the Buenos Aires public transport system. At least, I was pretty sure that's what they were discussing, hands flying in all directions.

I knew that, as with French, many Spanish words for political and community topics were similar to English, making guessing easier for me.

31

From their conversation I picked up words such as *federal, la política, el presidente, el parlamento, el congreso, el senado* and *el sistema de transporte público.* Had the conversation been slower, I would have understood more.

I stared through the glass wall at the passers-by. There was a never-ending stream of pedestrians – shoppers with trolleys, grandmothers pushing their grandchildren in prams, waiters delivering trays of coffee, young people darting through the crowd, and men carrying sacks of potatoes from a truck to the chute in the wall of the restaurant next door. The pedestrians all skirted a large block of concrete surrounded by a broken fence of orange plastic tape that warned of a pothole in the sidewalk. Cars, trucks, motorbikes, bicycles and the occasional in-line skaters raced along the one-way five-lane avenue. We were in a relatively quiet *barrio* of Buenos Aires, but there was more activity than rush hour in central Sydney. I felt like the foreigner that I was, staring at a strange new world.

Once we've looked at a few apartments it will feel more familiar, I thought.

Pedro and his new friend were now discussing music.

Elena stood, nodded to me and strode out the door, a large shawl around her shoulders. I hardly had time to register what was happening before she disappeared down the sidewalk.

'Come on, Pedro,' I said, grabbing his arm, glancing at his companion and saying, *'Perdón.'* 'She's half way along the block already.'

It was regrettable that I had to separate Pedro from his prey, but I knew he'd soon find another person to talk to. And I had no doubt that the elderly man would greet him warmly in the street if they met again. Pedro looked disappointed, but shook hands with his friend and we bolted out of the office.

Within minutes, Elena stopped outside a decrepit looking building and pressed a third-floor buzzer. After a conversation over the intercom and a five-minute wait, a man wearing a creased shirt and track suit pants shuffled across the foyer toward us, his slippers dragging along the floor. I assumed he was the owner. He took keys from his pocket to unlock the glass door.

I turned to Pedro. 'Wouldn't it be easier if he buzzed us in from upstairs? Why come all the way to the foyer?'

'He can't buzz us in. It's a lingering remnant of the 2001 crisis. There was a crime wave – "buzzing in" got too dangerous.'

'But that was fifteen years ago.'

'I suppose people got used to the security. I'm pretty sure this will happen with each inspection,' he said.

I sighed. I had seen this at the in-laws but hadn't known that it was widespread. House hunting felt slow even before it had begun.

I'd read about the economic crisis years before, but since meeting Pedro, I'd found out much more. Before the crisis, the value of one peso was one United States dollar and they were interchangeable – you could put dollars or pesos into your bank account and they would be registered as pesos. After the crisis, the value of the peso dropped to twenty-five United States cents. Many people who had put dollars into their bank accounts rather than pesos, found that the pesos were now worth seventy-five per cent less than the dollars they had originally deposited.

Added to this, runs on the banks led to the freezing of all bank savings, referred to as a *corralito,* or a 'corralling of savings.' Individuals could only access a certain number of pesos per month, leaving many people in terrible financial trouble. Businesses closed, many people lost their jobs and houses, and in provinces where cash ran out, the provincial governments printed IOU's. Barter became commonplace. It was a massive disaster. After the 2008 global financial crisis, parallels were drawn between the Argentine experience and developments in Greece, Spain and Portugal.

I'd heard Pedro and his Mum discussing a current crisis in Argentina, with import restrictions, two exchange rates for the peso to the dollar – one official, and one unofficial – and high inflation. I had tried, unsuccessfully, to grasp the causes and issues through Internet searches, and my attempts had simply made me dizzy.

But my mind was wandering again. Pedro and I were now in the single tiny elevator as it struggled to reach the third floor. I looked around me.

'This building's not only falling apart, but filthy,' I said to Pedro, pointing at the dirt in the corners of the lift. He nodded as the lift stopped, and he opened the door. We stepped into the corridor and waited for Elena and the owner, who would catch the lift once it arrived back on the ground floor. The corridor smelled of mould. When our companions arrived, we were ushered into a huge living room with wide cracks in the walls. The sound of a dog barking filled the space around us – it appeared to originate from the apartment next door. Our inspection was brief.

'You wanted unrenovated,' I teased Pedro, as we scurried along behind Elena to 'apartment number two' on the list.

But we spent less time there than in the first one. Many of the Buenos Aires apartments we had visited on our previous trips were small – much smaller than Sydney apartments – but this one was simply minute. Way too small to swing a cat.

The third one was exactly the size we were looking for.

Cayó como anillo al dedo.
It fitted like a ring to a finger.
Meaning: It was a perfect fit with our need.

Too big, too small, now perfect, I thought. *Like the story of the Three Bears. That was quick.* But when we turned off the lights we could hardly see a thing. There was no way to improve the light situation. There were too many

33

buildings in close proximity. Such a dark place would be overly depressing.

I dragged my feet as we trudged toward the fourth apartment on Elena's list, but I livened up when I saw the light and the proportions. Elena praised the heating arrangement, and Pedro helped me to understand what she said.

'There are two boilers downstairs, one for hot water, and one for central heating in winter.'

This must be the one, I thought. *No need to look further, surely. And no need to buy heaters.*

'Why don't you buy this one? It's within the budget,' I said to Pedro. 'And I wouldn't mind a break – let's stop for a coffee.'

But Pedro, with his endless energy, was keen to keep going.

'One more – please?' he said.

*

I relented, and we continued the inspections. Elena strode quickly ahead of us, but Pedro and I were drawn to the colourful and symmetrical fruit displays at each greengrocer's we passed. One mountain of strawberries was particularly impressive and must have taken hours to assemble. We stared at it, mesmerized.

I glanced into the shop, expecting to see order and tidiness. But instead, I saw a confusion of stacked boxes, a battered weighing machine that hung from the ceiling, and precariously stacked vegetables that looked as though they could be dislodged by any thoughtless movement. The chaos inside the shop matched an unruly streetscape – traffic bedlam, uneven sidewalks, and untidy cable television wires dangling between high metal posts and apartment buildings.

I became aware that Elena had slowed, and was looking at us. I nudged Pedro and we turned to follow her.

She repeated her usual pre-inspection mantra, 'You'll love the next apartment.' And added, 'Don't be put off by the foyer. They're going to renovate it – starting Monday.'

The owner approached the glass foyer door to let us in. He was tall and wore a grey suit, white shirt, and a striped red and blue tie. He ruffled his hand through his red hair as he unlocked the foyer door, and when he greeted us, I was surprised to see that his eyes were blue. Even though Pedro had blue eyes, I knew how uncommon they were in Argentina. We followed him into the foyer with its crazy-paving floor and multiple wall mirrors. It was a time warp from the seventies.

There were two elevators, a rare luxury. Pedro and I took one of them, Elena and the owner the other. Ours was lined with scratched and sagging imitation wood. We stepped out at the fifth floor, climbing up more than ten centimetres to the level of the passageway.

Our two companions had already arrived.

'If they're renovating the foyer, maybe they'll fix the elevators,' Pedro said to me quietly.

'Remind me why you didn't want to buy in a new building?' I responded, my mind blank as I tried to remember our 'criteria discussion' in that peaceful Sydney café, as well as yesterday's conversation with Clara. I was tired and hungry. I still hadn't recovered from jet lag. I'd been waking up at three in the morning, as bright as a button, and dozing off to sleep at four o'clock each afternoon.

I jumped back into the present when the owner opened the apartment door. Light flooded the corridor. My mood improved instantly, and Pedro and I moved toward the glass doors of the living room. We saw a narrow balcony with a glass balustrade, and from the top of the balustrade, a safety mesh that reached up to the base of the overhanging balcony.

Below us, a couple of back-yard swimming pools reflected the blue of the sky, and beyond them towered the rear walls of a continuous line of apartment buildings, with rows of windows and balconies. They were distant enough to allow streams of light to enter the apartment.

But the safety mesh made me cautious.

'It must be a dangerous neighbourhood if they're protecting the apartment from burglars – all the way up here on the fifth floor,' I said to Pedro.

He grinned. 'It's got nothing do to with burglars – it's for babies and kids – to stop them falling out. Imagine you were a thief – why scale up an outside wall when you can follow an unsuspecting resident into the foyer, take the elevator and pick the lock?'

'Oh,' I said, feeling stupid, but not entirely convinced. 'I suppose so.'

Elena approached us and said, 'There will always be light in the apartment. There's a huge patio on the ground floor, covering the residents' car park – nobody could block you in.'

Pedro opened one of the sliding doors to the balcony, and a hurricane swept through the room. Objects whirled through the air and dropped in new locations. Pedro glanced at me and closed the window.

'Nice cross breeze,' I whispered to him.

Pedro apologized to the owner and we returned objects to the places we thought they must belong. The owner shook his head, telling us not to worry.

Elena followed us into the main bedroom. Its walls were purple.

And into the kitchen. It was big compared to the other kitchens we had seen. A few more people could easily have joined us. But the cupboards sagged, the oven was ancient, and with each gust of wind, the windows rattled against their frames.

In summary, the apartment was exactly what we were looking for. Big kitchen, light, unrenovated, no cracks in the walls, located at the back . . .

But it was too expensive.

The price was twenty-five per cent over Pedro's limit.

> *No estaba para tirar manteca al techo.*
> He was not up to throwing butter at the ceiling.
> Meaning: He didn't have money to spare.

Even so, I wanted to linger a bit longer, and asked Elena if we could inspect the kitchen again. Pedro beamed.

*

In the kitchen, Pedro pointed to the solitary bench top. 'That's Carrara marble,' he said.

Wow, I thought, *real Italian marble,* before he deflated my enthusiasm.

'We'd have to get rid of it – look at the cracks . . . is that sticky tape?'

He peered more closely. I looked over his shoulder.

Elena hovered nearby.

'Yes, and silicone sealer,' he whispered.

He glanced up and jumped backward. I sidestepped to avoid losing my balance and sprawling across the floor. Elena looked startled.

'Oops, sorry,' Pedro said, in a detached voice. 'Look at this.' He was pointing at an ancient gas hot-water system. It hung giddily from a frame that listed to one side. I guessed it was this precarious object that had taken him by surprise.

'If the gas company saw this they'd cut supply to the apartment. Or to the whole building,' he said.

None of this sounded promising.

I was conscious of Elena's gaze as I ran my finger along one of the cupboard doors. It was heavily stained and scraped, though not enough to obscure a once-fashionable orange.

I felt sorry for Elena and her serious and zealous behaviour. I tried to cheer her up with a positive remark. 'Look, the cupboard doors match the green and orange tiles,' I ventured.

She smiled faintly.

I observed the rest of the kitchen. Against the opposite wall stood the oven, rusted by the years.

> *Estaba en las diez de últimas.*
> It was in the last ten minutes of its hour/its life.
> Meaning: It was on its last legs.

A lonely breakfast table stood against the wall on our left. Scattered nearby were two stools, two chairs, and a baby's high chair.

Elena saw me looking at the seating arrangement and piped up, 'The owners need to move because they've had a third child.'

I wandered over to a ramshackle corner of the kitchen where improvised walls and a door, made of sheets of polycarbonate, enclosed a miniature laundry area. A corrugated sheet of the same material functioned as a roof. I guessed that the area had once been a small balcony, open to the elements. Beneath a tangle of brooms was a severely pitted enamel sink. *A renovator's delight,* I thought.

Pedro turned to me, unfazed, and asked, 'What do you think? I could probably stretch the budget.' I wasn't sure what to say. I still thought that 'unrenovated' meant 'intact but needing a splash of paint and the replacement of missing door handles.'

'It's got potential,' I said, trying to sound positive. 'But the kitchen's more of a knockdown than a renovation. If we're not buying the fourth one we saw, why don't we look at a few more first?'

Privately, I thought, *A lengthy renovation is the last thing we need. We'll never find out what it's like to live in Buenos Aires. The one with central heating is much better.*

*

That night, when I told Pedro's mother that we'd found a great place with central heating, she quickly cautioned me. 'Each resident can elect to have the heating on, or off. There's generally only one temperature setting – unbearable.'

And when I told her that we'd seen another one that needed a kitchen makeover but was too expensive, she sighed. 'I'm sure you'll find what you want. It will simply take time.'

Our inspections took place every day except Sundays for three weeks. One apartment was memorable only because the owner lowered the foyer key from above, having placed it in a bag at the end of a piece of string. Another apartment overlooked a warehouse, which if sold to a property developer would presage a dark future for the living room. In another, the quarters for the live-in housekeeper could be made into a third bedroom, but the apartment was even darker than the dark one we'd seen on the first day.

It was a frustrating time. When we visited Pedro's relatives, they asked us, 'How's your house hunting going? Why do you want a big kitchen? Why not a big *living area?* Why don't you want to live closer to us? There's a beautiful house for sale around the corner . . .'

His cousin Felicitas was one of the few who stood up for us. One night at the in-laws, I overheard her speaking to cousin Rodolfo on her cell phone. 'Leave them alone. They don't need a family inquisition. Catherine will be put off Argentina. She won't want to have anything to do with you.'

No metas la cuchara.
Don't put your spoon in.
Meaning: Don't get involved where it's not your concern.

Pedro's Tía or 'Aunt' Diana was lovely. She said, 'I so missed Pedro when he left Argentina. How exciting to be looking for a home here. Make sure it's exactly what *you* want, and don't listen to any of the relatives. Of *course* you want a big kitchen. Of *course* you want to be in the city centre near the subway. Pedro was always different to the others, and they can't understand why he values things that they don't.'

Tía spoke slowly and clearly and I could understand most of what she said. I assumed that she was doing this on purpose, to help me to 'settle in.' She told me that none of the other relatives had lived overseas, let alone returned. 'They still see Pedro as the teenager he was when he left Argentina, living near them on the outskirts of the city, a clever student who unfortunately liked to skip his classes to go fishing. Not as a bilingual university scientist who lived in Australia, with a wife he's brought to a city she doesn't know. I myself can hardly imagine how his life must have been there, but I can see that you both know exactly what you want. As for Rodolfo, ignore him. He never gives up.'

Nunca se baja del caballo.
He never gets off the horse.

It was reassuring to hear Tía's view of the situation. I determined not to over-react to the relatives who tried to dissuade us.

When I phoned Annie in Sydney, she told me we were nuts. 'As I said before you left, I don't know why you want to even consider living in that country. Sydney is such a great city. I'm sure you could persuade Pedro to rent for six months and come home.'

That touched a raw nerve, seeing as I'd had exactly the same idea before Pedro had suggested buying a place.

Mum reacted in the same way as Tía Diana. 'I suppose he can always sell it later dear, if you don't like it. I'm sure you two will sort it out. When I bought this hobby farm, I didn't know if it would work out, but I love it now.' I was glad to have Mum's support, though I didn't want to imagine Pedro selling an apartment he hadn't even bought.

But right now, the relatives' remarks were academic. Because here we were, near the end of our self-imposed 'finding an apartment' phase, and we had not found the place we wanted.

> *Nos quedamos con el pescado sin vender.*
> We were left with the unsold fish.
> Meaning: We didn't achieve what we set out to.

Our plan was unravelling. The longer we took to find a place, the less time we would have to enjoy Buenos Aires from our own 'nest.' Were we being unrealistic?

*

Pedro came to the rescue. 'Let's stop and think for a moment. We're both exhausted. I'll take you to my favourite café in Buenos Aires – we can sit and think it through, far from the relatives.'

'The famous one?' I asked, hoping we were going to *Café Tortoni*. Pedro had mentioned it a few times, but we'd had no time to visit. He smiled conspiratorially, but said nothing.

We descended into the *Subte*, or Buenos Aires subway. I gathered that *Subte* was short for *Subterráneo*. I'd already found that the *Subte* was the only rapid form of transport available in Buenos Aires – if you discounted the Formula One inspired taxi drivers who raced along avenues in the early hours of the morning – the only time that the roads did not teem with traffic.

The carriage was crowded, but we managed to find two seats. I hoped a busker would pass through the carriage. We'd seen tango dancers, a magician and an accomplished saxophone player on our underground journeys.

A loud shout in my ear made me start, and I grabbed Pedro's arm, turning my head in the direction of the sound. A man with a thunderous voice moved toward us in a threatening manner. No one in the carriage took any notice.

'Calm down,' said Pedro, smiling. 'He's only trying to sell something.' I held on to Pedro's arm as I listened, shrinking closer to him until the man stopped shouting and gently placed a flashlight on Pedro's lap, and another on mine. And then on the lap of each commuter who sat near us.

'You see, it's simply a small flashlight,' said Pedro. I took a few deep breaths and soon recovered my composure.

'Do we need a flashlight?' Pedro asked. 'It looks okay. It's cheap.'

> *Cuesta chaucha y palitos.*
> It costs a bean and little cheese sticks – like the cheese sticks served free with a beer.
> Meaning: It costs very little.

'You want to buy it on the *subway?*'

'Why not?' Pedro asked.

I tried to think why not, but couldn't.

'And it's easier than searching for one in the shops,' he said.

I *had* been meaning to buy one. I agreed. It felt odd to be buying a flashlight randomly on the subway but, as Pedro had said, why not?

We arrived at our stop and climbed to street level. Pedro pointed across the road. A red-on-white *'Café Tortoni'* sign stood out against a glass and wrought-iron awning.

We entered the café world of the nineteenth century, where smartly dressed waiters moved with their trays of food and drink between patrons chatting at marble-topped tables. The high, wood-panelled walls were covered with drawings, paintings and photographs, and light entered through a beautiful stained-glass ceiling. A row of shining brown marble columns with white Corinthian capitals ran ahead of us along the length of the café, partly hiding a grand counter with a cash register from long ago.

Despite the hubbub of conversations, it was an oasis of calm after our fruitless search for an apartment, and after my recent overreaction to the 'travelling salesman.'

As we waited to be seated, Pedro told me that famous artists, writers, and politicians had patronized the café since it opened in the 1850s. Being close to the famous *Casa Rosada,* or presidential palace, and not far from the *Palacio del Congreso,* or 'Congress', it was easy to imagine major political strategies taking shape here over the years.

The waiter showed us to our table and left us with menus.

We both spoke at once.

I said, 'You know, that apartment we saw on the first day had potential. The hurricane's a positive. And a slap of paint can cover the purple walls. The kitchen's a disaster – but we – or should I say you – could renovate it. What do you think? Would it take long to do?'

As I spoke, I heard him saying, 'I want to make an offer for the one with the awful kitchen tiles and the ancient foyer. We'd need to be careful with that gas hot-water system.'

We looked at each other and laughed out loud. Pedro called over the waiter and ordered champagne. Then he grabbed a serviette and sketched out the kitchen. 'I've already worked out one way to rearrange the space, and change the laundry area. Have a look at this.'

I felt so relieved. The decision was made. As long as he made a reasonable offer, our house hunting would be over. And now we also had a *Serviette Plan* for the kitchen layout.

I felt only a mild flutter of uncertainty at the back of my mind, but I dismissed it. I'd never lived through a house renovation, but I could easily imagine the apartment in its final state. I was confident that our relationship was strong enough to withstand the experience, and not end up in 'renovation counselling.'

I thought of all the relatives' reactions to our 'trial period in Buenos Aires,' and my sister's belief that I could have persuaded Pedro to stay in Sydney. Perhaps I could have. But he would have been miserable.

Perhaps by spending this time in Argentina, a country so different to Australia, we would get to understand each other better, and plan a new and different future together.

Pollo a la cacerola — Chicken Casserole

Back at the in-laws' apartment, we decided it was high time for us to return their hospitality. Pedro took over their kitchen, relieved that it was modern and easy to work in when compared to the one in our chosen apartment.

He decided on a chicken casserole with a deep complexity of flavours. Pedro's stepfather was an atypical Argentine in that he didn't eat red meat, so chicken was a perfect choice. The only ingredient that was hard to procure was chilli, so Pedro left it out.

Pedro always delighted guests in Sydney with this casserole, and they came back for more and more. It was slightly different each time, but always delicious. We accompanied it with plain pasta such as fusilli or penne, though it was also yummy with mashed potato or plain white rice.

Friends who used this recipe varied it by adding more wine — one friend added half a bottle — or more mushrooms, or by leaving out the olives, or by adding different herbs. All were delectable.

Ingredients

3 medium sized carrots

1½ red capsicums (i.e. red bell peppers)

200g mushrooms, white or Portobello (Swiss brown) or a mixture of both, i.e. whatever you have in the kitchen

1 whole red chilli, finely chopped. Pedro usually uses a small hot chilli.

250g green beans

1 brown onion

3 large cloves of garlic

2 tbsp plain flour or more if required

2 kg chicken cut into small pieces, say 12-14 pieces.

Olive oil

100g tomato paste

1 cup red wine, or white wine if you prefer a lighter colour.

1 standard can crushed tomatoes

Generous quantities of herbs, in some cases even more than for the Bolognaise Sauce in Chapter 6. This can make a big difference to your chicken casserole.

Oregano: If you are used to using a pinch of oregano, this is the time to rethink. Pedro piles up dried oregano on the palm of his hand, so that the palm is completely covered and forms the base of the mountain of oregano

1 heaped tbsp thyme

A handful of fresh basil leaves, coarsely chopped.

2 bay leaves

1 rounded tbsp smoked paprika

3 cloves

1/2 tsp grated nutmeg

Other herbs as desired

Chicken or vegetable stock. Use a good quality stock or make it yourself.
12-15 pitted green olives, whole
Salt and pepper to taste

Method

I had never heard of a brunoise before meeting Pedro. A brunoise consists of finely chopped vegetables, added early in the cooking process to enrich the flavour. Hence the different sized pieces of carrot, mushroom and capsicum below.

To prepare the brunoise, chop 2 mushrooms finely into 2mm cubes. With 1/3 of a carrot, and about 1/4 of the red capsicum, julienne them and then chop them across to get them into 2mm cube sizes. To these, add the finely chopped chilli and set aside.

Cut the remaining vegetables — the carrots into bite sized sticks, the capsicum into strips 3-4cm long and 1cm wide, the mushrooms into halves or quarters depending on their size, and the beans into 5cm lengths. Mix together and set aside.

Finely chop the onion and garlic. The garlic is better chopped than squeezed through a garlic crusher — it will more likely burn if crushed. Set aside.

Flour the chicken pieces. An easy way to do this is to add a couple of tablespoons of plain flour to a plastic bag. Make sure there are no holes in the bag. Add the chicken pieces, twist the plastic bag closed, and shake. Flour the chicken when you are ready to cook it, otherwise, the flour will absorb the moisture, making the pieces soggy and sticky.

Take a big heavy saucepan, cover the bottom with olive oil, and brown the chicken pieces, a few at a time. If you do them all at once, they will boil in their own juice instead of going brown. Set aside.

Add more oil to cover the base, and heat up the saucepan again.

Add the onion and garlic, and cook till they are between transparent and golden. They should not go brown. Stir from time to time.

Add the brunoise.

Stir everything together, and let it settle for 2-3 minutes.

Add the tomato paste and mix it in thoroughly, stirring as it cooks, for 3-4 minutes.

Add the wine and stir in for 2-3 minutes.

Add the crushed tomatoes from the can and stir in for 2-3 minutes.

Add the herbs, remembering to be generous: oregano, thyme, fresh basil, bay leaves, smoked paprika, cloves and grated nutmeg.

Add the large pieces of vegetables and stir in.

Add the chicken pieces and the olives and mix thoroughly.

Add stock to almost cover the mix.

Season to taste with salt and pepper.

Cover with a lid, bring to the boil, lower the heat and simmer for 45 minutes, or until the carrot is fully cooked through.

Serves 6, or 4 if you are all very hungry.

Serve with plain potato mash or pasta. As a rough guide, for two people we use 150g of dried pasta, or 300g of fresh pasta.

4

PATAGONIA

'Left or right?' Pedro asked.

We were in the middle of Patagonia, and had not seen another car or human being in three hours.

I'd been delighted when Pedro's offer for the apartment was accepted. I always felt reassured when a plan worked out, and we were right on schedule.

It was even better to know that the architect, Andrés, had been granted access to the apartment. Pedro had tracked him down with the help of a few cousins, and Andrés had enthusiastically agreed to prepare alternative designs for the kitchen – after all, Pedro's *Café Tortoni Serviette Plan* was only one of the possible layout options. Andrés had undertaken to show us his drawings when we moved in, so that we could envisage them 'in situ.'

The in-laws had insisted we stay with them for the five-week property settlement period, but we'd already spent three weeks in their home. We didn't want to impose on their hospitality any longer, but if we moved out, Pedro said they'd be offended, and they'd ask, 'Why pay for hotel accommodation when you can stay here?'

It was only by leaving Buenos Aires for the full five weeks, rather than staying in a hotel in the city, that we could avoid the discomfort of offending them.

The solution was Patagonia. A few months before, Pedro and I had found that we shared a dream to visit that southern region. Now was the perfect time to explore it together.

We were sure that within five weeks, we could drive all the way to Ushuaia and back. We'd drive southwest to Bariloche, then pick up the *Ruta 40* or 'Route 40' and continue south. We'd cross into Chile to visit *Torres del Paine* national park, and continue down to Punta Arenas. From there we'd take the car ferry to Tierra del Fuego, then drive back north along the

Argentine coast. The *Ruta 40*, running north-south through Argentina and skirting the Andes mountain range, was described in many travel magazines as one of the world's most spectacular drives. Altogether we would drive at least seven thousand kilometres, nearly twice the width of Australia.

Pedro borrowed a 1989 Toyota four-wheel drive from one of his primary school friends, and we gathered the necessary gear. We'd been told that driving through Patagonia was like driving through the Australian outback – fraught with risk. Not only could we get lost or suffer engine failure, but the stony roads could slash a tyre to pieces. We'd equipped ourselves with reserves of additional petrol, spare parts, tyres, a compass, maps, and two large plastic drums of drinking water. And at all times we had enough food to last us a few days. We were ready for anything.

So there we were, in one of the most isolated regions of South America. The treeless stretches of red earth were reminiscent of the Simpson Desert in Australia, except that this landscape was flat. Flat as a red pancake.

And now we were faced with a challenge. The dirt road forked without giving us any clue as to which way to go. There was one road sign. It displayed a two-headed arrow informing us that we had to go either to the right, or to the left, but neither direction gave the name of a town.

To the right, an armadillo ran across the road, its carapace remaining level to the ground as its little legs flashed past each other in a haze. Then it hurried along the road, away from us.

I looked to the left.

Nothing.

The car engine hummed. Pedro switched it off. The desert air whistled around us, red dust rising in small clouds.

'It looks as though we're here.' I pointed to the map where a spidery line split into two. 'The road forks. The compass says left is east. That's where the next petrol station is – an hour's drive.'

Pedro leaned over to take a closer look.

'We've travelled two hundred kilometres, so it makes sense. The only fork for miles. So, left? Or follow the armadillo?'

'Left,' I said, hoping he was joking about the alternative.

He turned the key in the ignition, the engine hummed once again, and we turned left, leaving the armadillo silhouetted against the red earth.

*

A week later, having spent two days visiting the magnificent *Perito Moreno* glacier near Calafate in Argentina, we crossed into Chile at a mountain pass near the Chilean village of Cerro Castillo. That afternoon we drove into one of the most spectacular national parks in South America, *Torres del Paine*.

So far the trip had been fabulous. We'd driven through stunning and contrasting landscapes – the open *pampa* in Buenos Aires province, the beautiful lake district around the city of Bariloche, and further south, the wide-open plains of Patagonia fringed by the Andes Mountains to the west. We'd met friendly people, bought delicious fruits in the Rio Negro irrigation area and in Los Antiguos, and visited isolated one-horse towns such as Bajo Caracoles.

> *Había dos gatos locos.*
> There were two mad cats.
> Meaning: It was deserted.

In the less barren areas of Patagonia, we'd encountered large mobs of sheep, many with lambs – the famous and tasty *corderito patagónico*, or 'Patagonian lamb' – and from time to time we'd spotted *gauchos*, or 'Argentine cowboys,' herding cattle or horses.

In *Torres del Paine*, we would spend four nights far inside the park, at a campsite beside *Lago Azul*, or 'Blue Lake.'

I couldn't wait to see more of the park over the oncoming days – its wildlife, mountains, lakes, glaciers, and rivers. Since entering the park we'd seen herds of *guanacos* – cousins of the *llama* – grazing on hillsides, condors flying above, foxes crossing the road, and a lonely skunk strolling near the road toward a stream. Perhaps we'd be lucky enough to see a puma.

The only drawback was the fierce wind. At one point, I wanted to stop and take a photo, but the force of the wind made it impossible to open the car door. Pedro managed to open his door and take the shot. On the park's dirt roads, the car threw up huge clouds of dust. Occasionally, when we travelled in the same direction as the wind, one of those clouds would overtake and envelop us, obscuring the view.

By the time we reached the camping grounds late in the afternoon, the wind had abated. The grounds were deserted – the official holiday season didn't start until January.

We parked the car by the shore of *Lago Azul*, and carried our gear through a grove of Patagonian cypress trees to a campsite further along the lake.

Pedro set about preparing our dinner, and I pitched the tent. I took my time because the superb view was so distracting. Our campsite looked across the cobalt blue lake to the three colossal granite towers of the *Paine*. The towers soared majestically, flaunting their intense deep blue against a cloudless sky. It didn't surprise me that *Paine* was the word for 'blue' in the indigenous *Tehuelche* language. Or that these impressive towers gave their name to the national park. The towers dominated a chain of granite mountains beneath them, and in turn, the mountains dwarfed gentler hills of open heath and light woodland that stretched along the edge of the lake.

We ate our dinner by the campfire, watching the colours darken as twilight progressed. Shallow waves lapped the gravelly shore, a light breeze whispered in the trees, and a lonesome owl hooted nearby.

*

The next morning after breakfast the wind picked up again. We gathered objects that might fly away, and stored them inside the tent.

Looking forward to a day exploring the wilderness, we walked through the cypress grove to the car. Pedro settled into the driver's seat and turned the starter key in the ignition.

There was not a sound.

Oh oh, I thought.

'Damn. Battery's flat. The car's dead,' he said.

I'd already guessed as much. I shivered slightly, and glanced across the water. The towers were no longer an idyllic backdrop. They loomed menacingly over the landscape. The wind whistled madly around us. The branches above swayed ominously. Gusts of air flattened the grass near the lake in waves. I felt a sense of foreboding.

Pedro sighed. 'The battery's almost new,' he said. 'I must have forgotten to turn the lights off when we took out the camping gear.'

He fiddled with a few switches – lights, radio, the ignition again – and said, 'Yes, I think that's what it was. At least, I hope so – otherwise it'll be more complicated.'

His matter-of-fact voice and attitude contrasted wildly with my sense of apprehension. I didn't want 'complicated' engine problems. Not here, in the middle of nowhere. It was too easy to envision disaster scenarios, like being stuck for days, or weeks. Or being towed to civilization. This was the most isolated spot we'd stayed in. The nearest establishment was the park headquarters, about fifteen kilometres away. The nearest town was Puerto Natales, our next stop, over one hundred kilometres south.

Until now, I hadn't been concerned about the loneliness of the Patagonian landscapes, lack of human settlements, or our need for self-sufficiency. We always had enough food and water. And Pedro was a car lover and a great mechanic.

Un tipo tuerca.
A nut person – as in 'nuts and bolts.'
Meaning: A car-crazy person.

He tended to carry out intricate repairs on his car, or any car, and to check the instructions *after*. As he always said, 'I want to make sure I did it correctly.'

There had been only one mechanical problem on this trip, an unbelievable feat considering the thousands of kilometres of dirt roads. That was in Bariloche, where Pedro found an oil leak in the front wheel area, and took the car to a mechanic. Pedro determined the cause before the mechanic did. He told me later that it related to the front-wheel-drive locking-hub system, which meant nothing to me. But the mechanic was so impressed that he didn't charge us for the repair.

However, our current situation was potentially serious. I looked at Pedro, who looked at me in turn.

He said, 'We can't push-start the car from here, the ground's too uneven and it'd be uphill. It's too heavy anyway – almost two tons.'

Hiding my anxiety as well as I could, and trying to take my 'cool as a cucumber' cue from him, I answered, 'I guess we walk to park headquarters. And if it's only a flat battery, we have jumper leads.'

'Yep – hopefully a kind person will bring us back so we can use their car to jump start ours.'

*

We locked the car and set off with daypacks containing water, food, and our rain jackets, along the road we'd driven only yesterday afternoon. We figured that we could easily make the fifteen kilometres in three hours.

By the time we'd climbed two kilometres along the road that led out of the valley, my feeling of trepidation had lessened. There was sure to be someone at the park headquarters who could help, and Pedro was now more confident that our only concern was a flat battery. I felt a sense of purpose and adventure as we strode along. We were more exposed up here, and the wind almost bowled us over with each gust, but it was exhilarating to be breathing the fresh air, to be surrounded by amazing views and to glimpse herds of *guanacos* in the distance.

'Hey,' Pedro said, pointing at the next rise. An unruly dust cloud moved toward us. As quickly as it formed, it was dispersed by the wind.

'Look, we're in luck. I bet it's a car.'

We *were* in luck. The roof of a camper van nosed above the rise, and soon the whole vehicle came into view. Its dust cloud swirled and disappeared skyward as it slowed to a stop beside us. Four faces inside the car looked up at us – Mum the driver, Dad in the front passenger seat, and two daughters in the back. All had fair skin and blue eyes. The girls were aged about fifteen and ten, and the youngest had a sprinkling of freckles across her nose.

The mother rolled down her window, her brow furrowed, and said, '*Buenos días.*'

Pedro must have recognized an accent, because he answered, '*Buenos días*. Do you speak English?'

The creases in her brow disappeared and she smiled.

'Yes,' she said. 'I hope you can help us. Is there a campsite nearby?'

I recognized a Dutch accent. The family, we soon found, had escaped the cold of Amsterdam to drive through southern Chile and Argentina. They'd left one of the park hotels early to seek out a campsite, and were very pleased that we could help them – and that they could help us.

Back at the campsite, Pedro and the father, Daan, attached jumper leads from their battery to ours. I held my breath as Pedro turned the key in the ignition.

The engine kicked over and roared to life.

I sighed with relief and crossed my fingers whilst Pedro did further checks. When he gave the 'all clear,' I was overjoyed.

We invited our new friends to a fireside dinner to thank them, and to celebrate the revival of our engine.

*

For the next two days we explored the park, taking endless photos of the jaw-dropping scenery. The *Cuernos del Paine*, or 'Horns of Paine' – a group of jagged, snowy granite peaks over two thousand metres high – dominated the landscape. They were reflected in turquoise lakes, they provided a picture post-card scene against a blue sky strewn with gorgeous lenticular clouds, and they formed a perfect backdrop to herds of grazing *guanacos*. We drove to *Lago Grey* or 'Grey Lake' to admire icebergs broken off from *Grey Glacier* on its northern edge. The icebergs were sculpted into bizarre shapes by the wind, waves and rain. From time to time we stopped the car to watch condors soaring upward in expanding circles. And when we parked in a forested area for a walk, we immediately heard the rat-a-tat drumming of a Magellanic woodpecker, and caught glimpses of a male with its stunning red head feathers.

In the evenings we shared dinner and stories with our companions.

Too soon, it was the fourth morning after our arrival in the park, and time to strike camp. We regretfully bade our friends goodbye, and continued south to Punta Arenas.

*

In Punta Arenas late that afternoon, we cruised the streets looking for a hotel, as we had in many other towns. For someone who needed certainty as much as I did, this 'accommodation on the run' approach of Pedro's had been a new and unsettling experience.

Before leaving Buenos Aires, I asked, 'Shouldn't we book hotels for the first week? And week by week after that?'

Pedro gave me an incredulous look. 'But we won't have any flexibility. It would be too complicated, firstly booking, and then cancelling the bookings if we change our mind . . . do you really want to do that?'

'But I've never been anywhere without booking ahead,' I said. 'What if we don't find a place to stay?' I was way outside my comfort zone. I imagined us spending nights in the tent beside the road – not my idea of a holiday.

'We *will* find places to stay,' said Pedro.

I wanted to give him the benefit of the doubt, so despite my anxiety, I gave in. On the first night, in the town General Acha, we found a hotel immediately. The next night in San Martín de los Andes, we found a cabin outside town after half an hour. In Bariloche, it took longer but we found a clean, economical hotel and a room with a view of the lake. Gradually I became accustomed to his approach, even though my feeling of unease increased each time we rejected a hotel – it meant that the list of remaining hotels was shorter. And 'Pedro the thrifty' didn't always make it easy.

> *Era gasolero.*
> He used diesel.
> Meaning: He was thrifty.

'This is perfect,' I'd say, only to be met with, 'Nope, too expensive.'

> *Te sacan los ojos.*
> They take your eyes out.
> Meaning: Very expensive.

'But it's the equivalent of only five dollars more than last night,' I'd protest in vain.

Eventually I agreed to embrace Pedro's 'don't plan' and 'pay the least possible' approach. I told him that he could be the accommodation boss on one condition – I would be the undisputed food-timing boss. There would be no insubordination on either side.

> *Donde manda capitán no manda marinero.*
> Where a captain gives orders, a sailor doesn't.
> Meaning: The person in charge 'calls the shots.'

Regular meal times were essential for me. But Pedro often forgot that I needed to eat at lunchtime. Being a highly active person, he regularly skipped lunch and was ravenous by dinner.

*

In Punta Arenas, it took an hour to find a charming bed-and-breakfast run by a Croatian mother and daughter. They welcomed us into their home as though we were family, and recommended a restaurant that was cosy and inviting.

The restaurant offered a range of dishes including *guanaco*, ostrich-like *ñandú*, and *castor* or 'beaver' – introduced from Canada to Tierra del Fuego, where the animal became a major pest – and of course, Patagonian lamb. We settled into seats beside an open fire. It felt odd to have a roaring fire in the middle of summer, but the evenings were considerably cool. We were further south than the southernmost coast of New Zealand, and not far from Antarctica.

After the main course, I saw *leche asada* on the menu.

'What's *leche asada*?' I asked Pedro.

'It's like *flan* – you know, *crème caramel* – but it's baked in the oven instead of in a bain-marie, and ends up with a more solid top.'

'That's for me. I'm loving our holiday within a holiday, aren't you?' I said, as I examined the names of other desserts – in case I'd missed one. *Mote con huesillo* and *chirimoya alegre* sounded interesting.

Pedro wasn't responding.

I looked up and my eyes met his. He smiled.

'So am I. You've been incredibly relaxed on this trip. I can't believe it. You were stressed out of your mind at work. I was so relieved when you left that job,' he said.

'Was it *that* bad?'

He continued, 'Haven't you noticed that since we left Sydney, you've not once mentioned your work? As though it was never really a part of you.'

'Haven't I?'

I must have looked taken aback, because he dropped the subject. Even after a few years together, and our career conversations in Sydney before leaving, I wasn't used to talking about myself to Pedro.

As I dozed off that night, I asked myself whether Pedro was right. Was I relaxing? Maybe. Only a short time ago, I wouldn't have set off anywhere without planning all aspects of a journey, and yet here we were, arriving in strange towns without any idea of where we'd spend the night.

*

We took advantage of the tax-free zone in Punta Arenas to buy new tyres, having sacrificed three to the stones *en route* – one for every thousand kilometres of rough roads.

Leaving Punta Arenas, we caught the car ferry to Tierra del Fuego and drove along dusty roads to Ushuaia, the stepping-off point for Antarctic

51

tours. In Ushuaia, we took the boat trip on the Beagle Channel and chugged across the local national park on a steam train called the 'Train of the End of the World.' Pedro didn't mention my stress level again, and we reverted to our light-hearted camaraderie. I treasured our time together.

As we drove up the coast of Argentina, on our way to the Valdes Peninsula, I saw a label, *Monumento Natural Bosques Petrificados*, on the map. Neither of us had ever seen a *bosque petrificado*, or 'petrified forest', and we decided to investigate. We followed the signposts and turned off the paved road into a national park. A sign beside the dirt road told us that we needed to drive forty-five kilometres to the park headquarters, where we could walk to the 'forest'.

'How much further?' Pedro asked me, as another *ñandú* ran ahead of the car, diverting attention from its chicks. It must have been the tenth one that we'd come across on this out-of-the-way road. The *ñandú* ran frantically, grey feathers flaming out behind, and white under-feathers spreading out like the layers of a petticoat.

I checked the map. 'Should be half an hour or so. But it's late and the park may be closed.'

'Didn't the sign say it closed at five thirty?' Pedro said.

'Yes. It's a quarter to five already.'

Pedro 'alias Fangio' sped up, skidding around corners in controlled slides while my knuckles whitened on the door handle.

¡Agarrate, Catalina!
Hold on Catalina!
Meaning: Watch out! In the 1940s, a Buenos Aires circus audience would shout this to a trapeze artist, Catalina, because three of her relatives had died in trapeze displays.

Pedro had recently told me about Juan Manuel Fangio, Argentina's most famous Formula One driver, who'd won the World Driver's Championship five times. I tried not to think of him or the speed we were driving. Instead I tried to focus on the scenery – gently rolling hills covered by dry, red earth, with occasional jagged rocks rising up between clumps of scrubby bushes.

We arrived at the park headquarters intact. I knew nothing about petrified forests, but soon learned that they were extremely rare. Over one hundred and fifty million years ago, before the Andes Mountains were formed, a Jurassic forest of immense monkey-puzzle trees flourished under the rain that washed across from the Pacific Ocean. A few million years later, volcanic storms buried the forest under ash and the trees petrified. Gradually, erosion exposed them.

'Stand in front of that one,' I asked Pedro, and I levelled the camera. I couldn't believe the size of the tree trunk. It was one hundred metres long, with a diameter of over two metres. Annual growth rings were clearly delineated in contrasting hues of yellows and browns. Around the base of the tree were petrified wood chips. It was as though a woodcutter had only recently hacked at the tree and left the wood chips lying around the base, but when we picked them up they were solid stone. There were hundreds of trunks similar to this one. We could see the ends sticking out of the earth all around us. It was fascinating.

Back at the information shed, we saw the park rangers tidying up and building a fire for an *asado* or 'barbecue.' We were the only sightseers left in the park, and knew that it was time to get going.

In less than a week, our Patagonian adventure would be over. On the way back to Buenos Aires, we would stop at the Valdes Peninsula, made famous by David Attenborough's dramatic documentary of orca whales hunting sea lion pups. And two days later, we'd be back in Buenos Aires and moving into the apartment.

Patagonia had been all that I'd expected. It was vast, spectacular, and empty. We'd shared great times and challenges in one of the most isolated regions of South America.

> *La pasamos bomba.*
> We went like a bomb.
> Meaning: We had a fantastic time.

We had survived wayfaring, but would our compatibility endure renovating?

Flan con dulce de leche y crema – Crème Caramel with Caramel and Cream

In Punta Arenas, I had chosen _leche asada_ for dessert. It was similar to _crème caramel_, called _flan_ in Latin America. Pedro told me that _flan_ was offered as a dessert in most restaurants in Argentina. Other very popular desserts were _budín de pan_ or 'bread and butter pudding,' _panqueque con dulce de leche_ or 'pancake with caramel,' _ensalada de fruta_ or 'fruit salad' and _frutillas con crema_ or 'strawberries and cream.'

This is an easy recipe for _flan_. It can be served warm, or cold from the fridge.

Ingredients
600ml milk
250cc sugar
4 eggs
1 tsp vanilla essence

Method
Have your baking mould or moulds nearby on a wooden board so that you don't burn the counter. You can use 8 small individual moulds, 6 large individual moulds, or one large mould. If you use one mould it will need to contain at least 1.5 litres.

Prepare the bain-marie. A bain-marie means the following: get a roasting pan with a flat bottom with sides of 5-6cm or higher. Add hot water. Place an empty mould in the hot water to make sure that the water will come up to a quarter of the height of the mould when cooking. This method of cooking will mean that your _flan_ will cook uniformly due to the heat of the surrounding water. Remove the empty mould from the bain-marie.

Place the bain-marie in the oven at 120°C so the water remains hot.

Take half the sugar and heat it in a small saucepan, constantly stirring over a medium heat with a wooden spoon. Stir and stir and it will start to melt. Be very careful because the sugar will be much hotter than boiling water.

The sugar will start to turn brown, i.e. to turn into toffee. Many people stop here, but you can continue until the sugar is slightly darker. There's only a short space of time between 'darker' and 'burnt.' The dark sugar may start to boil and if so, it is a bit past the stage you want, but I prefer the taste – less sweet, and slightly smoky. Pedro prefers it to be less cooked and therefore sweeter. Very carefully pour it into the base of the mould or moulds.

In another small saucepan, add the milk and the rest of the sugar. With a wooden spoon, stir over a medium heat until the mixture is hot but not boiling. It must not boil. Remove from heat.

Crack the eggs into a bowl. If possible, use a bowl that has a lip for pouring. Lightly whisk until the mixture is a uniform colour.

Mix in the heated milk/sugar mixture.

Add the vanilla and mix in.

From the bowl, pour the mixture through a sieve into the mould or moulds. The sieve will catch any bits of egg that have not mixed in — the transparent bits that are best left out.

Take the bain-marie out of the oven, place the mould or moulds in it, and place the bain-marie back in the oven for half an hour. Pedro sets the oven at 150°C, so that the _flan_ boils, leaving small holes within the mass when it solidifies. I prefer it to be completely uniform and for this a lower heat is recommended.

If you've used one large mould, you will need to leave it for longer than half an hour. If the water in the bain-marie was cold, you will also need to leave it for longer.

You can tell it's cooked if you insert the tip of a skewer and it comes out clean.

Take the bain-marie out of the oven, remove the moulds and cool.

When ready to serve, get a knife with a thin blade and very carefully separate the _flan_ from the edge of the mould. Of course, this depends on your mould — if it's non-stick you should not have to do this. Hold the mould in one hand. Place a plate upside down on top of the mould, tight against the mould. Then turn the whole thing over. You should hear a 'plop' as it falls onto the plate. When you take the mould off, caramel sauce will flow down the sides.

Serve with cream, and, if you want to do the 'Argentine thing,' also serve with a dollop of _dulce de leche_ (see Chapter 14, Meringues with Caramel).

5

UNSTEADY BEGINNINGS

It was eight weeks after our arrival in Argentina, and three days after our return from Patagonia, when we moved into our home-away-from-home.

On the way from the in-laws to the apartment, we bought sheets and blankets and organized a bed and mattress for delivery that afternoon.

I could hardly believe my eyes when we saw the foyer of our building. It had been renovated in record time, and was light and airy and smart. Our spirits high, we took the elevator to the fifth floor.

But when we opened the door of the apartment, my heart sank. It was so, so small. The living room now struck me as tiny and drab, the parquet tired and stained, the walls dirty. The kitchen walls were greasy, the oven filthy, the laundry area a ruin. All the light fixtures were gone, as agreed with the previous owners. Not even a light bulb remained. That important criterion, 'unrenovated,' immediately lost its romance.

And not only that. We'd inspected a place with furniture, pictures on the walls, bookshelves, a television, even flowers on the table. A family home with a large bed in the main bedroom, two small beds and a cot squashed into the second bedroom, a high chair in the kitchen, and brightly coloured toys spilling from a basket in the living room. Now it was empty, hollowed out, cheerless.

Despite this, Pedro's step lightened as he sauntered around the living room. He whistled a few notes. He was home.

Our home in Sydney felt far away. I longed for that feeling of coming back to our cosy old apartment – the warm hues that welcomed us, my Granny's piano tucked into a corner of the living room, the familiar furniture, the comfortable sofa, the posters of art exhibitions we'd been to, the view of the harbour, the eucalyptus branches swaying outside in the breeze. Even our little kitchen with its battered saucepans and the colourful Italian platters hanging on the wall. On Saturday mornings, the familiar aroma of coffee, and of freshly baked bread from the French patisserie nearby. And on Saturday afternoons, the yacht races on the harbour. Meanwhile, the chit-chat with neighbours, and the proximity of family and friends.

We can go home now, we've had our holiday, I thought.

Pedro looked at me, obviously thrilled. But when he saw my face, his expression changed to one of concern, and he gave me a big hug. Then he grabbed my hand and ushered me out the door.

*

Down in the street, life went on as normal, and I cheered up. The farther we walked from our building, the more I saw the apartment for what it was – a place to stay when we visited from home. All we needed to do was to change its drab emptiness into a cheery welcoming space. I told myself to be positive.

Usually I daydreamed as I walked, but today I made myself notice my surroundings. As part of my being positive, I wanted to get the feel of our city block – the sooner it became familiar, the easier it would be to settle in.

At the base of the building next door was a butcher, and next door to that, a baker, and then, instead of a candlestick maker, a lamp shop. On the other side of the road I saw a hairdresser, a stationery shop, and, interestingly, a luthier's workshop. We crossed over to have a look. There was a sign on the door saying, *'Vuelvo en media hora'* 'Back in half an hour.' Through the dusty window, we saw flat wooden violin shapes hanging along one of the walls, and rows of shelves and tools along the others. A polished violin was propped on a central workbench. How marvellous to know there was a music maker close by.

We crossed back to our side of the road, passed a greengrocer, and arrived at the corner ice cream shop. We must have been thinking in tandem, because we gravitated in unison toward the door. We stepped inside. It was busy, with all the tables occupied – couples canoodled, babies cried, retired friends reminisced.

Pedro knew how to lift my spirits. I loved chocolate ice cream, and there were fifteen chocolate flavours to choose from. Three of those flavours were plain – milk chocolate, white chocolate and dark chocolate. To make six more flavours, either almonds or rum-soaked raisins were added to each of those plain flavours. Then there was *chocolate rocher*, containing hazelnut, or *marroc*, a mixture of white and milk chocolate mixed with peanut paste, or *mousse de chocolate* containing eggs, sugar and vanilla. And the list went on.

I was in heaven. I chose a cone with *chocolate oscuro con almendras* or 'dark chocolate with almonds,' and Pedro chose *crema de higo con nuez* or 'fig cream with walnuts.'

57

In no time, we were laughing and joking with the shopkeeper. He told us that Italians had introduced ice cream to Argentina, though I was sure Pedro already knew this.

As we left the shop with our ice creams, I grabbed one of their home-delivery leaflets.

'Let's take the long way home,' Pedro said. 'We can walk around the block and explore the neighbourhood.'

I murmured agreement as I skimmed through the leaflet.

'I can hardly believe there are sixty flavours.' I said. 'What's *quinoto*?'

'Just as it sounds,' he replied. 'It's Spanish for the Italian *chinotto*. Let me see and I'll tell you the others.' I handed him the leaflet.

Pedro became engrossed in the translation exercise saying, 'Cumquats with whisky, zabaglione with chocolate-coated almonds, banana split, yoghurt with mixed berries, candied chestnut, caramel with chocolate chips . . .'

We heard a voice say, *'Buen día.'* We both looked up in surprise, and I recognized the elderly man that Pedro had met in the real estate office. He nodded and kept walking.

'We're already part of the neighbourhood,' said Pedro proudly. 'Soon people will think we live here permanently.' He was elated, as though he'd already settled in.

'Perhaps,' I answered, thinking that it would be a long time before I'd feel 'settled.' I saw myself as a visitor, learning more about my husband as I tried to understand his country, its society, its history, and its idiosyncrasies. And its ice cream.

A few minutes later, we saw a fabulous one-storey house. 'Look Pedro, Art Nouveau. Lovely.'

We stopped to admire it. Seven-storey apartment buildings hemmed it in on either side. As with almost all the houses and apartment blocks I'd seen in Buenos Aires, and in typically European fashion, its front wall followed the building line. The pattern on the wrought iron outer door was of three curved and 'flowering' lines that joined as a curved triangle. Above the door was a face carved in stone, with flowing hair. A huge arched window comprised three vertical sections, each surrounded by gently curved wooden frames.

'I wonder who lived here,' I said, 'and how life was, in those old cobblestone days.'

'I wouldn't mind living there myself, right now,' said Pedro. 'As for who *used* to live here, I'm sure you'll unearth stories about buildings here, as you do whenever we travel,' he said.

I hoped so. I longed to see more of Buenos Aires and its famous buildings, but that was unlikely in the near term, whilst we were busy renovating.

I was day dreaming again. The ever-practical Pedro brought me down to earth.

'By the way, we need light bulbs,' he said.

We arrived back at the apartment tired and happy, armed with light bulbs. After our short excursion, the interior didn't look so forbidding.

*

The next morning, we woke up to the insistent ringing of Pedro's cell phone. He reached out to answer. It was his Mum.

He said, 'Is it ten o'clock *already*? You must be joking. It can't be *that* late.'

I jumped up and opened the external shutters a crack. Blinding light flooded the room. No wonder we'd slept in. It wasn't only because the room was pitch black when the shutters were down – it was also because it was so quiet, being at the back of the building. We'd slept through rush hour.

Shading his eyes from the glare, Pedro glanced over at me. 'Yes Catherine's fine . . . Yes it's all good. Pillows would help but . . . No, it's okay, we'll buy them today, we're going shopping, you don't have to lend us any . . .'

As he hung up, Pedro said to me, 'We can expect a few more of those calls from the relatives. Let's get going before they start. Or should I turn the phone off?'

'And offend them? I don't think so. And you need to call the architect – his name was Andrés, wasn't it?'

After a decent night's sleep, my usual optimistic mood had returned, and it improved further when Pedro told me that Andrés would come by later in the day.

We split the shopping list between us. Pedro's list included furniture and saucepans. Mine included pillows and crockery. We set off, and at the entrance to the bed-linen shop, we agreed to meet in an hour. Pedro went on his way and I stepped inside.

*

Within thirty seconds I knew that a solo shopping trip was a disastrous idea. Yesterday it had been easy. Pedro had done all the talking.

I asked for *almohadas* or 'pillows.' The helpful sales assistant pointed toward shelves stacked with pillows and related items, all protected in plastic wrapping. She retrieved one of the packets and said, *'También tenemos almohadas con xxx xxx xxx pero xxx xxx.'*

I must have looked puzzled, whereupon she said, *'Xxx xxx xxx y xxx.'*

59

Era chino para mi.
It was Chinese for me.
Meaning: It was all Greek to me.

I was clearly out of my depth. I didn't want to risk buying seven duvet covers and twenty pillowcases, then asking Pedro to sort out the whole sorry mess.

Sacar las papas del fuego.
To take the potatoes out of the fire.
Meaning: To get someone out of trouble.

I chickened out of my pillow-buying task.

Me fui al mazo.
I folded – as in a deck of cards.
Meaning: I chickened out.

'*Gracias,*' I said. '*Lo voy a pensar*' 'I'll think about it.'
My luck improved at the crockery shop. I managed to ask whether saucers were included in the set.

'*Voy a averiguar,*' said the assistant, frowning, and disappeared into the back room.

A few weeks earlier, I would have been concerned that I had offended him, and that that I'd never see him again, because '*averiguar*' sounded menacing with all its four syllables. It would have been way out of my league of Spanish verbs and I might have assumed it was an insult or jibe. However, I was in luck – and it was all due to Agatha Christie. On our Patagonia trip I'd attempted one of her novels translated into Spanish, and the detective had spent his time *averiguando* or 'enquiring.'

I waited hopefully.

The sales assistant came back with a saucer and said, '*Si, y xxx xxx xxx. Xxx xxx*' 'Yes, and . . .' Whereupon he tightened his grip on the saucer and whacked it against a steel post. I winced and closed my eyes, waiting for a thousand saucer pieces to hit the floor.

Nothing happened. I opened my eyes to see an intact saucer in his hand. I figured that he'd been extolling its strength. I bought the set.

I may be okay at shopping after all, I thought, *but only if I concentrate on physical demonstrations.*

Pedro found me before the hour was up and dragged me along to see the antiques that had engrossed him for all that time. He pointed to a sagging sofa and two matching armchairs. They were covered in faded and torn green velvet. Each piece of furniture tilted at a different awkward angle.

Como alpargata de pobre.
Like a poor man's slipper, or espadrille.
Meaning: Very worn and torn.

'Aren't they fantastic?' he said. 'Look at the woodwork, it's so intricate. They're antiques in their own right, walnut, from the early twentieth century, copies of a late eighteenth century style.' He was bubbling over. 'And they're small and delicate, so they won't crowd out the living area.'

His eyes followed mine and he said, 'Don't worry, they're sound. Once we recondition and re-upholster them, they'll look fantastic. They're well priced.'

I put on a bright smile, not wanting to be negative – perhaps they *would* look beautiful *one* day, but at present, they wouldn't exactly brighten up the drab and uninviting feel of the place.

On the other hand, I was well aware that Pedro's antique furniture influence had considerably improved our apartment in Sydney. We'd pooled our furniture resources at first, but subtle changes soon took place. A notable disappearance was my dining room table, a sturdy old office table with metal legs and no aesthetic appeal. A beautiful, one-hundred-year-old, oak table with barley twist legs had appeared in its place. Remembering this, it didn't take me long to relent on the sofa and armchairs, though I covertly decided to drape them with lengths of colourful fabric until they were rejuvenated.

We also bought a bookcase I admired. 'For all the books you're always reading,' said Pedro, 'and because we're going to need temporary shelves in the kitchen.'

When we'd paid for the furniture and organized delivery, Pedro spotted two antique Rembrandt floor lamps.

'Look at these. They'd be a good match with the sofa and armchairs,' said Pedro. They were attractive, and the brass stands and 'candle holders' were all intact.

'They would. But right now, let's get the basics like pillows. We can come back for them when there's room in the apartment – after the renovation. Or get similar ones. It'll only be a few weeks,' I said.

He didn't look particularly convinced, but he dragged himself away to help me with a re-run of the 'pillow-purchase.'

The sales assistant and I greeted each other, and I pointed to Pedro. She turned to him and spoke at a rapid pace. I didn't understand a thing.

Pedro replied as rapidly, and in no time we left the shop with our pillows. It was the first time that I hadn't understood one word of a Spanish conversation. I felt as though my grasp on Spanish was going backward.

'You can't tell me that you were speaking *Spanish* in there,' I teased Pedro.

He grinned, 'I was waiting for you to mention it. I can't believe how much slang she used – even *I* had trouble with a few expressions. I guess the language keeps evolving, and I've been in Australia a long time.'

How long would it be before I'd understand a person speaking quickly in colloquial Argentine? Years? Pedro and I always talked to each other in English. Spanish conversations required so much more concentration and quick thinking in real time, something I took for granted when speaking English. And even though my reading comprehension of Spanish was progressing well, my ear was not accustomed to *hearing* the words. I needed to make the effort, but it wasn't easy.

Saucepans were next on Pedro's list, and with my own list complete, I joined him. But unlike the easy pillow-buying re-run, saucepan buying was a challenge. Pedro, the 'kitchen maestro,' was the chief decision maker, and he knew exactly what he wanted – excellence at the lowest price. It wasn't easy to come by.

I discovered that a saucepan quest was one way to explore the city. That day we tried five homeware shops – two nearby, two downtown, and one in the wealthy *barrio* of *Recoleta*.

> *Más vueltas que un perro antes de echarse.*
> More turns than a dog makes before lying down.
> Meaning: To make something complicated.

In the end, we had to rush back to meet the architect, no saucepans in hand.

*

We ran from the bus stop and arrived as Andrés pressed the buzzer to our apartment. He was smartly dressed in a suit, with an open-necked shirt, his hair fashionably dishevelled, and his beard neatly sculpted.

We greeted him, and Pedro unlocked the foyer door. Pedro and Andrés immediately became engrossed in a political conversation that continued as we waited for the elevator, and then as we travelled to the fifth floor.

My mind wandered, and within seconds I was contemplating the relatives' reactions to our renovation plans. The Sydney relatives were blunt, saying things like, 'Renovation's hard enough in your hometown, especially with a kitchen. You say it's a total knockdown. Why don't you have a nice holiday in Peru instead?'

> *El que mucho abarca, poco aprieta.*
> He who embraces too much, holds little.
> Meaning: Don't bite off more than you can chew.

The Argentine relatives were hardly more supportive. 'Surely you're not going to ruin the rest of your time in Buenos Aires with a renovation?' Some of them started to call our 'trial' the 'ordeal.'

But Pedro and I remained undeterred.

Reading between the lines, my Sydney relatives were probably concerned with my well-being – not only were we 'trialling' a country that was foreign to me, far from family and friends, but we were also embarking on the sort of renovation that could put a relationship through its paces.

Annie had phoned me in Patagonia, one night after she'd been surfing the net. She'd accidentally found an article that linked renovation with divorce rates, and sounded excited when she told me about it. 'It mentions this survey – I don't know how many people it covered – but anyway, it says that over ten per cent of couples have separated or divorced after renovating. And you're doing it in a foreign country! Not only do you *buy* instead of *rent*, but you renovate as well. What's *happened* to you?' I'd raised my eyebrows but I hadn't responded. Annie loved melodrama. It was inconceivable to me that our relationship could fall apart over a renovation.

The elevator arrived at our floor.

'We're keen to see your drawings,' Pedro said as we stepped out.

Andrés smiled his charming smile and patted his briefcase. But in a change from the intense conversation in the elevator with Pedro, he barely looked either of us in the eye. His mixed signals gave me a feeling of foreboding.

When Andrés unfolded his drawings, my heart sank. I blurted out my disappointment. 'It's only one design, and it's not any different.' As I spoke, I despaired of the basic state of my Spanish speaking skills, because I was unable to say what I wanted to, which was, *'You've provided only one design when we expected a number of options. And the design that you provided is exactly the same as the current layout of the kitchen.'* But it was clear that both Pedro and Andrés understood exactly what I was trying to say.

Andrés was unmoved. He said, 'I'll project manage the job for free, but I'll need to add ten per cent to the cost of the materials we choose.'

'But . . . Catherine and I can choose the materials. And I can find the best prices,' Pedro said, nonplussed. 'I do that all the time at work.'

I felt rudderless. Pedro and I looked at each other. How could we have been so wrong? The new Andrés was completely different to the old Andrés. Sadly, we had to tell him that we could not engage him. He left, unperturbed. Pedro's efforts to find an architect, many weeks ago, had been in vain and the exercise had been a complete flop.

Fue como gastar pólvora en chimangos.
It was like wasting gunpowder on *chimangos.*
Meaning: A wasted effort. The *chimango* bird was all feathers and no meat.

Later we heard that Andrés had been asked to design a multi-storey building, with excellent remuneration and bonuses.

> *Le ofrecieron el oro y el moro.*
> They offered him the gold and the Moor.
> Meaning: They offered him the moon and the stars. Rhyming slang.

Pedro's cousins told us that Andrés was ecstatic about his new job, which was understandable, but I couldn't fathom why he hadn't told us earlier that he was no longer available. For us it was 'back to the drawing board.'

*

I didn't know what to think. We had four months left in Buenos Aires. The plan was looking impossible. Were the relatives right, after all?

Pedro was reluctant to discuss it. Frankly, so was I.

I wanted to have a long conversation on a completely different topic. However, Pedro was not being talkative. Perhaps I could call a friend in Sydney. I opened my computer to see who was on Skype. But then I calculated that it was five-thirty in the morning in Sydney, and much too early. Even if friends were awake, they'd be preparing for work.

Hmm. What to do? I needed to feel positive.

I gazed across the centre of our city block to the rear faces of the apartment buildings opposite. The concrete jungle of Buenos Aires continued beyond them, one multi-storey block after another. Along with the bitumen, concrete, and cobblestone roads and paved sidewalks, the buildings formed a massive heat sink that absorbed the sun's heat during the day and held onto most of it overnight, compounding each day's level of heat. I longed for rain.

Rows of balconies adorned the apartment buildings. On one balcony, clothes flapped on a drying rack. On another, a woman sunbaked on a reclining chair. And on another, a man polished a sliding glass door. My eyes followed the line of rooftop terraces and encountered two parallel ropes hanging down the side of a six-storey building. One of the ropes led to a wooden abseiling seat at the level of the fourth storey. The wooden seat was a little crowded, considering that it was shared by a man in overalls, wielding a paintbrush, and a huge can of paint. The second rope seemed to be a safety line, with a knot each few metres. To the left of the painter and above him the wall was white instead of yellow. From time to time he maneuvered the seat down the wall, and his brushstrokes continued.

His seating looked extremely precarious. But it gave me an idea. I would draft a newsletter to my friends, telling them a few odd or lesser-known Argentine facts, and how different it was here to life back home. I'd add humorous stories from our Patagonian trip. Hopefully this would prompt replies from friends, and set up those lines of communication that so far had proved elusive.

I'd omit the 'lack of architect' issue in my covering notes for Mum and Annie. I didn't want Annie to write back with an '*I told you so.*'

*

It took less time than I expected to find topics in my notebook. I'd jotted down details from recent conversations, and from Pedro's comments as he discovered more about Argentina. I wished I knew more, but I was confident that what I described would be interesting.

Not many of my friends would have been aware of Argentina's scientific achievements. Hence my first topic was the launch in September 2015 of a geostationary communications satellite, the ARSAT-2. It was designed, built and operated by an Argentine state-owned high-technology firm. ARSAT-1 had been launched in 2014, and Pedro told me that at least two more satellites were planned. ARSAT-1 and ARSAT-2 were used for telecommunications, data transmission, telephone and television services in Argentina, Chile, Uruguay and Paraguay.

More familiar to friends was Argentina's role as an agricultural powerhouse, but even so, it would have surprised many to know that it was the world's biggest producer of fresh lemons, and the leading exporter of lemon juice. They may also have been surprised to know that Argentina produced more wine than Australia. The country was home to one of the top ten wine-producing companies in the world, *Grupo Peñaflor*. And in 2014, the French Winemaker's Association had awarded 'Best Dry Red' in the world to an Argentine wine, the *Famiglia Bianchi Malbec 2012.*

As for red wine more generally, I'd seen people drinking it with ice. Pedro assured me that the wine in that case would not have been the best dry red in the world, and that people did this because the weather was hot and humid.

I'd also seen people drinking red wine with soda, which reminded me of Spanish sangria. This led to my next topic.

Near our apartment building, there was a shop that sold only two products, the first being fire extinguishers, and the second being soda water in metal siphons. Pedro, the scientist, informed me that this curious association was not as odd as it sounded, considering that they both worked on the principle of pressurized liquid. Fire extinguishers were common because they were compulsory for all cars in the country.

I probably noticed items like fire extinguishers because Pedro loved hardware shops and we always wandered into them, rather than *past* them. One hardware shop offered tools for anyone to use on their purchases before they left. The tools included a saw to cut up lengths of wood, a drill, and a light bulb tester. In the Australian state where we lived – New South Wales, sometimes referred to as the 'nanny state' because of its highly protective legislation – it would have been deemed too dangerous, and too fraught with potential liability, for a business to allow clients to use saws and drills 'on site.'

I took this 'hardware' opportunity to write about the man who was painting the outside of the building opposite.

Moving on to a new topic, lifestyle, the in-laws had told me that many well-heeled *bonaerenses,* or 'people from Buenos Aires,' owned houses in gated communities outside the city. Protected by a perimeter fence and strict security, they breathed in the fresh country air as they played golf, rode horses, or visited the shops on site. There was always a separate entrance for 'the Help.'

I found myself adding a note about pet dogs. I was astounded to see so many of them. There were pet shops everywhere. We saw an advertisement for dog *pan dulce* or 'panettone.' The panettone was beautifully packaged in clear cellophane, with a ribbon.

After listing these observations, I added our stories of the car dying in the middle of Patagonia, and of Pedro and I speeding toward a petrified forest.

*

I polished the words, finalized the newsletter, and sent it off with personalized cover notes.

I sat back, satisfied. But seeing Pedro's gloomy face, the pleasurable feeling faded, and before long I was mulling over the implications of being far from familiar surroundings.

First, there was a time difference with Sydney of thirteen hours, limiting the opportunities for spontaneous interactions with friends. And second, I wasn't used to depending so much on Pedro. He helped with the shopping, with directions, with finding the architect, with everything. I was used to being in charge of my surroundings.

In general when I felt gloomy, I needed to switch off, and my favourite way to achieve that was to find a book and curl up on a sofa. But the sofa was falling apart and I'd read the three books I'd brought from Sydney. Although I'd recently bought another Spanish book to read, right now I wanted one in English. I wanted the familiarity of my own language. Where would I find one? Or would I need to curl up on the sofa with a cold electronic book reader? No, there had to be English books in the city. After all, I imagined that it was similar to London, where you could find anything if you searched for long enough.

I shrugged, tried to clear my thoughts, and resolved to make the most of the remaining four months in Buenos Aires. It was no use wishing we were back in Sydney – no point in regretting the 'trial period.'

Agua pasada no mueve molino.
Water that has passed does not move the mill.
Meaning: It's no use crying over spilt milk.

I'd simply have to get used to calling friends and family at a reasonable time – for them. And I'd get hold of an electronic reader and buy books online – however much I preferred physical books.

In this positive mood, I fell back on my love of classical music, and searched the Internet for cultural events in Buenos Aires. *There must be a concert somewhere in the city*, I thought, sitting on the tottering green sofa, hoping that it wouldn't tilt too much. I had visions of it collapsing to the side and sending me flying onto the balcony, prevented from falling five storeys by the childproof wire mesh.

I held my trusty computer carefully on my lap, and scanned a few Buenos Aires tourist websites, in English. I soon found it more useful to search in Spanish.

Pedro moped around.

'By the way, what's the famous theatre, the one you said had great acoustics?' I asked.

'The *Teatro Colón*, in English that would be the *Columbus Theatre*, after Christopher Columbus, but nobody ever calls it that.'

'Ah, that explains why it keeps popping up. Hmm . . .' I narrowed in on a classical music site called *Cantabile*. It listed the *Teatro Colón's* opera, concert and ballet performances for the month.

'They have free concerts one Sunday each month,' I said.

Pedro brightened up, and came over to have a look. 'Yes, of course. Let's go to one,' he said. 'We need to pick up the tickets on the Friday before.'

'That's right, it says so here, how do you know?' I asked.

'Oh, they've had those free concerts for as long as I can remember. We used to go when I was a kid, learning the violin.'

'I assume the musicians get paid?'

'Of course. Argentine governments have subsidized classical music for decades – and not only those Sunday concerts. I told a friend in Sydney about it last year. He assumed they were rehearsals – being free. Not true.'

I browsed an article in one of the *Cantabile* magazines.

'Huh, did you know that music here is different?' I asked Pedro.

'How so?'

'Well, the first three notes just happen to be, Do Re Mi, like in the song. Not C D E.'

'Like in Europe,' he said.

'Yes, I guess it never entered my mind before.'

I read a few more articles, and investigated the *Teatro Colón's* own website, resolving to pick up free concert tickets one Friday and surprise Pedro. And to see this famous theatre for myself. On our European trips, we'd toured opera houses such as the *Palais Garnier* in Paris and the *Scala* in Milan, and it would be interesting to compare them.

On a more practical note, I determined to figure out the subway and bus systems, instead of following Pedro and waiting until he paid, and then waiting for him to announce where we had to get off. Millions of people used the system, so it couldn't be too hard.

One thing at a time, I thought.

*

The next morning that positive mood persisted. I toured our little apartment and concluded that things were going well for us. After all, we'd found pillows, we were eating off unbreakable crockery, and we had furniture that would one day be comfortable. *And* we were spending time together and not working. All was not lost.

My positive state of mind must have sparked different neuronal pathways in my brain, because now I remembered Pedro telling me of a building project he'd completed at work.

'Do we *need* an architect?' I asked him, as he made our breakfast coffee. 'We already have your *Serviette Plan*. And didn't you project manage the building of that suite of multi-purpose laboratories at the university? Wouldn't it be easy enough to project-manage a kitchen?'

Era pan comido.
It was eaten bread.
Meaning: It was a piece of cake.

Pedro's brow furrowed. 'You know, I've sort of been thinking the same thing. I don't know how time consuming it'll be, or how long it'll take.'

He added, 'But if we can find a builder to organize the plumbing, labouring and electrics, I'm sure that I could manage all the rest – carpenter, windows, bench tops.'

'So all we need is a builder, right?'

'Yes.' With his voice sounding ever more confident, he said, 'And I know exactly where to look for one. Have you noticed the rubble piling up in that skip outside?'

I hadn't of course, but I agreed to loiter with him near the skip after breakfast, in the expectation that a helpful building-type-of-person would turn up, and hoping that no one would think we were odd or crazy.

We hung around near the skip for half an hour before a man appeared from the foyer of the next-door building, pushing a wheelbarrow full of rubble. Pedro introduced us both, and mentioned to him that we were looking for a builder.

'Come up and see us when the boss arrives at ten o'clock tomorrow morning,' the man advised.

So we did. The next day, we followed our new wheelbarrow friend to the service entrance of an apartment, and before we knew it, we were introduced to José, the builder. We found ourselves looking down at a smiling face with a large moustache. But not for long. The face suddenly disappeared in a puff of smoke. José apologized and knocked the ash from his pipe into a sink that lay on the floor.

I could imagine his stocky frame stepping out of a village in Cantabria, pipe in hand. His mop of fair hair contrasted with his dark blue beret, betraying his northern Spanish origins.

Sensing a new client, José launched into a marketing pitch. I understood most of it, though not the technical terms, which Pedro later clarified for me. José said, 'We take off the old tiles, remove the lead pipes and replace them with high-pressure plastic ones, build a plinth for the cupboards, plaster and paint, and so on. Also the electrics.'

'But please put new cupboards in,' he added. 'My client here is saving money – he's putting back the ugly, battered old cupboards when I've finished all this work. It will look horrible.'

'They will definitely be new,' Pedro said. 'It's a complete renovation – nothing stays.'

José beamed up at us, his beret flopping backward as he raised his head. His eyes sparkled, his eyebrows rose, and the edges of his moustache twitched.

Pedro and I glanced at each other. I saw enthusiasm in Pedro's eyes – I could see that he would get on well with José. It looked as if he had indeed found the very man for the job.

As we were leaving, José picked up a strange looking potted plant. 'It's carnivorous,' he explained, when he saw me eyeing it curiously. 'Tiny, isn't it? With the dengue scare, they say we have to get rid of house mosquitoes, and the kids saw a plant eating an insect – on television. I want to show them how small the plant is, and how many you'd need in our house.'

I was fascinated. He continued, 'My analyst says he only needs one of these plants to get rid of mosquitoes. But I'm not convinced – he must live on an upper floor, or keep the windows closed.'

I could hardly believe my ears. When José referred to his shrink, I felt as though I'd been transported to the New York set of a Woody Allen movie. I'd read that Argentina had more analysts per head of population than any other country globally, and now I'd met my first 'patient.'

We said goodbye and Pedro whistled a tune as we took the elevator to the ground floor.

A few days later we saw some shabby old cupboards being hauled into the next-door foyer. We guessed they were to be fitted into a sparkling new kitchen.

> *No comían huevos para no tirar la cáscara.*
> They didn't eat eggs so as not to throw out the shells.
> Meaning: They were tight with money.

José was overseeing the operation. He stepped aside to chat with us, and recommended a carpenter.

'The carpenter is trustworthy,' he said.

> *No te va a meter gato por liebre.*
> He won't give you cat instead of hare.
> Meaning: He won't trick you.

At last we had progress. We had a builder *and* a carpenter.

But still no saucepans.

I was delighted that Pedro had found a builder so easily, but apprehensive about the random way in which we'd found him. After all, Pedro expected him to transform our 'renovators delight' into the holiday home of our dreams. It reminded me of the 'accommodation on the run' approach to our Patagonian trip.

Though I suppose if that worked out, I guess this will, I thought. *So I may as well agree to step off another cliff into the unknown.*

Risotto de pollo y champiñones con ensalada — Chicken and Mushroom Risotto with Salad

Risotto de pollo y champiñones
Chicken and Mushroom Risotto

Now that we had both a builder and a carpenter, it was time for a celebration. We borrowed a wide-based pan from the in-laws and tested our dilapidated kitchen by preparing Pedro's chicken risotto, a dish he'd developed in Sydney as a 'failsafe' quick-to-prepare guest dinner. It was failsafe because, if friends dropped in unannounced, all the ingredients were usually to hand — dried mushrooms could replace fresh ones, and a frozen piece of chicken could be thawed in the microwave.

We bought fresh chicken at one of the three local chicken-only shops, and whilst we chatted to the shopkeeper and other customers I felt again the villagey atmosphere of the <u>barrio</u>. We bought mushrooms and fruit at the greengrocer's, and when I asked for parsley, I was given a bunch for free. Pedro's Mum had told me about this parsley-give-away approach, but I hadn't quite believed it. She'd told me that the amount you were given depended on three things: how much parsley there was, how many items you bought, and how generous the greengrocer felt.

Tonight, in a change from our usual practice, I was the executive chef and Pedro the sous-chef. He prepared the ingredients on the small, cracked marble bench in the kitchen, and handed them to me as I stirred. From time to time, he fetched an item from the bookshelf we'd bought at the antique shop. Its shelves were protected by layers of newspaper, so we could use them to store condiments, onion, garlic, tea, coffee, rice, flour, oil, wine, our cutlery and of course the unbreakable plates. The kitchen cupboards didn't inspire enough confidence for food storage. I imagined gradually filling the bookshelf on our future visits to Buenos Aires, with novels, art books, architecture books, music books, cooking books, travel books . . .

It was lovely to sit for dinner together at the fold-up metal table we'd borrowed from one of the cousins, knowing that in a couple of weeks the renovation would begin.

First, prepare the chicken and marinade.

Ingredients
2 chicken breasts, opened flat to a consistent thickness. You may need to slice the thicker area horizontally with a sharp knife and unfold.
Marinade:
2 tsp soy sauce
Juice of half a lemon
3 tbsp olive oil
Seasoning
2 tsp dried thyme, or fresh thyme

Method

Add the marinade to the chicken and leave in the fridge for half an hour, or more if you have time.

Take from the fridge, let the juice drain from the chicken, and brown the meat on either side. Put in a bowl and set aside.

Then, prepare the rest of the dish.

Ingredients

2 tbsp oil and 30g butter
1 brown onion, finely chopped
1 large clove garlic, chopped
2 cups arborio or carnaroli rice
1 cup white wine, or similar alcohol – see comments in Method
4 cups sliced mushrooms, or 5 cups if you love the flavour. If you can, use a mix of white button mushrooms and Portobello mushrooms. The Portobello mushrooms add a lovely earthy flavour, and this is accentuated in mature mushrooms. When the ring protecting the spores breaks and you can see the 'gills,' the mushrooms lose moisture and this concentrates the flavour.
1 litre warm chicken or vegetable stock. If you use a stock cube, use a quality one and add a little more water than the packet indicates.
½ cup grated Parmesan
3 tbsp parsley
Salt and cracked pepper

Method

Heat the oil and butter in a wide-based pan.

Add the onion and stir until it is covered with the oil, sauté on a medium heat, cover and leave it simmering in the oil and steaming in its own moisture for 3 minutes. You want the onion to be see-through and not brown. You will have to adjust the temperature depending on your own cooktop and pan. A pan with a thick base is best.

Add the garlic, sauté and cover for another 3 minutes. It should not go brown. If you add the garlic at the same time as the onion it will burn, as it cooks faster than the onion.

Add the rice and stir for a few minutes until it goes white.

Add the wine or other alcohol. One cold winter's evening in Sydney we came home tired and hungry. It was already dark outside when we found that we didn't have any white wine for our risotto. Pedro offered to go out and buy some, but although the supermarket was only 3 blocks away I proposed we use a different type of alcohol. We settled on Pisco, a wine-based brandy popular in Chile and Peru. It worked well. You can skip the alcohol and add stock instead.

When you add the wine, the rice releases a creamy substance. Stir for 1-2 minutes.

When the alcohol evaporates, you are ready to start adding the stock, a ladle-full at a time. Stir constantly.

Add salt, but remember that the chicken, the stock and the Parmesan will also have salt so don't overdo it. About 20 minutes after you start to add the stock, you will find that the rice is nearly cooked. If you run out of stock use warm water.

Keep stirring. This not only cooks the rice evenly but makes it creamier.

At this point you have risotto bianco, a basic risotto, and you can add almost anything to finish off the cooking to your taste.

You can add the sliced mushrooms at any stage. I add the mushrooms gradually once the rice is half cooked, i.e. 10 minutes after starting to add the stock. Pedro tends to add them as soon as he starts adding the stock.

Quickly slice the cooked chicken into bite-sized pieces and add to the risotto mix along with any chicken juices.

Give a final stir, and turn off the heat.

Add the Parmesan, parsley and cracked pepper and stir in.

Serve with a knob of butter on top and with grated Parmesan on the table.

Serves 4.

Ensalada
Salad

This is our favourite salad to accompany the risotto.

There is a reason for not making the standard Argentine ensalada mixta or 'mixed salad,' which invariably comprises iceberg lettuce, tomato wedges and sliced raw onion — often, red Spanish onion — with a balsamic vinegar, oil and salt dressing. It's simply because Pedro doesn't like raw tomato or raw onion.

Ingredients
4 handfuls wild roquette
1 small avocado, cut into 1cm pieces
2 mushrooms: one may be a Portobello mushroom. Slice thinly.
¼ red capsicum, sliced thinly and cut into 3-5cm lengths
5 walnuts, each broken into 3-4 pieces, or half a handful of roasted pine nuts
1 dried fig, cut in small cubes

Ingredients for the dressing
Juice of half a lemon
Dash of caramelized balsamic vinegar
1 tsp sugar
Salt and pepper
Small clove of garlic, crushed
Dashes of olive oil

Alternative dressing

Juice of half a lemon
½ tsp mayonnaise
½ tsp sugar
¼ tsp Dijon mustard
Salt and pepper
Small clove of garlic, crushed
Dashes of olive oil

Method

Add salad ingredients to a bowl, and cover with all the dressing ingredients except the oil. Mix lightly. If you add the oil first it will cover the ingredients and they won't take up as much of the flavour from the rest of the dressing ingredients.

Add the oil and toss.

If you want to roast your own pine nuts, heat them in a frying pan and stir constantly until they are a very light brown. Take them out and spread them on a paper towel on a plate, to cool. They will keep cooking for a short while and go a bit browner. They add a lovely nutty flavour and crunchy texture.

Serves 4

6

UPHEAVAL

Our kitchen renovation was about to commence. It was less than two weeks since our hanging-around-the-skip-and-meeting-José morning. José was now officially our builder, and the trustworthy Santiago was officially our carpenter.

We'd been in Argentina two months and three weeks, just shy of the half way mark in our trial period. It was the first week of January, and it was even hotter and more humid than December.

I recollected the events of the last ten days. The in-laws had invited us for dinner on Christmas Eve – the time that Christmas was traditionally celebrated in Argentina. The dinner table was laden with food, and because of the hot weather, all the dishes were served cold. Pedro's Mum made her speciality, an *empanada gallega*, or 'tuna fish pie', and Tía Diana made the traditional *vitel toné*, or 'vitello tonnato'. There was an *ensalada rusa* or 'Russian salad' – a potato salad with peas and carrots – and an *ensalada mixta*, with lettuce, tomato and onion.

Family members arrived in waves, adding more platters to the feast. Children ran around the apartment in all directions. Pandemonium reached crescendo levels just before we sat down to eat, at exactly the time that I'd planned to call home.

Despite the chaos, I carried out my plan, because the time difference was important – it was Christmas morning in Sydney. I wanted to hear Mum and Annie's familiar voices. It was Annie who answered.

'Oh, it's you. I'm putting the ham in the oven, it's a bit awkward to talk now. What's that *noise*? Mum's not here yet. I'll call you later.'

I felt a flash of panic, the severing of familiarity.

'Wait . . .'

But there was nothing I could do. We agreed on a time the next day, and I hung up.

I took a deep breath. It wasn't as though I was unhappy. I was simply flailing about for something familiar.

Australia felt immeasurably distant, the links increasingly tenuous. In Buenos Aires, surrounded by high-rise buildings in the sweltering heat, it was hard to imagine the Sydney beaches, the blue of the harbour, the sea breeze in the evenings, prawns from the fish market for Christmas lunch, or the reverberating *chop chop chop* of propellers on Boxing Day, as news helicopters hovered over the departing yachts in the Sydney to Hobart race.

Apart from the Christmas dinner, Pedro and I spent the time on our own, settling into the apartment and exploring the *barrio*. Greengrocer shops displayed piles of cherries, reminding me of December in Sydney, and I bought a few each time we went out.

It was two weeks since I'd sent my newsletter, and no one had responded except Sarah, with a quick one-liner. Annie and Mum had mentioned the email in our phone call. But none of them had read the newsletter itself.

The New Year crept up on us. Most of Pedro's family and friends had left town early for their summer holidays, and we spent New Year's Eve in the apartment. I left voice messages on Australian phones and sent emails with best wishes for the coming year.

No one replied. I felt cut off, with only a fragile lifeline to home, like one of those astronauts who venture from their space station into a starlit vacuum, attached by a flimsy cable to their companions, the voice connection gradually failing. 'Catherine to base . . . Come in base . . .'

At five minutes to midnight on New Year's Eve, Pedro dragged me up to the terrace of the building. And exactly at midnight the whole city erupted in a cacophony of explosions. Fireworks shot up from family groups gathered at ground level, or on the terraces of other buildings, brilliant colours against the black sky. An amazing exuberance of noise and colour.

I silently wished my family and friends a happy New Year.

*

And in no time, the renovation was upon us.

For the first three days of the first week, José and Santiago measured and tested the walls and columns, and confirmed that the *Serviette Plan* was feasible. They had one big disagreement regarding the dividing wall to the living room. But Pedro resolved the problem over a coffee, and the *Serviette Plan* became the blueprint for our new kitchen.

On the Wednesday, as we dragged the bookshelf out of the kitchen, Pedro dropped the bombshell.

'José told me that it will take eight weeks to gut the kitchen and rebuild.

I can't wait. What do you think?'

I was stunned.

I forgot my usual 'I beg your pardon' stalling tactic. I sank to the floor and leaned against the dividing wall.

Pedro steadied the bookshelf and smiled down at me. He must have thought I was tired, rather than flabbergasted. He radiated enthusiasm. I hadn't seen him as pleased with any 'work' for a long, long time.

Eight weeks was a hell of a long time for Pedro to be working on a renovation. I had thought, probably stupidly, that it would be over in three weeks, at most four. I didn't speak for a minute or two, then . . .

'All day . . . *every* day?' was all I could manage. It came out as a mumble. A surprised mumble.

Pedro's smile faded. He leaned his weight to the bookshelf and pushed it toward the kitchen, saying, 'Grab the other side and we'll have it there in no time.'

'What are you doing?'

'We're moving it back. I can tell from your face that eight weeks is too long.'

How could he tell that from my face? I thought.

'It's not that, it's just that . . .'

'No, it's okay,' said Pedro. 'I shouldn't have even considered it. I'm sorry. We can renovate another time. I'll tell José and Santiago. I got carried away.'

'Wait, wait,' I said. 'Let me think.'

He stopped and looked at me, confused, his forehead crinkled.

I had to close my eyes to think clearly. It was definitely a shock. Two months of renovating, with Pedro caught up in measurements and materials. Two months of me pretending to be interested in a world that was totally alien.

He'd be engaged in the work, and I'd be bored. Not a little bit bored. Really, really, really bored.

Then it dawned on me. Perhaps . . . I tilted my head back, and opened my eyes, meeting his gaze. Perhaps I too could find an activity that I enjoyed – a creative one. The type of activity that I had rarely given myself the time to do. Maybe this was the perfect opportunity. I depended on him way too much. And he'd looked so, so enthusiastic a few minutes ago.

'I think it'll be okay,' I said, smiling involuntarily, though I could feel my smile was tinged with uncertainty.

'Are you sure?'

'Yes.'

'Definitely?'

'Yes,' I repeated, not knowing what I would find to do, but conscious that it was the only way forward, the only way that I would have a chance to really know Buenos Aires on my own terms.

*

And so it was . . . that we proceeded with the renovation.

On Thursday morning, the manual work started. Three of José's men trooped in at eight o'clock, and in no time, two of them were prizing off the green and orange tiles, pounding hammers against chisels against unyielding cement. The third man began to break up the floor with a pickaxe. The reality of living through a renovation hit home – literally.

A cloud of dust gently billowed through the kitchen doorway into the clean but cluttered living area. Pedro and I glanced at each other, and he disappeared into the kitchen. There was a lengthy conversation and I heard a few laughs before Pedro returned, shutting the kitchen door behind him, saying, 'They've agreed to keep it closed.'

I smiled, but soon found that closing the door meant an end to the cross-breeze in the apartment. My smile disappeared. With no air conditioning, the heat was stifling.

Strangers tramped in and out of the apartment all morning with wheelbarrows and buckets and hammers. I hadn't reckoned with the fact that our space would not be 'ours' for eight weeks.

Pedro was immune to the noise and to the lack of privacy, dealing with practical issues as they cropped up. I looked on for a while, trying to show interest, but it wasn't 'me.'

> *No le pidas peras al olmo.*
> Don't ask the walnut tree to produce pears.
> Meaning: You can't make someone an expert at something for which they have no ability.

I felt at a loss. I'd agreed to proceed, and I'd planned to find an activity, but Pedro was already organized and busy, and I was 'at sea.' What sort of activity could I get involved with? I was stumped.

It was strange to feel like a 'hanger on.'

> *Estaba al divino botón.*
> I was there to the divine button.
> Meaning: I was hanging around doing nothing. This expression may refer to using rosary beads without thinking.

I stared at the jumble of items that Pedro's relatives had lent us, including fold-up chairs and the metal table, an old television, and a teapot. They were crammed into a corner to make way for boxes of tools.

The hammering was driving me nuts. I developed a headache. I tried to

78

escape the noise, but it followed me into the second bedroom, which, already minuscule, was now dwarfed by the unsteady antique furniture. I dismissed any thoughts of settling to read a book, went into the main bedroom where it was quieter, took out my diary and wrote the two words UPHEAVAL STAGE.

Then I went for a long walk. Hopefully the fresh air would help me to work out what to do while Pedro enjoyed himself.

In Sydney, we'd always spent our free time together, whether it was a visit to the movies, dinner with friends, or the weekly shopping. If Pedro went to a hardware shop or I went to a bookshop, we'd make it part of an outing. Even when he tinkered with his car, I sat nearby on the lawn reading a book. We were inseparable.

Éramos carne y uña.
We were like flesh and nail.
Meaning: We were joined at the hip.

But now our lives had changed. We were in Buenos Aires rather than Sydney, we were renovating rather than 'working,' and Pedro was busy and unstressed. I was anxious, and needed a friend to talk to.

*

On Friday Pedro proposed an outing. He was perturbed by my long absence the previous day.

'Why don't we go out this afternoon and buy a roll of electric cable? There's a place I found on the web, it's an hour's bus ride.'

I imagined the bus ride to a faraway outer *barrio*, loitering in a hardware shop whilst endless useful objects caught Pedro's eye and he explained their function to me, and a return journey where we'd leap off the bus whenever he saw another hardware shop.

Before I could voice a tactful reply, he launched into one of his technical explanations.

'The builders will need it soon. We'll need a separate circuit for the air conditioner, and because it'll draw more current we need a six-millimetre cable from the ground floor. The cable for the circuit needs to be four millimetres. We'll set it up in parallel rather than in series.'

When he paused for breath, I said, 'I wish I understood all that, darling, but I'm afraid I don't. How about *you* go, and I hang around the bookshop on the avenue, buy a book, and practice reading Spanish in the corner café?'

'But don't you want to come along, and see more of Buenos Aires?'

I imagined a trek similar to the saucepan search, but in uninteresting parts of town.

79

'No, sorry. There's that distant Buenos Aries *barrio* – that area of hardware shops – that you've described to me. And there's elegant Buenos Aires – where we went on the hunt for saucepans. I prefer the elegance.'

He looked surprised. He was interested in *any* part of Buenos Aires, a city that he hadn't explored since his teenage years.

But he soon brightened up, probably because it meant he could avoid a bookshop visit. Perhaps he also thought that he'd get more done on his own. In any case, he agreed.

'Maybe we shouldn't have decided to renovate?' he said.

'No, I'm okay with it. And seeing as the kitchen is already a disaster zone, we have to finish what we started.'

> *Ya que estamos en el baile, bailemos.*
> Now that we are at the dance, let's dance.
> Meaning: We are already in this, so let's finish it.

He persisted, 'We can scale back the renovation and do a basic kitchen, and finish the rest in the future. That may only take four weeks. In fact . . .'

'No, we'll go ahead. I'm sure it'll work out.'

Did many other couples cave in to each other, as we did? I had no idea. For me, it was fantastic to see him motivated, especially after his difficulties at work. And he was so concerned about my lack of interest in the renovation that he would have turned back time if he could. What I loved in our relationship was that we always tried to see each other's point of view, at least in relation to matters that were resolvable.

But not so much on BIG matters like moving countries, uprooting our lives, ending our careers . . .

*

By the start of the second week of the renovation, we'd become used to waking up at the uncivilized time of seven thirty, and having a quick breakfast of coffee and toast. We'd made sure to set up the refrigerator, coffee maker and toaster in the living room for exactly this purpose. At eight o'clock we met José or Santiago and their employees. Occasionally we slept in, in which case we'd greet the workers and then have breakfast at one of the many local cafés.

> *Al que madruga, Dios lo ayuda.*
> God helps early risers.

Seven thirty in the morning felt early because, for many *bonaerenses* I'd met, the working day commenced late. This was possibly because dinner was eaten so late. Restaurants opened between eight thirty and nine in the evening, but didn't fill up until nine thirty or later, and it was common for restaurant kitchens to stay open until at least one in the morning. If we visited Pedro's friends or relatives for dinner, we often returned home after midnight. One memorable Saturday night, we ate at two o'clock in the morning. Luckily, no one heard my stomach gurgling because of the loud music. After that experience, I made sure to snack before we left home.

As we waited for the renovating team on the Tuesday morning, I reminded myself of all that had transpired since we'd arrived. Pedro had bought an apartment – easy in hindsight. We'd holidayed in Patagonia – idyllic and quiet in contrast to our construction, or rather, *destruction*, zone. We'd found a builder and carpenter – serendipity. Last week we'd finalized the plan for the kitchen – relief. And Pedro had announced the renovation timetable – shock.

Now Pedro could enjoy his time renovating, I could organize myself – soon, I hoped, with some sort of activity – and we should have the odd day here and there to share.

I found myself thinking of friends and family, as I often did lately, and how I'd miss them if we moved to Argentina. I also found myself remembering that I'd lost some friends as a result of my years in London. During that time away, our respective lives, like train tracks, had diverged. Not all those tracks had converged when I returned.

As for my family, I was close to my Mum, who always encouraged and supported me. She lived alone on an isolated hobby farm near Newcastle, north of Sydney.

En medio de la nada.
In the middle of nothing.
Meaning: Isolated.

She was practical and self-reliant, fixing fences and water pumps, growing her own vegetables, and caring for a herd of alpacas. She loved her independence and the freedom she felt, living out there. We talked regularly by phone, and I always felt that she was nearby. When we drove up to visit her, we'd turn off the main road and onto the gravel track leading to her farmhouse, and the dog and cat would run out to welcome us. Mum would appear and wave. She'd make tea – or coffee for Pedro – and offer us a slice of cake she'd baked that day.

But now the closeness of friends and family was stacked up against Pedro, the love of my life. I'd never met anyone like him. I could see how contented he would be here, even if I'd be cut off from everything familiar.

*

The ringing of the doorbell jolted me from my reverie. It was the workmen. Someone must have let them in downstairs. They greeted us as they trooped through the living area into the kitchen, closed the door behind them, and resumed the seemingly endless task of prizing tiles off walls, and opening up the floor. The whacking threatened to bring back last week's headache.

From under the closed door, the habitual early morning film of dust crept into the living area, obscuring the floor we mopped each night. To minimize the dust invasion, the wall between the kitchen and living room was to be demolished at the last possible moment.

One of the men pushed a wheelbarrow out of the kitchen, fighting to balance the rust-bucket oven perched on top, and leaving a tyre tread of fine cement particles in his wake.

I was a poignant moment, since the oven had served us well. But it had 'had its time.'

> *A cada chancho le llega su San Martín.*
> *San Martín* day catches up with every pig.
> Meaning: Everyone's time will come. On *San Martín* day it was common to eat pork.

When José arrived, he and Pedro disappeared into the kitchen to check on progress. The noise stopped. A few minutes later they re-appeared and the racket and wall shuddering resumed. They were covered in a layer of grey, and shook their clothes to loosen the dust. José took off his beret and whacked it against his leg, creating a powdery cloud that settled around his feet. It was the first time he'd removed the beret in our presence. He placed it back on his head in exactly the same position and shape as before.

'We've started to remove the old lead pipes,' he told me.

I'd learned that in Argentina the kitchen and bathroom pipes were in the floor, encased in compacted loose fill that was topped with a layer of cement. To change the pipes, the cement had to be removed, and the loose fill had to be dug out.

As José explained technical details to Pedro, Santiago buzzed the street door. I went to collect him. Just as José always wore a beret, Santiago always wore a jacket, even in the blistering heat. It hung loosely on his gaunt figure. He held his drawings in one hand, and over his shoulder was draped a bag with bulky contents.

José and Santiago nodded to each other, each saying, *'Buenas.'* Argentines tended to be very courteous people.

Santiago unfolded his drawing for us all to see, and José inspected it before moving toward the kitchen to double-check the measurements. The wind direction must have changed because when he opened the kitchen door, clouds of powdery particles flew around the living room. When he opened the door again to re-join us, he formed the epicentre of a dust cloud, reminding me of a sandstorm attack I'd seen in the film 'The Mummy.'

As the dust settled, he repeated his beret-whacking performance and turned to me.

'Have you chosen the tiles?' he asked.

'Yes, white.'

'No! Not *white*.' José and Santiago exclaimed in unison.

José said, 'Not in your own *home*.'

And Santiago said, 'It would be like living in a hospital. You need to have colour.'

They clearly thought I was crazy.

> *Está media tócame un tango.*
> She is half 'play me a tango.'
> Meaning: She's a little bit crazy.

Despite their protestations, I couldn't help smiling. It was funny to see Santiago and José in agreement, especially after the previous week's 'dividing wall' episode where they'd held such divergent views.

Santiago saw my smile and became defensive. He explained, 'White tiles have no soul. The kitchen will look like a canteen. Come to my workshop and I'll show you how much better it is to have colour.'

We were tired of negative remarks from many of the relatives, and now even our own contractors were disagreeing with us.

Pedro came to my rescue, and in a constrained voice he repeated, 'White.'

He added, 'All the way up to the ceiling.'

José was aghast. 'What, like a *butcher's shop*?'

Before either of us could reply, we heard a knock at the front door.

I looked through the peephole and recognized a woman with whom I'd exchanged greetings in the foyer. My smiling *'Buenos días,'* as I opened the door, was met with a seething *'Buenas.'*

She was not pleased. Not pleased at all. The others looked at her with trepidation.

The *señora* – we subsequently learned that her name was Adriana – launched into a tirade. Her voice shook. Her face reddened, and her hands flew through the air in one rapid gesticulation after another. She said, 'My father is unwell. He's in a very delicate condition. His doctor told him he has to be careful. Your noise is driving him crazy.'

She stared at Pedro, then José, then me, then Santiago, clearly not sure to whom she should direct her complaint. Her glare settled on Pedro.

'Twice he's limped home from the doctor at five in the afternoon, and they're still smashing the floor above him. And as if that wasn't enough, they pushed rocks through our ceiling when he was boiling water in a saucepan and one landed in the water. It's lucky he wasn't burnt. He should be resting as much as possible.'

Urk, I thought. *What a way to meet the downstairs neighbour.*

The others turned to José and I followed suit. Feeling weak-kneed, I put on a blank expression, determined to look as though I didn't understand any Spanish.

It took me a couple of seconds to figure out that José had come to the rescue. He'd embarked on a charm offensive to draw Adriana's attention from Pedro. It was a side of José that we had not seen.

José offered profuse apologies, and undertook to have a look 'right now.' He disappeared into a dust cloud as he opened the kitchen door. The hammering stopped, then resumed as José reappeared within another dust storm.

He told Adriana that he was revising his schedule. 'This week we'll only work until four in the afternoon, and next week there'll be less noise.'

Adriana calmed down. She and José left the apartment to inspect her kitchen and to clear the 'rocks' – hopefully only one or two tiny pieces of cement.

*

Santiago had been silent throughout the visit except for the compulsory greeting. He now turned to Pedro and me, impressed.

'Smart man, José,' he said. 'What he didn't tell Adriana was that the worst of the noise will be over by mid-week anyway – so it'll stop earlier than she expects.'

Santiago placed his mysterious bag on the table and took out a thermos and a pouch of *mate* leaves. At last I knew what the bag contained.

I hadn't tried *mate* – a popular green tea – but I'd seen plenty of people drinking it – stallholders at a local market, shopkeepers, even Pedro's mother and a few of his cousins.

It looked as though Santiago planned to settle in for a chat.

'Do you drink *mate*?' he asked, loudly, to counteract the noise from the kitchen.

'Yes,' said Pedro, before I had a chance to answer, 'but weak, with sugar.' I had never seen Pedro drink *mate*. It was clear to me that he was being polite. The only tea Pedro ever drank was *boldo*, a South American herbal tea, popular for stomach upsets. I guessed he'd asked for sugar to overwhelm the *mate* taste.

I repeated, 'Yes, with sugar,' for solidarity.

Santiago hesitated. He said, 'Hmm, I guess I could have it with sugar this time.'

The ritual commenced. First he placed the *bombilla* or 'metal straw' in the *mate*, or 'cup.' The *mate* cup was a scraped-out and dried pumpkin gourd. It was slightly larger than a teacup. Next, he filled the *mate* cup with *mate* leaves and covered them with hot water from the thermos. The *bombilla* was for drinking the *mate* out of the *mate*. This nomenclature could be confusing for the unwary.

By now Pedro had found the sugar dish. Santiago added a spoonful, and took a sip. He said, 'It's better with sugar. Don't tell my wife though – she says sugar's bad for me.'

> *No levantes la perdiz.*
> Don't make the partridge fly up.
> Meaning: Don't let the cat out of the bag. The expression related to hunting with guns and dogs.

He took a few more sips, added more water, and passed the *mate* to Pedro. In the *mate* ritual, each person drank from the same cup, using the same *bombilla*. I watched in admiration as Pedro sipped without grimacing.

The noise from the kitchen subsided, causing Pedro to say, 'They must be stopping for *their mate*.'

Santiago settled into his chair.

'Ah, silence at last. We can talk more easily. About the building work – so far so good,' he said, as Pedro passed the *mate* to me. 'There aren't any surprises – apart from your neighbour's complaint.'

I took a sip. It was strong and bitter with a welcome sweetness from the sugar.

He continued, 'Now, tell me about Sydney. It must be lovely to drink *mate* at the beach after a day at the office.'

Neither of us answered immediately.

Santiago searched Pedro's face and then mine, and his brow creased in comprehension. He turned back to Pedro. 'Do you *have mate* in Australia?'

'No,' I said, too bluntly.

Even though my Spanish continued to improve, I found that I couldn't think quickly enough to respond to such surprising or unexpected questions with more than a 'yes or no' answer. I would have preferred to be more tactful. Luckily, Pedro said, 'You can buy it in Australia, but it's not a common drink, as it is here.'

If Santiago wanted to know why Australians didn't have *mate*, he kept the thought to himself. He moved to another line of questioning. 'You must find it chaotic here . . .'

But he didn't seem to be expecting too much in the way of an answer.

He chatted for half an hour, describing his children's careers and discussing the state of the world.

His comments were directed at Pedro rather than me. My comprehension of the written language had increased since that day at Clara's real estate office, when I'd undertaken to improve my Spanish. Over the weeks since then, I'd bought and read a few Spanish books, including the translated Agatha Christie that had helped me when buying crockery.

Ratón de biblioteca.
Library mouse.
Meaning: Bookworm.

Two of the books were by the Argentine author Pedro Mairal, one being a collection of short stories called *Hoy temprano* or 'Early Today,' and the other a novella, *La uruguaya* or 'The Uruguayan.' And since finding the *Cantabile* classical music website, I'd read a number of the longer articles.

But I seemed to have a mental block where *conversations* were concerned. I could understand more spoken Spanish than when we'd first arrived, but I couldn't easily answer back. There was always a point in a conversation where I couldn't find the correct word, and where my conversational partner would wait expectantly for an intelligible comment or response. I *was* capable of buying bread at the bakery, and vegetables at the greengrocer's, and carrying on a simple, 'Hello how are you very well thanks,' conversation. On the other hand, discussions concerning society, politics and religion were merely an aspiration.

I *did* keep trying, by attempting to construct Spanish sentences in my head – sentences that often lacked key words. For example, right now I was working out how to say to Santiago, 'I drink tea and this *mate* is excellent. I'd like to drink *mate* regularly.' But once again, I couldn't think of all the words.

I resolved to start reading the local newspapers. Perhaps, by choosing a particular news topic, and learning the words associated with it, I could initiate and continue more conversations.

Despite the drawbacks of my conversational Spanish, I was proud of my newly discovered ability to detect quirky Argentine words and phrases. We had recently visited Pedro's brother, Jorge. At one stage he referred to an annoying person as a *perejil* or *gil* for short. I had asked what *perejil* was, and Pedro had explained that literally, it meant 'parsley,' but also referred to a 'stupid person.' I thought that was funny, especially as another herb, 'dill', was sometimes used in Australia to describe a silly person.

Jorge's son Esteban was a chip off the old block as far as interesting expressions were concerned.

De tal palo, tal astilla.
From such a log, such a splinter.
Meaning: A chip off the old block.

He invoked vegetable, fruit, or charcuterie terminology to refer to stupid people. His favourites were *zanahoria* or 'carrot,' *papa frita* or 'fried potato,' *nabo* or 'turnip,' *zapallo* or 'pumpkin,' and *salame* or 'salami.'

But if Esteban showed off too much, and told everyone how good he was at using Spanish expressions, Pedro would ask him, *'¿No tenés abuela?'* 'Don't you have a grandmother?'

I asked Pedro what he meant, since I knew perfectly well that Esteban *did* have a grandmother. Pedro explained that it was a common Argentine expression, and was based on the assumption that grandmothers doted on their grandchildren and were always complimenting them. The logical outcome was that, in the absence of a grandmother, one had to compliment oneself.

Soon after, I noticed that Pedro teased his other nephew, Mario. When Mario told Pedro that he'd been studying at a friend's place, Pedro mocked him, saying, *'Estabas paseando los libros'* 'All you did was take your books for a walk.'

I thought this was very funny, but was lost when Mario protested, *'No, me rompí el mate estudiando.'*

Pedro had to explain to me what Mario meant, which was, 'No, I broke my head studying.' I pulled out my notebook and wrote it down. I was fascinated that the *mate* cup was used to describe a person's head. I also recorded the 'grandmother' question and the 'walking the books' expression.

I made a habit of recording odd words and sayings, and before long Pedro's friends and relatives would stop the conversation when a quaint expression came up.

'Hang on, this one's for Catherine – where's your notebook?'

My collection grew rapidly. I found that some sayings reflected local history, and others the Argentine way of life, and that yet others were simply colourful and fun. I also noted a few expressions that had clearly originated in Spain, especially within Pedro's largely Spanish family.

Pedro nudged me as Santiago stood to leave. I had drifted right off into quirky-phrase-land.

Estaba en Disney.
I was in Disneyland.
Meaning: I was daydreaming; I was in another world.

Pedro said to Santiago, 'You must be a busy man. Thank you for stopping to share a *mate*.'

Whereupon Santiago responded, *'Me organizo muy bien. También he encontrado la forma de mitigar la angustia de la existencia'* 'I'm very organized. Also, I've found the way to mitigate the anguish of existence.'

There was a pause. Pedro was evidently lost for words. As for me, the sentence circled in my mind until I understood it, whereupon I assigned existentialist conversations in Spanish to a future beyond society-politics-and-religion conversations.

Finally I broke the silence by saying, *'Qué bueno'* 'That's good.'

Pedro and I accompanied Santiago to the foyer. Santiago and I kissed on the cheek and Pedro shook his hand.

'What a morning,' I said to Pedro as we took the elevator back up. 'We get browbeaten by the neighbour, *you drink tea – congratulations,* and we find that we have an existentialist carpenter. How nice that he stayed for a while.'

The elevator doors were opening. On a whim, Pedro pressed the ground-floor button saying, 'Let's not go in. José has it all under control. Why don't we shop for tiles? White or non-white?'

'I have an open mind if you do. Let's see what's available,' I said.

Anything was better than the whacking of the hammers and the shaking of the walls.

Salsa boloñesa de cerdo – Bolognese Sauce with Pork Mince

There were three reasons for having pasta with Bolognese sauce that night. The main reason was that pasta with Bolognese sauce was a comfort food, and we needed comforting after the fiasco with the downstairs neighbour, not to mention the continuing invasion of our space by strangers.

The second reason was that we we'd been invited to the in-laws for dinner, and Pedro had offered to cook the meal – in their kitchen. He chose to make this dish because it was one of his Mum's favourites. Though, once again, the only ingredient that he couldn't find was chilli.

And the third reason was that we'd discovered a fresh pasta shop nearby, and we wanted to try the *ñoquis* or 'gnocchi.'

Whilst we were buying the pasta, the shop assistant told us that on the twenty-ninth day of each month, many Italian-Argentine families gathered to eat *ñoquis*. She said the tradition was so important that the shop always opened on the twenty-ninth, even if it was a Monday – when the shop was usually closed. There was always a long line, which was understandable considering that over half of Argentina's population was of Italian descent. I recalled that an Argentine had once said to me, 'We Argentines are really just a bunch of Italians who speak Spanish.'

On the way to the in-laws with our pasta, Pedro elaborated on the *ñoqui* theme. He told me that in Argentina the word *ñoqui* was used to describe government employees who sat around doing little in the way of work, and waited for their pay cheque on the twenty-ninth day of the month. And that the word was also used to describe people who took advantage of the system.

Ingredients
5 medium-sized mushrooms
1½ carrots
½ large red capsicum
1 large brown onion
3 garlic cloves
10 pitted green olives
1 tbsp capers
Olive oil
500g pork mince, i.e. minced pork, or ground pork. Pork gives the sauce a sweeter flavour than beef.
400g canned tomatoes
½ chilli, optional
100g tomato paste, depending on your taste
1 cup red or white wine
Salt and pepper to taste
Generous quantities of herbs. Don't hold back:
Oregano: Pile dried oregano in a mountain whose base is half the palm of your hand.

Thyme: a smaller mountain where the base of the mountain takes up one third of your palm.

Others of your favourite herbs if you wish, such as fresh basil or sage. For fresh basil, use a handful of leaves, coarsely chopped.

2-3 bay leaves

Cloves, nutmeg and paprika to be added separately:

3 cloves

½ tsp grated nutmeg

1 rounded tsp of paprika, or for a smoky flavour, use smoked paprika

Method

Prepare a brunoise in the same way as for the Chicken Casserole (Chapter 3). Chop a mushroom finely into 2mm cubes. Take 1/4 of a carrot, and 1/5 of the red capsicum, julienne them, and chop them across, to end up with 2mm cubes. Set aside.

Chop the remaining vegetables and place them in a bowl, the mushrooms into slices, or into halves and then slices, and the carrots and capsicum into bite-sized cubes of 1cm. Set aside.

Finely chop the onion and garlic. Set aside.

Cut the olives into slivers by slicing them along their length. Set aside.

Rinse the capers, chop them roughly and set aside with the olive slivers.

Add a couple of tablespoons of olive oil to a large saucepan. Put the saucepan on a high heat, add the meat and brown it. If very fatty, remove some of the fat and add olive oil to continue the browning. Set the meat aside in a separate bowl.

To the saucepan add oil and cook the onion and garlic until soft and very slightly brown.

The chilli can be added at this stage, if you want to include it.

Add the brunoise to the onion and garlic, and sauté until the capsicum softens and slightly changes colour.

Add the tomato paste and stir.

Add the wine and mix, cooking for a couple of minutes to let the alcohol evaporate. The flavour will release and the mixture will thicken.

Add the other vegetables and stir, cooking for 2-3 minutes.

Season and add the herbs — but not yet the cloves, nutmeg or paprika — and cook for 2-3 minutes.

Add the browned meat and cook for 2 minutes on a low to medium heat, stirring until it is well coated with the mixture.

Add the following, leaving a minute or two between each step to allow the flavours of each ingredient soak in. First the olives and capers, then the cloves, then the nutmeg and finally the paprika.

Add the can of tomatoes.

Add a can — the volume of the tomato can — of water to the mixture, bring the heat to maximum and bring to the boil. Once it reaches boiling point, cover, turn the heat down and simmer for half an hour, stirring occasionally until the vegetables are soft. You can leave it simmering for longer allowing the flavours to become richer, e.g. 1 or 2 hours at a very low heat, ensuring you add liquid to attain the desired consistency.

Season to taste with salt and pepper.

Serves 10

Pasta

As a rough guide, use 200g of fresh gnocchi per person.

7

EXTREME RUBBLE

It was the Thursday evening of our second week of the renovation. More than half of our time in Argentina had raced past. I imagined that if I blinked, my eyes would open to see familiar Sydney landmarks. Argentina would have been a dream.

For Pedro the renovation was not only fun, but also a source of local knowledge. He said, 'It'll give us an idea of what to expect if we spend time here, and I do this for a living. I can figure out how people network, and how to deal with local construction issues.'

'I suppose so,' I said, hearing the strain of boredom in my voice, and realizing it was high time to find an activity of my own. As for exactly what that could be, I still had no idea. But I knew who could help – Sarah, my closest friend. I grabbed the computer, and called her cell phone number on Skype. She answered immediately.

I knew I'd been missing friends, but I hadn't realized how much. When I heard her voice, tears sprang to my eyes. It wasn't as though Pedro and I had been away for a long time – three months. And four days. But it felt much longer with the renovation upheaval, and with the unfamiliarity of Buenos Aires. Patagonia was a lifetime away.

Sarah was on her way to work. I'd forgotten that I should only phone people on my Friday or Saturday nights.

> *Tenía memoria de pez.*
> I had the memory of a fish.
> Meaning: I forgot everything straight away.

And I also kept forgetting that my friends back home worked long hours, and probably assumed that we were having a fabulous time in Argentina.

'I'm on the bus – it's running late. I'll have to run for the ferry when we get to the wharf. By the way, you sound tired,' Sarah said, concern in her voice.

'I'm fine. The renovation started last week. What about you?'

'Oh the usual, going to the beach on the weekend. Movie last night.' She paused. 'Are you sure you're okay?' She must have detected a tone of resignation in my voice.

I thought enviously of an evening at the cinema. Both Pedro and I enjoyed art house films, but in Argentina they were in Spanish. In Australia, of course, Spanish movies had sub-titles. As yet my Spanish wasn't up to scratch.

'I guess so. I don't regret coming over here. But there's dust all over the place, and we can't prepare meals. The kitchen's non-existent. We're eating out, or getting takeout, or going to Pedro's Mum's.'

I glanced over at Pedro, who'd looked up from the book he was reading, and winked at him as I said, 'And the furniture's falling to pieces.'

'What? Didn't you buy *new* furniture? What've you *done* to it?'

'I'm kidding. It's antique furniture that we'll fix up. We can sit on it without breaking it. By the way, any chance you can bring saucepans when you visit?'

Sarah was the only friend who had booked a flight to Argentina after we'd announced our temporary move. She'd spend a few days in Buenos Aires at the end of our stay.

But she was already 'switching off.' 'Er, okay. But . . . Sorry, I've gotta go – we're at the wharf. I'll call you on a weekend. Keep happy.'

'Stop! Tell me what I can do while Pedro's busy with the drains and dust.'

'Do what you always did. You used to get out and about in the old days . . . By the way I still need to read that email attachment you sent. MUST go.' She hung up.

I thought of Sarah going to her office and greeting her colleagues, and felt odd. I missed that regular interaction with workmates. I didn't miss the job itself, but the truth was that work had always provided me with a social context, giving order to the day.

And of course she was right about what I should do – those activities I'd put aside because of my busy job. Why on earth hadn't I thought of that before? I made a mental list. Painting – maybe a class, so I could meet locals. A writing group or book club . . . or maybe not, because they'd be in Spanish. Piano lessons . . . but practice would be hard with a renovation in train, not to mention the lack of a keyboard. So . . . Spanish lessons. I definitely needed to work on my conversational Spanish, even if only to better interact with the relatives on future visits to Argentina. A course on Buenos Aires architecture, if there was such a thing. Yoga . . . There was much to investigate.

These activities, I thought, *will help me to discover how people live and interact in the city.*

And I'd be killing two birds with one stone – I'd recreate the social context I missed, and I'd avoid the noise and dust.

> *Matar dos pájaros de un tiro.*
> Kill two birds with one shot.

*

Meanwhile, the noise continued. Pedro said this 'rubble' phase would last for two more weeks. Added to the ongoing demolition process, old pipes were being disconnected and new pipes chased. Brand-new pipes lay on the floor of the living room – for water, gas, drainage, and electrical wiring. The old pipes piled up on the mountain of ex-wall-tiles and old cement, in the crater that was once a kitchen.

From time to time, I opened the kitchen door to have a look, and a piece of floating grit would catch in my throat. I coughed my way out, none the wiser for the experience. The pages of my diary now had a new heading, which was EXTREME RUBBLE PERIOD.

The remains of our old kitchen migrated from the rubble mountain in the kitchen into rubble bags, and the bags piled up along the wall outside our front door. José refused to order a skip until he could fill it.

'Or other people will fill the skip and we'll be paying to remove *their* rubbish,' he explained.

Our front door was at the end of the corridor, so our neighbours were not inconvenienced. But Pedro, José, the builders and I squeezed along in single file to reach the elevator. One night, I dreamed the rubble grew so quickly that it buried the building.

As well as rubble in the corridor, there were piles of new tiles on the balcony. There was no other place to store them. José was adamant that they be kept safely within the property. As he said, 'If you leave these tiles in the corridor they will disappear one by one. I call it, "The march of the ants." '

> *El ojo del amo engorda el ganado.*
> The eye of the owner fattens the livestock. In other words, the wolves will not attack them.
> Meaning: Keep an eye on things and they will remain safe.

'But you will never grab the thieves in the act,' he added.

> *Nunca vas a agarrarlos con las manos en la masa.*
> You will never grab them with their hands in the dough.

94

There was a downside to the piles of tiles on the balcony – they blocked access to our clothesline. Pedro informed me that the BLOCKED BALCONY PERIOD would continue for at least a week after the EXTREME RUBBLE PERIOD ended.

The washing machine had been sitting in the living room, inert, since the start of the renovation. Pedro's Mum had insisted we wash our linen at her place. But I didn't want to be even more beholden to her – she'd been kind enough already.

It was time to outsource the clothes washing. I overcame my daydreaming self to look for a laundry, and to my surprise, I found at least one in each block. I tried the closest one to the apartment and was pleased to find that the owner, Daniela, was friendly and efficient.

She waved to us whenever we passed by, and from time to time, we stopped for a chat. On our first visit, on the Friday of that second week of the renovation, we hauled bags of groceries and vegetables as well as laundry. We were on our way to the in-laws where Pedro had offered to cook dinner for the second night in a row.

As Daniela filled out the docket for our washing, she asked where I was from. When I said Sydney, Australia, her eyes lit up and she said, 'I met many Australians in Cuzco – where I grew up. My Mum had a laundry near the centre of town, and lots of tourists brought their washing. The Australians were always friendly.'

Daniela herself was friendly, and she was patient when I spoke to her in my halting Spanish. I found it was easy to talk to her. I felt encouraged to ask her about the Australian tourists.

'Did they speak Spanish?' I asked. 'Or did they make hand signs?'

'Oh yes, most of them spoke at least *some* Spanish. They practiced on us. We had plenty of laughs. I learned quite a lot about your country. I'd love to visit Sydney – and see the Harbour Bridge.'

Soon her curiosity got the better of her. She looked at our bags of vegetables and asked Pedro, 'What did you buy?'

Pedro sighed, 'Everything except what I most wanted – chillies.'

'Chillies? Are you joking?'

¿Me estás tomando el pelo?
Are you pulling my hair?
Meaning: You're kidding me.

She asked, 'What sort of an Argentine are you, eating spicy food?'

I knew that Peruvians loved spicy sauces, but we were discovering that many Argentines couldn't handle any spiciness in their food. Most of

Pedro's cousins and friends avoided cracked pepper because it made the meal too 'hot'.

And last night, the meal that Pedro had cooked at the in-laws was only mildly spicy, with two drops of a bottled chilli sauce. But his mother and stepfather had coughed and spluttered, tears in their eyes, after one mouthful. They drank water to try to get rid of the chilli effect, even though we told them it was pointless. We had no idea that they'd react so strongly. We probably put them off chillies forever.

> *El que se quema con leche ve una vaca y llora.*
> He who is burnt by milk, sees a cow and cries.
> Meaning: Once bitten, twice shy.

Pedro told me afterwards that he would continue to use chilli in the meals he made at his Mum's, but he would only add it to our servings, not theirs.

We rarely found spicy sauces in restaurants. One exception was a Mexican restaurant where the chilli sauce was clearly marked, in order to warn mild-flavoured-food lovers. In our excitement at finding the sauce, we'd splashed it over everything.

'Australians love spicy food,' Pedro told Daniela. 'Thai food – almost always spicy, and sometimes *very* spicy – is common in Australia. As common as pizza is here.'

Although Daniela had met all those Australians years before, she wasn't aware of the Asian influence on our food. Pedro told her how difficult it was to find chilli, but that he knew where to buy it. He'd enquired at one of the local Taiwanese-owned supermarkets, though the Taiwanese lady he spoke to wasn't exactly talkative.

'Excuse me, do you sell chillies?' Pedro had asked.

'No.'

'Could you please tell me where I can buy some?'

'Barrio chino' 'Chinatown.'

'I'm guessing that you use chillies when you cook?' Pedro asked.

'Yes.'

'Where do you buy yours?' Perhaps Pedro hoped they had chilli bushes at home and could sell us a few private chillies.

'Barrio chino,' she said.

Pedro told Daniela that we had not yet visited *barrio chino*. When he asked Daniela whether she cooked Peruvian food at home, they launched into a cooking conversation worthy of a television chat show. This shared love of cooking must have inspired her because she disappeared to the back of the shop and came back with a plastic bag full of chillies, insisting we take them without any payment.

*

The days of rubble blended together. In the mornings I planned my activities. I learned how to use the bus and subway system and found a website outlining the quickest method of transport from A to B. I even learned the history of the subway. It was built by the British in the early twentieth century – which was why the subway trains 'drove' on the left side, even though cars drove on the right. This had probably intensified my utter confusion when I'd been following Pedro around town.

I found the different ways to track down classes. It was easiest to ask about painting groups by enquiring at art supply shops. Some classes took place at the back of those shops, some had their own 'shop-front' premises, and yet others were more private, taking place in the teacher's home, or in houses that had been converted to offices and studios.

The Spanish classes I sought were informal, one-on-one conversation classes, rather than those offered by language schools. These informal classes were advertised through leaflets on noticeboards in supermarkets and in local shops, and were more common in nearby, touristy *Palermo*.

Whilst some yoga groups were advertised by shopfront signs, most were easier to find on the Internet. That was because many groups met in converted apartments in residential buildings. The only other ways to know of their existence were by word of mouth, or observation – from time to time, groups of people gathered outside the foyer door of a building, yoga mats at the ready.

Also on the Internet was a course on Buenos Aires architecture, but it was in Spanish. I remained hopeful of finding a tour of one of the fabulous Buenos Aires palaces.

My search for activities bore fruit in the middle of the third week of the renovation, when I met my Spanish conversation teacher, Nora, at a local café. Nora was about forty. Her long black hair was held back in a ponytail. She was dressed in a black strappy T-shirt and black slacks, set off by a red handbag, and red belt and sandals. I decided to dress more smartly the next time we met.

Nora was impressed with my construction words, such as *taladro, lijadora, desagüe, pastina* and *losa* or 'drill, sanding machine, drain, grout and cement slab,' but agreed that they had limited use in day-to-day conversations. When I told her that I enjoyed classical music, art, and literature – and that, by the way, I also loved Argentine colloquial sayings – she was delighted, saying, 'We're going to get on well.' We agreed on two lessons each week.

*

On the Friday of that third week, Pedro's cousin Felicitas dropped by.

Pedro had told her that I wanted to see more of the 'real' Buenos Aires, and she offered to take me to a meat and vegetable market, the *Mercado del progreso,* in the nearby *barrio* of *Caballito.*

Felicitas insisted on first visiting the apartment, not that she had any interest in renovations or rubble – she simply wanted to have the latest information when the relatives gossiped about Pedro's kitchen. She took photos with her cell phone and off we went, leaving Pedro with the builders.

I'd hardly talked to Felicitas before. Even though we saw her from time to time at the in-laws, there were always other cousins dropping in. She was my age, and we soon found that we laughed at the same funny situations. She was gregarious, with an outgoing personality, and I warmed to her immediately. I remembered that she'd supported us when we were searching for an apartment, telling Rodolfo off for giving us a hard time. Rodolfo was low on the list of twenty of the seventy cousins that were in regular or sporadic contact with Pedro, probably eighteenth in importance. Felicitas was second or third, the first place being reserved for a cousin in Brazil.

We travelled back in time as soon as we stepped through the market entrance. Steel frames soared above the hubbub of the crowd, holding the roof at bay.

'This market has been in continuous operation since 1896,' Felicitas said. 'The produce is fantastic, even though the place could do with a thorough facelift.'

Delicious cooking aromas surrounded us. A butcher walked past with a suckling pig carcass slung over his shoulder. A stream of merchants pushed trolleys piled high with boxes of fruit or vegetables, skillfully maneuvering between lines of customers. The market was divided into different areas – red meat butchers, poultry and other meat butchers, fruit sellers, vegetable sellers, delicatessens. There was a constant chatter from stallholders spruiking their wares, fiercely competing with nearby stalls. It was reminiscent of market scenes in the movies 'Oliver Twist' and 'Irma la Douce.' I was captivated.

I imagined the customers who'd stepped across these same flagstones over the last hundred and twenty years. The women in the 1890s with their long dresses and gigot sleeves, in the 1920s with their drop-waisted dresses and bob hairstyles, in the 1950s with their full skirts and rounded shoulder lines, gradually giving way to jeans and casual contemporary fashions. They would have admired the colours of seasonal fruit and vegetables, enjoyed the aromas of cheeses and hams and been impressed by the freshness of the meat, and would have taken part in the same lively banter as today.

Towers of *milanesas* or 'Vienna Schnitzels' took pride of place at butchers' stalls. *Milanesas* were common on restaurant menus.

One of the stalls caught my eye. But Felicitas disappeared into the distance, talking to me as though I were still beside her.

I ran up and grabbed her arm.

'Hold on – come back. Let's have a look at this – please?' I asked her. I'd noticed a butcher preparing batter for the *milanesas*. He took eggs, two at a time, from a *maple* – a cardboard tray that held thirty eggs. An egg in each hand, he cracked them simultaneously into a huge baking dish. A mountain of breadcrumbs sat in another baking dish.

'Ask him how many eggs he makes in each batch,' I said to Felicitas.

'You ask him – you need to practice your Spanish. I'll listen – and help if you want.'

After the usual *'Buenos días,'* he answered my question without interrupting the egg-cracking rhythm. 'Let's see, I use three *maples*, so three times thirty.'

The answer was easy. The three of us chorused, 'Ninety.'

Ninety eggs – to make mountains of *milanesas*.

As we thanked him, his colleague opened the door of a large oven, and levered out a huge tray of *empanadas*. The air around the tray shimmered, and the rows of swollen, semi-circular golden pastries, with their hidden fillings, released a scrumptious aroma.

Empanadas were a common savoury snack in Argentina, and consisted of a circle of pastry folded over a large spoonful of filling to make a bulging semicircle. The pastry along the curved edge of the *empanada* was crimped in different styles depending on the filling. The most common filling was mince – ground beef – along with an olive, and pieces of chopped hard-boiled egg.

Felicitas too, had noticed the aroma saying, 'Let's line up. Have you eaten *empanadas*?'

'Of course. But why do they have sugar on them?'

'You haven't *lived* if you don't know. Those ones have sultanas in the meat mixture – and the sugar adds a delicious touch.'

My mouth watered as we joined the line. The customer in front of us ordered, *'Cincuenta milanesas, por favor'* 'Fifty *milanesas*, please.' No wonder there were such huge piles of *milanesas* in the market. Perhaps she ran a restaurant.

At the front of the line the owner told us, 'We have two butchers making *milanesas* all day. They make at least two large batches and we sell every one.'

Se venden como pan caliente.
They sell like hot bread.
Meaning: They fly out the door.

Ignoring the line behind us, he added local colour, saying, 'In the old days, the stallholders delivered meat from horse-drawn carriages. There's a photograph showing one of the carriages over there – taken in the 1930s.'

He nodded toward the wall beside the café.

After paying, we took a closer look at the photograph. Felicitas pointed to one of the buildings in the background. 'Look, this is the old house around the corner near the bus stop. All the rest have been demolished to build apartment blocks.'

It was depressing to think that the elegant houses were gone forever. The road where Pedro and I now 'lived' was experiencing a similar change. Santiago, the carpenter, had nostalgically shown us photos of our street from thirty years ago. Lining the street were lovely houses from the early twentieth century, in a mixture of art nouveau and art deco styles.

I loved admiring the old one- and two-storey houses in our *barrio*. Their street-facing walls were made of *piedra París* or 'Paris stone,' a mortar of cement, sand, and ground minerals like dolomite or calcite. *Piedra París* was developed by Italian craftsmen to resemble the stonework of Paris buildings. Grooves were drawn in the mortar to simulate large stone blocks.

The ceilings were high, in order to enhance airflow in the hot summer months, and the doors and windows were elegantly tall. The doors were beautifully carved, and many framed a narrow translucent window barred with wrought iron. The windows had external shutters and wrought iron Juliet balconies. Peeking inside an open door, one could glimpse a gorgeous stained-glass wall at the end of the entrance passageway, allowing light to enter the house from an inner courtyard.

But not everyone shared my sorrow at the speed of change. Pedro's sister-in-law had told us how much smarter our street looked with each new apartment block. I would never understand that point of view.

*

It was time for a coffee. We took our *empanadas* to the café, a raised area of the market, and chatted until the waiter returned from delivering drinks to one of the stalls. Felicitas instructed me to order, and I asked for two '*cafés con leche.*'

The waiter looked puzzled and I hesitated. Felicitas said, 'You need to speak up. Do all Australians speak softly? Here in Argentina we have loud voices. Your Spanish was perfect but he didn't hear you.' I repeated the order in a louder voice – success!

Felicitas spoke elementary English, and we muddled through a conversation.

'I don't know why you want to move here, even if it's only for a few years,' Felicitas said, bluntly. 'Surely you find us disorganized? All we have are strikes, power shortages, demonstrations and in recent years, social problems with drugs.'

Once she started, she couldn't stop listing the ills of Argentina. 'It's a naturally rich country, but there are too many people who are very poor. They are the ones who suffer most when we have an economic crisis – which happens every ten years. You must have noticed the people collecting cardboard on the streets? That never happened before 2001. And the middle class is always badly affected by a crisis. And the inflation rate is astronomical. As for our politicians and the way they duped the population before 2001 . . .'

> *Nos vendieron espejitos de colores.*
> They sold us little coloured mirrors.
> Meaning: They deceived us. Early settlers, in their trade with indigenous groups, traded cheap trinkets for more valuable items.

I managed to get a word in. 'We haven't decided to move yet. Pedro wants to of course. And you're not the only country with problems. Australia also has drug problems, and it's hard to admire politicians. Many make promises that come to nothing.'

> *Los políticos, como los peces, por la boca mueren.*
> Politicians, like fish, die by the mouth.
> Meaning: The words that politicians use can cause their downfall.

I loved Australia – it was such a fantastic country. But even so, I recognized that it had its own problems, as did all countries. I tried to think of how to describe my concerns about the direction Australia was taking. They included the increasing gap between the 'haves' and 'have nots,' the lowering of educational standards and the piecemeal approach of successive governments to innovation in industry. But it was too hard in Spanish. I found it easier to talk about Argentina.

'Argentina is an amazing country. I'm impressed with your free university education and free health, and Pedro told me that it's free for foreigners as well. That's incredible.' I said.

But Felicitas was on a roll, or else she hadn't understood what I'd said.

'Argentina takes things to extremes,' she said. 'Let me give you a simple day-to-day example. A few years ago we didn't have a proximity card for bus fares – we had to pay for buses with coins.'

'Not notes?'

'No, only coins – you had to put them into a machine on the bus. People hoarded coins and a coin shortage developed. I don't know why it all started. We all had our 'coin box' at home. Greengrocers gave you a lemon or an orange for change, instead of coins. If you bought an item for seven pesos, you had to give the shopkeeper a ten-peso note and a two-peso note so you could get a five-peso note in change. If you only gave them a ten-peso note they were stuck, because they had to give you a two-peso note and a one-peso coin. It was easier for everyone if no coins changed hands. How mad is that?'

I tried to imagine Australia running out of coins, but I couldn't. Then I tried to imagine it happening in Argentina, and oddly enough, I *could*. *Argentina's idiosyncrasies must be infiltrating my mind*, I thought. I asked Felicitas, 'Is that why they introduced a proximity card?'

'Probably. But before that, the government passed a law to stop dishonest people from selling coins in bulk for more than they were worth.'

A río revuelto, ganancia de pescadores.
A turbulent river is a fishermen's gain.
Meaning: When there is uncertainty, those who are knowledgeable in the area can take advantage.

'How could they get away with selling money for *more* money?'

'People were pretty desperate – they had to get to work – they needed coins. Simple as that. The central bank set up desks at two main railway stations – they swapped twenty pesos worth of coins in return for notes – the lines were endless.'

'Did you ever run out?'

'Yes, many times. I took more taxis than ever before. One day, I had no change, and I saw a woman at the bus stop rifling through her handbag. She found a handful of coins – I envied her. Nowadays, I think how heavy it must have been.'

Contar plata en frente de los pobres.
To count money in front of the poor.
Meaning: Showing off what you have – money or other possessions – in front of those who have nothing.

I felt comfortable with Felicitas, who ignored my Spanish mistakes. She was friendly, and genuinely concerned about my happiness. 'Don't you miss your family and friends?' she asked.

'Well, yes I do. But one of my closest friends will visit before we go back. Other friends said they'd come, but so far nothing.'

Despite sending those emails a month ago, only three more people had responded and no one had read the attached newsletter. *Do people always ignore attachments?* I asked myself. *Or are they all busy on summer holidays, or busy at work?* Whatever the reason, for most people, Pedro and I were 'out of sight, out of mind.' A few more signs from home would have been welcome.

'Hmm, frankly, I couldn't do it,' said Felicitas. 'But I suppose if I met an Australian man – and he wanted to live in his own country – I'd be in the same boat as you.'

Estaría en la misma.
I would be in the same.

We talked for ages, not noticing the time, and Felicitas gave me some useful tips on how to survive in Buenos Aires. One of them was surprising to me. She said, 'We all learn English at school. You'll find that lots of people speak at least *some* English – they're simply too shy to practice on a native speaker. If you're ever in trouble and can't think of the Spanish words to use, just ask anyone, "Do you speak English? I need help please!" You'd be amazed how many people will be able to assist.'

All too soon it was one o'clock in the afternoon, and the market closed. It would open again in four hours. I thanked Felicitas and we separated at the market exit, each to catch a different bus home.

*

I walked for a block, and stopped at a pedestrian crossing to wait for the traffic lights to change.

A hand grabbed my forearm in an iron grip.

I jumped out of my skin.

Me pegué un jabón.
I hit myself a piece of soap (i.e. a meaningless literal translation).
Meaning: I got the fright of my life.

I'd been jittery ever since we'd arrived in Buenos Aires, due to the media feeding frenzy that followed each major crime, detailing the minor points over many days.

Nerviosa como perro en bote.
As nervous as a dog in a boat.

My eye followed the arm and I saw an elderly lady half my height, pointing with her walking stick to the far side of the road. *'Por favor ayúdame a cruzar la avenida'* 'Please help me to cross the avenue,' she entreated. She must have assumed that this giant could safely cross five lanes of traffic.

I smiled at her and nodded, relieved she wasn't a criminal.

I'd easily understood her Spanish, which surprised me. Even though her request was simple, the strong Argentine pronunciation, and the fact that her voice quavered, would have utterly confused me when we first arrived. I looked forward to Nora's conversation classes, and to further improving my comprehension of spoken Spanish.

The pedestrian lights were displaying a red 'do not walk' figure. When it disappeared and the white 'walking' figure appeared I announced, *'Ahora'* 'Now,' and together we struck out for the other side.

Having seen my companion safely across the road, I approached the bus stop. Thinking back to my first bus trips in Buenos Aires, glued to Pedro's side, I couldn't understand why it had been so perplexing. I now knew that bus commuters in Buenos Aires were highly organized. There was no pushing or shoving.

There was a well-defined protocol. The first person to arrive stood by the pole or number that indicated the bus stop, and the second person stood behind them. It was clear who had the 'right' to get on the bus first. The protocol was blurry on exceptionally hot days, when some commuters stood away from the line in the shade, or on rainy days when they stood under awnings. In such cases, each person arriving in the line registered who had priority.

But more surprising than 'hot day' and 'rainy day' behaviour was the effect of Argentine courtesy. Women and elderly people were given precedence. In this case the line consisted of two men, a woman and me.

The bus arrived. The two men who arrived first gave precedence to the woman who arrived third. But at that exact moment, an elderly man and his grandson arrived, and *she* gave way to *them*. Then *she* got on. Then, the chivalrous two men nodded to me, and I thanked them and boarded. As a result of all this polite behaviour, the straightforward arrival order of 'first arriving person through to sixth' became the 'getting on' order of 'fifth, sixth, third, fourth, first and lastly, second.'

*

When I boarded the bus, the driver looked at me and immediately pointed to the proximity sensor where my transport card should register. I wondered why he'd indicated it to *me* – and not to the person ahead of me – until I grasped the fact that he was helping me. I covered up my confusion, and thanked him.

It was then that I understood I would always look like a foreigner in Buenos Aires. My height, blue eyes and fair hair would betray me. Despite this fact, I determined to try and integrate as best I could, to learn the Argentine codes and follow them, and to 'live like an Argentine' as much as possible.

On the way back to the apartment, I stared out of the bus window at the endless streams of cars, and the crowds of pedestrians on the sidewalk. I reflected on the generosity Felicitas had shown me with the market visit, and Daniela's friendliness whenever we stopped to drop off our laundry. Both of these women – in their own ways – had helped to make me feel more comfortable in Buenos Aires.

I knew we'd eventually have a circle of friends here if we stayed, but right now I found myself feeling lost socially. I'd seen people interacting in ways that I didn't understand, and hoped that it was not too long before I'd understand a joke, or a clever pun.

My mind wandered back to the apartment and I sighed. I wondered how long Pedro and I would be living in a renovation zone.

That night I dreamed of dust storms blowing through columns of tiles.

Empanadas – The South American Meat Pie Equivalent

The delicious meat _empanadas_ that Felicitas and I ate at the _Mercado del progreso_ were smaller, but similar in shape, to a Cornish pasty or an Italian _calzone_. The name _empanada_ came from the word _pan_ or 'bread,' and could be interpreted as 'contents surrounded by bread or pastry.' _Empanadas_ were a very common snack, and were sold in many shops, including _pizzerias_, _empanada_-only shops and _panaderías_ or 'bakeries'.

Empanadas probably originated in Persia. In the Middle Ages, travellers in Europe and the Middle East found that meat wrapped in pastry was easy to handle when travelling, and lasted for a few days. _Empanadas_ in Latin America were derived from these European and Middle Eastern foods, the influence having spread through the south of Spain, particularly Andalusia, and arriving with the Spanish Conquistadores.

Often, when we arrived for dinner at the home of relatives or friends, there was no sign of food. We chatted for ages, usually until nine-thirty or ten o'clock, and then our host would say, 'So, what will we get delivered? Pizza? _Empanadas?_' A lively discussion followed, the food was ordered, and the beer was taken out of the fridge in readiness. The idea of dinner together was exactly that – dinner _together_. The social aspect of the gathering was more important than the process of preparing or cooking food, and more important than impressing the guests with culinary skills.

A pizza order often included portions of _fainá_, a chickpea flatbread originating in Genoa. Like many Argentines we met, Pedro liked to eat a slice of pizza topped with a piece of _fainá_.

The _empanada_ fillings varied, and included chicken, ricotta and spinach, ham and cheese, tuna fish, or other mixtures particular to the supplier. The leftover _empanadas_ could be stored for a couple of days in the fridge, and eaten as a late-night snack.

This is Pedro's recipe for sugar-sprinkled _empanadas_.

Ingredients
Puff pastry
Mince (i.e. beef mince, or ground beef) mixture from the recipe for Sweet Corn Pie (Chapter 9)
Green olives, pitted
Raisins
Hard-boiled egg, sliced into 8 pieces containing both white and yolk

Method
Cut the puff pastry into rounds of 12-15cm. Or buy ready-made rounds of _empanada_ pastry.
Make sure that the mince mixture is completely cold.
Place a tablespoon of the mince mixture, 1 or 2 olives, a few raisins and pieces of hard-boiled egg on one of the rounds.
Run your finger under the tap or dip it in a glass of water. Rub your wet finger around the edge of a pastry round, but only a semi-circle.

Bring the semi-circle with the dry edge over the filling so that its edge meets the semi-circle with the wet edge.

Squash down the edges with the prongs of a fork, or crimp them as preferred.

Cook in a hot oven – 180-200°C – for 5 minutes. It is not uncommon to deep fry the <u>empanadas</u>, but if so, a different pastry may be used.

Sprinkle the top with white sugar.

Note

The sugar on the cooked <u>empanada</u> can burn your mouth, so wait for them to cool a bit before eating.

For a different flavour, leave out the raisins and the sugar.

8

THE COVER-UP

At last the rubble was gone. The dust bowl was history.

We were exactly half way through the eight-week renovation, and three months and three weeks into our trial period.

Pedro proudly told me that the worst was over, and that the cement floor slab would be laid next week.

'Once the slab is dry they'll do the plinths for the cupboards, render the walls, and tile. All that should take two weeks,' he said.

The COVER-UP PERIOD was upon us, and it was easier to imagine the transformation of the empty space into a functioning kitchen.

According to Pedro, all was on track except for a minor issue with the air conditioner. The split-system external unit had not yet been properly fastened onto the metal supports on the outside wall. As long as there were no strong winds, it was quite safe. I couldn't wait for the day we could switch it on – each day was hotter and more humid than the last. The air outside was very still, and even with the kitchen door open, there was no cross-breeze to alleviate the sauna-like atmosphere inside the apartment.

Pedro ignored the heat and hummed to himself, or whistled a lively tune as he organized the next stage of the renovation.

Contento como perro con dos colas.
As happy as a dog with two tails.

The 'Three Amigos,' Pedro, José and Santiago, were a cheery band and they worked well with few disagreements. This was reassuring, especially after the arbitrary way that Pedro had engaged José.

With the time and distance, my stress continued to recede. I saw my career in perspective and planned to find a more satisfying occupation back in Sydney. As for my activities, I now had a yoga class one morning each week, and painting classes twice a week. And I was enjoying my Spanish conversation classes with Nora, who lived nearby.

My painting classes took place in an art deco house in *Palermo*. I loved the feeling of entering a calm oasis, escaping the noise of constant traffic, and picking up my paintbrush. From time to time I'd gaze around the room at the Oregon pine floorboards, the moulded and panelled walls that soared up to the high ceiling, and the beautiful carved doors. The ceiling was in *bovedilla* style – rows of steel beams supporting an arched brick structure.

I was copying a medieval painting of a pageant, practicing with acrylic paints. The teacher told me the scene was difficult, and that I might become frustrated with the detail. But I was relishing the challenge of producing a range of ochre-like hues for the walls in the background, and the strong colours of the banners and festivities in the foreground. I wanted to test various effects, to help with my next painting, which was to be a present for Pedro.

The class was casually organized, and the teacher moved between students to provide advice, borrowing a paintbrush from time to time to demonstrate the effect of a simple dark line, or a brushstroke of a contrasting colour.

The students chatted about their paintings, about day-to-day activities, and about cultural events. Two of them attended tango classes and entertained us with stories of the tango scene in the *barrios* of *San Telmo* and *Almagro*. In this friendly space, I was comfortable with speaking in Spanish about topics I loved, and I joined in the conversations on theatre and art. I took advantage of one of the music conversations to ask about the free Sunday morning concerts at the *Teatro Colón*.

All of my fellow painters knew about the concerts. One of them said that it was best to arrive early, way before the box office opened at nine-thirty, because long lines could form.

Another said, 'They give out tickets to the stalls first – they're the best seats, and with them, you can use the main entrance – very grand,' and added, 'Oh, and they give only two tickets to each person.'

'Why not go next week?' a third said. 'There's a choir and a small orchestra, and they're performing pieces by Argentine composers. Plus, the theatre was renovated a few years ago and it's magnificent – it was built in 1908, when Argentina was very rich.'

I decided to whip in to the box office before next Friday's class and surprise Pedro with tickets, as I had resolved to do some time back, when Andrés the architect had disappointed us.

As for seeing a play, I couldn't wait until my Spanish was more fluent. I was, of course, practicing Spanish whenever I went out, but many expressions were still baffling. At yoga, the teacher used familiar Sanskrit names for the poses, but that didn't mean I *always* knew what to do. The first time he said, '*Boca arriba,*' which literally meant 'Mouth upward,' I involuntarily looked up, assuming we had to have our heads tilted back. But out of the corner of my eye, I saw the other students lying down. I determined that it meant 'Lie on your back.' I found out later that '*Boca abajo*' or literally, 'Mouth downward,' logically meant 'Lie on your stomach.'

The yoga classes were linguistically instructive in other ways. Where else but in Argentina would the yoga teacher say, 'Imagine your spinal column as a *bandoneón?*' A *bandoneón* was a type of accordion essential to tango music. And where else but in the Americas would he say, '*Boca arriba con brazos tipo cactus*' 'Lie on your backs with your arms like cactus branches.'

I gradually settled into a routine. And even though I knew from my London experience that not all – or possibly any – of the people I met were likely to become lifelong friends, I felt a little less lonely.

I sent off a second newsletter, covering various aspects of music, and, for contrast, a couple of paragraphs about sport.

The first topic was the *Carnaval* of late February, where troupes danced in the streets in brightly coloured satin suits. We'd recently seen groups practicing for *Carnaval* to the drumming of the *murga* rhythm, a beat that originated in Cadiz in Spain, and was transformed by the African slaves of the early colony.

I then described one of the many folk music rhythms of Argentina, the *malambo.* This rhythm originated in the centre of Argentina, and was usually played with drum and guitar. There were no lyrics. The music accompanied a powerful and energetic male-only dance. The performers often demonstrated their expertise with *boleadoras* – a weapon originally used by indigenous groups in Patagonia, and adopted by *gauchos* to capture running cattle. The men wore a traditional 'Sunday best' *gaucho* costume of black or grey *bombachas de gaucho*– loose long trousers – and matching shirts, with white scarves, wide brimmed hats and riding boots.

The music theme continued with a description of four famous Argentine classical musicians, past and present. Two musicians from the past were Alberto Ginastera and Astor Piazzolla. Ginastera was one of the most important twentieth-century composers of the Americas, and Piazzolla, the tango composer and *bandoneón* player, was one of his students. Piazzolla created *nuevo tango* or 'new tango,' incorporating elements from jazz and classical music into the traditional tango. Moving to the present, I mentioned Martha Argerich, the classical concert pianist, often referred to as the best pianist in the world, and Daniel Barenboim, pianist and orchestra conductor, and one of the founders of the West-Eastern Divan Orchestra based in Spain.

I couldn't let the list of musicians stop there though, because I'd found out that an Argentine musician, Gustavo Santaolalla, had won two Oscars for 'Best Original Music Score' – one in 2006, for *Brokeback Mountain,* and one in 2007, for *Babel*.

And then, in a complete change of topic, I turned to sport, describing the roar that swept across Buenos Aires during a major soccer game whenever a goal was scored. Our *barrio* erupted into cheers of '¡Gol! ¡Gol!' or shouts of pain, accompanied by a cacophony of barking dogs. It was as though every single person were watching the game on his or her television, and needed to shout out.

Also on the topic of sport was the fact that polo games were commonly shown on television in Argentina, something that was unusual in Australia.

I'd started reading local newspapers, and despite my limited interest in sporting events, it was hard not to notice an equestrian sport called *pato*, or 'duck.' I discovered that *pato* was the national game of Argentina. In colonial times, rather cruelly, a live duck was placed in a basket with handles attached. The game was played by two teams, each consisting of four horsemen. Team members would toss the basket between them, or grab it from the other team, with the aim of throwing it into a goal – a vertical ring – at the end of the field. In the 1930s, the 'duck basket' was officially replaced by a leather ball with wooden handles.

I added one or two amusing stories about our experiences, and sent off the newsletter, hoping it would elicit those much-desired responses from friends.

*

The next Friday, before my painting class, I picked up two tickets for the Sunday morning concert at the *Teatro Colón*. I told Pedro we were celebrating the end of five weeks of renovating and the laying of the cement slab.

On the Sunday morning we left home at ten o'clock, with plenty of time to spare before the eleven o'clock start of the concert. We took the subway into town and walked for a short way along *Avenida Corrientes*. Being Sunday, there was barely any traffic and only a few pedestrians. Unlike those cities in the world where Sunday was a day for walking or shopping or going out to eat, most *bonaerenses* were sleeping in, after a late night on Saturday. Or they were preparing for the customary large meal – an *asado*, where a variety of meats were barbequed over red-hot coals – at home with the family. Or, in our *barrio*, families and friends were picnicking at *Parque Centenario*, a huge park with a central lake.

But this commercial area on the *avenida* was dead. Shops were hidden behind metal roll-down shutters covered in graffiti. The stillness was a complete change from the frenetic crowds and traffic noise only two days previously when I'd dodged my way along the sidewalk.

'I can't believe the number of theatres I saw on this avenue on Friday,' I said to Pedro. 'It's like Broadway – or the West End in London. And endless bookshops. At least three specialized in politics, five in children's books and at least two in second hand books. All in Spanish – of course.'

'Mum says they close ten blocks of this avenue one Saturday night each year for the "Night of the Bookshops," ' said Pedro. 'She said you'd enjoy it. The shops are open until one in the morning – there are tours and street theatre. And story telling for kids.'

He added, 'And she told me there's an international book fair in April or May with over a million visitors.'

Damn, we won't be here for the fair, I thought. *We need to visit one year in April or May.*

'One day we should go to *El Ateneo* bookshop in *Recoleta* – it's a converted old cinema, and supposed to be one of the most beautiful bookshops in the world,' he said.

'I'd love that,' I said, thinking it would be a perfect topic for a newsletter.

Holding hands, we turned off the avenue into another incredibly quiet street, and soon the multi-storey buildings gave way to a vast green area the size of two city blocks.

Ahead and to the right, beyond the park and its skirting road, I immediately recognized the *Teatro Colón*. Taking up a whole city block, it was an imposing, very grand building – though not beautiful – in an eclectic architectural style. The three-storey frontage was as high as the seven storeys of the modern office building to its left. On the terrace above the third storey, and set back from the façade, was an additional level with a triangular pediment roof. The symmetry of the building, and its pediments and columns, hinted at an Italian neoclassical style, whilst the façade displayed the charm and variety of French architecture with its arches, architraves and mouldings.

Trees dotted the lawn, and a fountain played to our right. In an open area in the centre of the park, the statue of a nineteenth century military officer crowned a twenty-metre marble column. I guessed that the officer was one of Argentina's national heroes.

'It's so peaceful,' I said. 'On Friday I could hardly see these lawns until I was almost on top of them. The traffic was pandemonium – horns honking, cars and buses squeezed into one lane because a delivery truck was double parked.'

I recalled sidewalks buzzing with office workers, and cafés and restaurants bustling with patrons at outdoor tables, shaded by umbrellas. Smartly dressed men and women sweltered in the heat, many of the men wearing suits and ties, and in one case, instead of a tie, a fetching canary-yellow cravat. A row of kiosks sold law books – stacks of them, with names such as *Jurisprudencia, Derecho* or 'Law,' and *Leyes* or 'Laws.'

The kiosks, cafés and restaurants were now closed.

I thought of the law books and said to Pedro, 'I gather there's a court house near here?'

He pointed to our left, 'Right there. It's the Supreme Court.'

The building was so imposing that I wondered how I could have missed it on Friday – as with the *Teatro Colón,* it took up a whole city block. Maybe I'd been too preoccupied with getting tickets, or skirting the crowds.

The style of the building was monumental neoclassical. The first floor with its high arches, and the second floor with its attractive columns, were united in the centre of the façade by a row of huge, tapering square columns that detracted from its appeal. I assumed it was built to impress upon citizens the importance of the justice system.

'Remember that movie we saw in Sydney, *El secreto de sus ojos* – "The Secret in Their Eyes?" ' Pedro asked me. 'A few scenes were filmed inside the courthouse. We can visit on weekdays – I'll check it out.'

'If you have time between tile laying and grout purchasing,' I said. I *did* hope he'd find out, but I wasn't holding my breath – the renovation took up so much of his time.

'And what's that building over there, to the right of the theatre? The one with the row of statues above the columns, sort of Greek Revival style?' I asked.

The building boasted a beautiful portico with four ionic columns and two lateral square columns of grey granite, their dark colour contrasting with the pale sandy colour of the walls. A row of six caryatids, one above each of the six portico columns, supported the base of a triangular pediment roof. I loved the gracious lines.

'Oh, it's a high school,' Pedro said.

'A *school*? In that fabulous building?'

'Yes – one of Argentina's presidents – in the mid nineteenth century – said that school buildings were part of the education process, and should be grand, bright, airy and beautiful. They should have a positive effect on the student. My own school was once a lovely old mansion.'

'I can't imagine going to school in such a wonderful building. And looking out over this park and those palm trees – marvellous.'

We walked across the lawn and I breathed in the fresh weekend air. It was so calming to be surrounded by grass and trees. A lonely bus left its stop nearby, the sound of its motor barely breaking the silence. We heard the muted voices of a small group of people near us. They were strolling in the direction of the theatre, as were the other few groups we saw. There was one exception, a woman with a bible under her arm who ran toward the bus, waving frantically for the driver to stop.

*

Along with other concertgoers, we climbed the steps to the theatre entrance and soon found ourselves in a grand foyer. Cream and rose marble columns surrounded us, and way up above us, light shone through a beautiful octagonal stained-glass window that filled the ceiling.

Pedro interrupted my awestruck gazing. 'The tickets aren't numbered – so I'll grab a couple of seats whilst you look around. There's no interval, and I doubt we can loiter after the concert. Come up here.'

And he sprang up a flight of marble steps flanked on either side, at floor level, by a sculpted lion's head, toward what I assumed was the concert hall. I ran up behind him and he stopped and pointed to an area above the foyer, at the front of the building. 'Go up there to have a look at the *Salón dorado* – the 'Golden Room.' Have your phone ready for photos. Quick! See you inside.'

I raced up the side stairs and through a gallery, and almost tripped over myself as I entered a sumptuous salon that took up the width of the building. From its high ceiling hung a row of massive crystal and gold French Empire chandeliers, their reflections repeated forever in wall-high mirrors at either end. The hall was lined with arched windows separated by cream coloured columns, the base of each covered with floral and leaf encrustations in gold. The opulence reminded me of the rooms in the Palace of Versailles. It took my breath away.

The bell rang to remind the audience to be seated, and I dragged myself downstairs to find the concert hall. I took a few steps into the hall and stopped dead. The hall was magnificent, a sea of red velvet chairs surrounded by six tiers of golden balconies arranged in a horseshoe shape facing the stage. Plush rose and beige curtains with embroidered panels framed the entrances to the theatre boxes. Above the red velvet stage curtain, the cream ceiling and wall were covered in gilt reliefs. The ceiling painting surrounded a massive hemispherical chandelier and depicted strolling medieval minstrels in pastel hues against soft blues.

The concert hall was similar in style to many of the traditional European theatres we'd visited, but more opulent, more luxurious.

Someone bumped into me and I came down to earth. '*Perdón*,' they said, looking at me with concern. I automatically responded '*No, no es nada*' 'No, it's nothing' – the mandatory response for an Argentine. I looked around and saw Pedro waving at me from halfway down the stalls. The hall was packed, with almost all of the two thousand five hundred seats occupied.

We settled into our seats and the curtain rose. I loved the two songs by Carlos Guastavino, '*En los surcos del amor . . . donde se siembran los celos*' 'In the furrows of love . . . where the seeds of jealousy are sown,' and '*Se equivocó la paloma*' 'The dove made a mistake.' The lovely music, the clarity of the sound, and the opulence of the hall were intoxicating.

As we applauded the first piece, I whispered to Pedro, 'I see what you mean about the acoustics. I can hear the notes so clearly.'

'They say it has the best acoustics of any concert hall in the world,' he said. 'When Pavarotti sang here, his only complaint was that the acoustics were too perfect – the audience could hear the slightest mistake.'

What could I say? We were in one of the most magnificent theatres in the world, listening to superb music. With our own pied-à-terre in Buenos Aires.

*

Later in the afternoon, Pedro stopped humming one of the tunes we'd heard and said, 'You know how I mentioned those other free classical music events? Why don't we go to one?'

Why not indeed, I thought. I grabbed my computer and searched for concerts. But it was not as easy as I'd expected, and from time to time I almost gave up. It was remarkably difficult to find useful information, unless it was about the *Teatro Colón*.

But I persevered, determined to find out. After half an hour of searching, I came upon the first few hints of free concerts, and soon found that we were spoilt for choice. The *Mozarteum Argentino* offered free concerts on Wednesdays, the Stock Exchange on Fridays, and the Faculty of Law and the Museum of Decorative Arts on Saturdays. Concerts given by the *Orquesta Filarmónica de Buenos Aires* were free when it performed away from its base, the *Teatro Colón*. The huge old *Correo Central* or 'Central Post Office' building, recently converted into the largest cultural centre in Latin America, housed an acoustically impressive auditorium. That auditorium was now the home of the *Orquesta Sinfónica Nacional*, with all performances free.

'Looks as though we're going to be busy,' I said. 'There's so much to choose from.'

As I searched I found that the *RadioARG* app gave access to Argentine radio stations online – including our favourite stations *Amadeus* and *Nacional Clásica*. And I also found that there were a large number of music conservatories in Buenos Aires city, and many more in Buenos Aires province.

Having listed the free classical music venues for future reference, I changed the search completely, in order to find other music options in the city. Tango of course, popped up all the time, with countless venues and mentions of the *Tango Buenos Aires Festival* in August each year, and the *Tango Dance World Cup*. I knew of these, but it was unbelievable to see the extent and diversity of jazz, contemporary, rock, Argentine *música folklórica* or 'folk music,' even gospel and ragtime, all involving both local and visiting professionals. There were five opera companies as well as two 'Off *Colón*' groups called *Sol Lírica* and *Lírica Lado B*. There were many music festivals in Buenos Aires and throughout Argentina, including classical, rock, pop, electronic, indie, blues, folkloric, and country. And interestingly, major ballet companies in London, New York and Paris had Argentine principal dancers.

Then I broadened the search to theatre and plays. After seeing all the theatres on *Avenida Corrientes*, I shouldn't have been surprised – but I was – to find that at least three hundred plays were performed in Buenos Aires each week – political plays, comedy and stand-up, musicals, classics including Shakespeare – in Spanish – and 'off Broadway.'

By this time, I was cross-eyed and stopped searching.

'I'm beginning to see what you mean about Buenos Aires being cultural and vibrant,' I said to Pedro. 'But it's not as though it's promoted strongly, especially classical music.'

'True,' he said. 'And tourists don't seem to pick up on it. Tango, yes. Meat and Malbec, yes. Economic crises, often. I suppose it could be a language issue – lots of tourists don't speak Spanish. Or maybe it's a belief that tourists aren't interested.'

I recalled a book I'd seen in France, showcasing the beautiful opera houses of the world. The *Teatro Colón* wasn't even mentioned, despite its magnificence and its world-class acoustics.

'Oh well,' I said, 'Whatever the reason, let's enjoy it.'

*

On Monday we reverted to renovation mode. The sixth week of the renovation became the ALMOST FRUITLESS SHOPPING WEEK.

In the mornings, José and Pedro organized the timetables for plinth building, rendering and tiling. The dividing wall would be removed within the next week.

Our afternoons were spent in homeware shops, looking for appliances for a finished kitchen. In these shops, Pedro's thriftiness, his excellent memory, and his enquiring approach all shone brightly together, driving shop assistants – and me – to distraction.

We inspected skimmers – to skim off the fat in casseroles – in four different shops before Pedro settled on one in the fifth shop because it was as suitable as the third one, but a few pesos cheaper. A garlic crusher needed six conversations with shop assistants on aspects of manufacture and efficiency, before Pedro told me that chopping garlic with a knife was preferable to crushing it. The pepper mills needed three discussions on strength and reliability before he rejected all of them.

It was the same in Sydney when we went shopping – Pedro became distracted because of his positive interest in practically every item in the shop. And if he wanted to *buy* an item, he investigated it thoroughly, reducing the chance of being sold a 'dud.'

¿A mamá mono con bananas verdes?
Would you offer a (wise old) mother monkey green bananas?
Meaning: There is no way you can fool him.

During these business negotiations, I stood on one foot and then another, trying not to tear my hair out.

Aburrirse como un hongo.
To become as bored as a mushroom.

If it were up to me, we would have finished all the shopping within a fraction of the time – except that if Pedro were with me he would ask, 'How can you tell that it's the best one?' 'What do you know about its functionality?' 'Why didn't you ask more questions about how it works?'

It was thanks to our even temperaments that we remained calm during these, in my view unsuccessful, and apparently in his mind, constructive, shopping trips. The odd coffee stop helped.

Toward the end of the week, he *did* buy a set of 'not quite reliable enough' saucepans to tide us over until Sarah arrived. The kitchen would be finished by then, and Pedro couldn't imagine it without saucepans.

'These ones are okay – they'll do for now,' he said, 'But good quality ones are incredibly expensive – *way* too expensive.' Then he saw some cooking knives, and said, 'Look at these, they're fantastic quality, from Brazil – just across the border. But in Australia they're half the price. Just as well we have some knives already.'

In that same shop he found a large circular Pyrex dish that he could use for a tuna fish pie, like the one his Mum had prepared for Christmas dinner. Whilst Pedro ruminated on the benefits of the Pyrex dish, I ducked out of the shop to buy figs from the greengrocer's next door. I'd seen open boxes of them, their alternating stripes of pastel green and grey-brown calling out to be tasted. I was becoming used to the seasonal abundance of fruits here – first strawberries, then cherries, and now figs. I wasn't sure why the fruit drew me in more than it ever had in Sydney, where the seasons were the same and the fruit as delicious. Maybe the fruit reminded me of home and I was more homesick than I cared to admit. Or maybe I was more relaxed.

The fig purchase was only a short respite during those endless and mostly fruitless shopping afternoons – fruitless except for the figs of course, and except for the purchase of a skimmer, the not-so-reliable saucepans and a Pyrex dish.

I reflected back on our first shopping outings when we quickly bought items for the apartment including a bed, linen, pillows, and the dilapidated antique furniture. How was it that we bought all those articles so quickly? Then I remembered the futile 'saucepan hunt.' I concluded that kitchen appliances demanded Pedro's close attention more than any other household item.

There was one big positive to the week, and that was music. Now that I knew where to look for free concerts, I found three to choose from, and I researched the performers. On Friday, *La Barroca del Suquía* orchestra would play at the *Correo Central* cultural centre. It was one of the first baroque orchestras formed in Argentina, and was based in Córdoba, a city to the northwest of Buenos Aires. On Saturday, the *Orquesta Nacional de Música Argentina Juan de Dios Filiberto*, or simply *La Filiberto*, would play at the Faculty of Law building. The orchestra was dedicated to Argentine music and composers, and was named after a famous Argentine violinist, conductor, poet and composer. Later on Saturday, the *Cuarteto Petrus* or 'Petrus' Quartet' was to play at the Museum of Decorative Arts. This string quartet was led by Pablo Saraví, the first violinist of the Buenos Aires Philharmonic Orchestra, and recognized as the best Argentine violinist of his generation. The name of the quartet, *Petrus*, was a Latin version of the Italian name *Pietro*, and was chosen in honour of Pietro Giovanni Guarneri, who in 1690 made the violin played by Saraví.

I was astounded at the quality of the free concerts, and was determined that we would attend at least one of them.

*

Another positive was a big day out. After the ALMOST FRUITLESS SHOPPING WEEK, I needed a break. I'd discovered a tour of one of the grand palaces of Buenos Aires. Pedro joined me in a rare break from his renovation duties.

We took a taxi, but before flagging one down we made sure that its windows were closed – an indication that it would be air-conditioned. Better than slow roasting in a non-air-conditioned bus.

The driver chatted with Pedro as I leaned back into the seat. Being in a car was luxurious.

I noticed two little bobble-head plastic dogs sitting on the dashboard, one white, and one with tiger-like colouring. They nodded whilst the driver and Pedro talked, as though in agreement with their remarks. I gazed out of the window, half listening to the conversation.

But I jolted forward when the driver said, 'I'm having a cataract operation next week in my left eye. I can't see a thing. When I get over that one, they'll do the right eye.' The plastic dogs nodded wisely.

We survived the trip.

118

Pedro winked at me as he closed the door. 'Safe and sound?' he asked. 'Next time we'll ask the driver to take a sight test before we get in.'

*

The taxi sped off, and we turned to face a grand arch framing the beautiful wrought iron gates of the *Palacio San Martín*, a magnificent and imposing building dating from 1909. The Argentine Government acquired the building in 1936 to house the *Cancillería* or 'Department of Foreign Affairs'.

I'd read about the palace and the Argentine history of the era. In the early part of the twentieth century, Argentina's wealth led Europeans to coin the phrase, 'As wealthy as an Argentine.'

> *Tenían un vagón de guita.*
> They had a wagonload of cash. In the old days, a special train carriage was set aside for transporting cash.

Many wealthy families had amassed their vast riches through land grants and land grabs in the nineteenth century.

> *La época de vacas gordas.*
> The era of fat cows.
> Meaning: A time of abundance.

They competed with each other in displays of wealth, ostentatiously building grand palaces. The *Palacio San Martín* was no exception.

In stark contrast, many people lived in crowded and squalid conditions in areas such as the *Boca* district on the other side of town. They had to take any work available.

> *Cuando hay hambre no hay pan duro.*
> When there is hunger there is no stale bread.
> Meaning: Beggars can't be choosers.

The *Boca* was immortalized in the tango *'Caminito,'* named after one of its roads. The famous Argentine artist Quinquela Martín, born in the *Boca*, was the driving force behind the group of artists who painted *Caminito's* houses in bright colours, attracting tourism to the area.

*

Our English-speaking tour guide met us in the main foyer. 'This fabulous palace was built by the Anchorena family in the Beaux-Arts style,' she said. 'It was designed as three separate homes, one for the widow, and one each

119

for her two children, not to mention one hundred and fifty servants.'

'One hundred servants would be enough for me,' I heard in a Scottish brogue behind me. 'Or even fifty,' someone else countered, also in English, his Spanish accent only faint. 'I can already list enough jobs for ten.'

Pedro and I smiled at each other and turned around to see two men, one tall with red hair and freckles and the other shorter with dark hair and a neat beard and moustache.

'Maybe you can give *us* a job,' said Pedro. 'We're moving to Argentina for a few years.'

Pedro smiled his cheeky smile at me, but I had no chance to respond because the guide continued, 'One of the most beautiful churches in Buenos Aires was built with an Anchorena family donation. The widow used to love gazing at the church – it was on the other side of that park, *Plaza San Martín* – from one of the palace windows. In those days there were no trees in the park, just grass.'

The guide pointed to where the church was supposed to be, but I couldn't see a thing. Was it hidden behind the huge trees? Or did I need a new prescription for my glasses?

> *No veía una vaca dentro de un baño.*
> I couldn't see a cow in a bathroom.
> Meaning: I was very short sighted.

'When her son fell in love with the daughter of the "less noble" Kavanagh family, the widow forbade the romance. Corina, the girl's mother, was outraged.'

'He made her change her mind?' asked the Scottish voice.

'Quite the opposite. Corina understood there was never going to be a marriage. She wanted vengeance. Land in front of the church came up for sale, and even though the Anchorena widow was interested, she went to Europe on holidays. It was a careless move.'

> *El que se fue a Sevilla perdió su silla.*
> He who went to Seville, lost his seat.
> Meaning: Leave something unattended at your peril. Rhyming slang, often used by children.

'Corina swooped in and bought the land. Within fourteen months she had built the largest reinforced concrete structure in the world at the time – the thirty-one-storey Kavanagh building. It blocked the widow's view of the church forever. Clearly the widow underestimated Corina's resolve.'

'Well done Corina.' It was that Scottish voice again. I couldn't help grinning. 'I'm guessing you're from Scotland?' I asked.

'Glasgow. Alastair,' he said, 'Are you . . .' But the tour guide resumed her speech and we turned to listen, and to follow her to another room.

When the tour was over, Alastair suggested the four of us go for a coffee. A café was easy to find, not only because we were in *Recoleta*, the refined, smart, and elegant *barrio* of well-heeled old money, expensive shops and restaurants, but also because, as far as I could tell, there were cafés all over Buenos Aires.

It turned out that Alastair had arrived in Buenos Aires two years previously, for a three-month break, met Matías, and stayed. Now he was, as he said, 'A happy part of the landscape.'

'I'm trying to persuade Catherine to do the same – to settle here – for a few years. Please only say positive things,' Pedro entreated.

It was interesting to meet a foreigner who'd made the move and who enjoyed living in the city. We talked for half an hour, and then Matías remembered a meeting he had to attend. 'I need to hurry to get there on time,' he apologized.

Alastair looked at his watch and told us that he too needed to leave, and I wasn't able to ask him all my questions about living in Buenos Aires as a foreigner. We all agreed to meet again soon, and exchanged contact details.

*

I wanted to prolong my day with Pedro, so I said, 'Why don't we visit Tía Diana? She told us we should. And you're obviously her favourite nephew.' Whenever Tía and Pedro met at the in-laws, they became involved in long conversations.

'Let's buy sandwiches and eat them on the way,' I said.

Pedro brightened up. 'We can tell her all about the renovation.'

Then he must have registered the sandwich issue.

'Are you hungry *already*?' he asked. Pedro had forgotten – again – that I needed to eat regularly.

'I *will* be by the time we arrive. Isn't it a long way on the bus? Doesn't she live in *provincia*?' *Provincia* was what *porteños* or 'Port people,' the inhabitants of inner Buenos Aires, called the outer areas of the city.

> *Donde el diablo perdió el poncho.*
> Where the devil lost his poncho.
> Meaning: A long, long way away.

It didn't take long to find a bakery – as with cafés, they were omnipresent. They all sold *miga* sandwiches, a snack I'd discovered on our appliance-seeking treks around town. The sandwiches were made each day, piled up in refrigerated glass-fronted counters, and covered with a slightly damp cloth to keep them from drying out. They had three thin layers of crust-less bread and two separate fillings, altogether being fifteen to twenty millimetres thick. There was always 'ham and cheese,' but my favourite was 'ham, roasted capsicum and egg.'

I ate my sandwich on the bus, daydreaming about those heady years of Argentina's great wealth. I imagined a city where one elegant house merged into another as far as the eye could see. Where motor vehicles, trams and a few horse-drawn carriages travelled along wide Parisian-style avenues. Where architectural fantasies were expressed in amazing buildings such as the *Barolo*, whose every feature reflected aspects of Dante's 'Divine Comedy.' Where the dazzlingly beautiful stained-glass windows of *Palacio San Martín* were covered with fabulous tapestries because the windows themselves became 'common' when the European artisans who created them moved to Argentina. Where the intricate wall panelling of whole palaces was sent to Buenos Aires from Europe, to be installed in new mansions.

> *En esa época se decía que ataban a los perros con longanizas.*
> In that era it was said that they tied up dogs with strings of sausages.
> Meaning: It was a time of plenty; of opportunity.

And where Corina built a multi-storey building to cut off the view of another.

Even though I'd read so much about the city, I'd so far seen only a fraction.

Empanada gallega y postre de higos con mascarpone – Tuna Fish Pie from Galicia, and a Fig with Mascarpone Dessert

Empanada gallega
Tuna Fish Pie from Galicia

Tuna fish pie was one of Pedro's favourite dishes as he grew up, and he loved to make it. Although it was a large pie, it shared the description _empanada_ with the small pastry-wrapped snack described in Chapter 7.

On the day that Pedro bought the Pyrex dish, I hadn't realized that the dish was to be used for dinner that same evening. In a welcome break from our usual dinner routine of buying takeout roast chicken or pizza, or having a cheap restaurant meal, we'd been invited to the in-laws – as long as Pedro cooked the meal. He'd decided on _empanada gallega_, in the hope of gleaning some new cooking tips from his Mum.

Pedro's Mum was the _empanada gallega_ specialist in the family, even though she was not from Galicia in Spain but from Cantabria. Pedro said that she always took one of these pies to family gatherings – as she had for the Christmas meal. And although she had a perfectly good dish for making the pie, Pedro had wanted to buy one for our future kitchen, and to test it out that night.

In Sydney, when Pedro prepared this pie for lunch with friends, we served it with a mixed green salad or roasted Mediterranean vegetables, accompanied by chilled Sauvignon Blanc or Pinot Noir. A guest once insisted that it was a chicken pie – probably because the onion caused the tuna to lose its 'fishiness.'

This is Pedro's version of _empanada gallega_.

Ingredients
Red or Spanish, and brown, onions in equal quantities. As a rough guide the onions should be the same weight as the tuna, i.e. 800g or so.

½ large red capsicum or a whole small one

2 x 400g cans tuna. The tuna should be chunky and of good quality, in oil. It should not be shredded tuna or sandwich tuna.

Olive oil

2 cloves of garlic, roughly chopped

10-12 green olives, pitted and sliced lengthways into 4 to 6 slithers

5 tbsp tomato purée, or a finely chopped tomato with all its juice, or a hydrated sun-dried tomato to give more sweetness.

Salt and pepper

1 heaped tbsp of oregano

¼ tsp of thyme

2 heaped tsp smoked paprika. Apart from the flavour, it gives the pie a lovely red colour. If you prefer, use mild, or hot, paprika.

2 x 25cm diameter layers of puff pastry. Follow the packet directions for when to remove it from the freezer. Taking it out too soon makes it sticky and difficult to handle.

3 hard-boiled eggs, the yolks separated out and crumbled and the whites cut into slithers and kept apart from the crumbled yolks

Method

Feather or julienne the onions. To feather the onions, cut off both ends, then cut the onion in half along the root-to-stem line. Slice thinly to achieve long thin semi-circular shaped strips – these are the 'feathers.' If available use a mandolin, employing the thin slice section.

Lengthwise, cut off one third of the capsicum. Cut it into brunoise size pieces, i.e. 2mm squares. See Chicken Casserole at the end of Chapter 3 for brunoise.

Cut the rest of the capsicum lengthwise into thin slithers and cut the slithers in half.

Open the cans of tuna and drain the oil.

In a large frying pan, put up to 100ml olive oil, place on a medium heat and add the onion, garlic and the small squares of capsicum. Sauté for at least 3-5 minutes.

Add the strips of capsicum and sauté 5-7 minutes or more, until the onion is slightly transparent. Stir occasionally so the onion cooks evenly and does not stick to the pan.

Add the lid, lower the heat, and allow to sweat until the capsicum is soft – up to 10 minutes. Check a couple of times and stir. Don't allow it to dry up. If you need to, add more oil. Once this is cooked, add the tuna and some olive oil. Make sure that the tuna is broken up and mixed with the onion.

Add the olives. Add the tomato purée. If it is drying out at this stage you could add say 50ml of water.

Season, add the oregano, thyme and smoked paprika, and cook for a further 3 minutes to draw the flavour of the herbs into the mix.

Turn off the heat, and let it cool.

Take the puff pastry out of the freezer and allow it to defrost.

Preheat the oven to 200°C.

Gently lay a sheet of puff pastry across the base of a 24-centimetre circular pie dish to check whether it covers the base and walls. Then take out the pastry and smear some oil on the base and sides of the pan. If the pastry was the correct size, lay it back in the dish. If not, roll it out with a rolling pin to the correct size. Or if you are daring, stretch it with your hands and hope it doesn't break.

Tip the cooled tuna and onion mix into the pie dish. Distribute the slices of the white of the egg over the top, and add the crumbled yolk.

Add the lid of the pie and seal the edge, cutting off excess pastry.

Paint the top of the pie with beaten egg if you want it to become golden and shiny when cooked or, if you prefer, with milk. In the latter case it will not go golden and shiny but will help the pie to retain moisture.

Cut a cross in the centre of the top to allow steam to escape.

Place the pie in the centre rack in the oven and cook for 20-30 minutes. You may need to adjust cooking time and temperature or to move the pie around depending on your oven. When the pastry is golden brown and to your liking, the pie is ready, since everything inside is already cooked.

Take it out, allow it to cool slightly and remove it from the pie dish.
Serves six to eight depending on appetites.

Variation

This is a versatile and accommodating dish. Variations could include the following.
If you prefer a sweeter flavour, use only red onions.

Save the capsicum until later in the process. If you do this, layer sliced roasted capsicum over the top of the egg before adding the top layer of pastry. Incorporating the capsicum into the tuna mix makes it sweeter and moister but adding the capsicum later makes it more colourful. You can do both of course.

Substitute other herbs or use them in larger quantities. For different flavours you could add chilli at the capsicum strip stage, or fresh parsley at the end, when preparing the filling.

Add the eggs a different way. Don't slice and crumble them. Instead, when the tuna mix is in the pie, make say 5 depressions evenly around the pie, and crack an egg into each. The yolks will stand out in the cooked pie.

Higos con mascarpone
Figs with Mascarpone

This yummy dessert (also mentioned in Chapter 2) followed the <u>empanada gallega</u>.

Ingredients

4 small figs or 2 large ones (or, for a variation, use juicy peaches instead of figs)
20g butter
1 tsp extra virgin olive oil
Cognac or brandy
100g mascarpone
2 tbsp sugar for the mascarpone, and 1 tbsp for the figs
1 tbsp coarsely chopped pistachios for each serving, or if you don't have pistachios, a mix of almonds and walnuts, or just walnuts

Method

Cut the figs in half along the stem line.
Whisk the mascarpone with the sugar and set aside.
Place butter and oil in a frypan and cook the figs with the flesh side down until they go golden brown. Turn over.
Add the sugar to the pan, and a little splash of cognac or brandy, and cook until the figs are soft, the alcohol has evaporated and the sugar is caramelizing.
Turn heat off.
Place figs on plates with open side up, add a couple of dollops of mascarpone, sprinkle over the nuts, and drizzle with juice from pan.
Serves 2

9

TOM-TOMS

Tía Diana lived in a street devoid of apartment blocks. The open view of the sky was a novelty for me. It made me nostalgic for our neighbourhood in Sydney and its low-rise skyline. Some houses in the street were stand-alone, but the façade of Tía's house was continuous with those on either side. Pedro told me that she shared a common entrance with two houses to the rear of her property. The other two houses had been built when the original property was subdivided.

Pedro pressed the buzzer.

'Watch that curtain, it'll twitch when she checks who we are,' he said. Sure enough, her face appeared in the window, and she waved. We heard a key turning in a lock, and footsteps.

Tía opened the street door and we entered an open-air passageway that stretched ahead of us for at least thirty metres. The right hand wall of the passageway was two metres high, and was the boundary of the next-door property. Along the passageway on the left was an entrance that I guessed was Tía's front door. Further along on the left was an open courtyard, after which another door on the left was the entrance to the second house. At the end of the passageway was the entrance to the third house. The property size was narrow though deep, and I deduced that the houses were each about the same size as our apartment. It was as though someone had sliced horizontally through an apartment block to remove one storey, and had placed it at ground level, leaving the common areas open to the sky.

The smell of bleach escaped from her house, a telltale sign that Tía had been washing the floor. I'd heard that she put all the relatives to shame by doing this each morning.

It was family lore that Tía dressed impeccably regardless of her choice of activity – cooking, cleaning, or simply sipping *mate*. And today I could vouch for the truth of those stories. In fact, I had the weird sensation that the floor had cleaned itself. There was not a crease to be seen on either of Tía's perfectly matching skirt or blouse. Not a hair of her perm escaped. I hoped she never dropped in on us when we were cleaning our apartment, wearing old shorts and sloppy t-shirts, dripping with perspiration in the heat.

Before we stepped into the house, we kissed and hugged and she asked us about the renovation.

'So they're tiling already? Have you chosen the cupboards? Felicitas told me that the external unit of the air conditioner is falling off the building,' she said.

Pedro rolled his eyes. The family tom-toms had been busy, as usual.

Tía Diana led us into the house and removed her apron. As she closed the screen door, she turned to me. 'Do you see that hole in the mesh of the door? When Pedro was three years old, he used to swing on the door. He'd stand on the frame and hold on to the handle as he told me about his adventures. His little shoes pushed the screen out – from all his swinging back and forth. I could never bring myself to fix it.'

'*Qué tierno*,' I said, mimicking a remark of Nora's as she watched the cute antics of a child, in our 'Spanish lesson' café. I assumed it meant something like, 'How sweet.' Tía smiled and nodded, so it must have been correct. Emboldened, I decided that from now on I'd keep throwing myself into the language – and see how I fared.

I was trying to imagine Pedro as a young child when the phone rang.

'Felicitas, hello. Yes, Pedro's here. Yes, Catherine too. Yes, of course he's going to tell me about the cupboards . . . The air conditioner? Oh, I know all about that!'

> *Chocolate por la noticia.*
> Chocolate for the news.
> Meaning: That's not news.

She listened for a while and said, 'Okay, I'll tell you the latest when they've gone . . . Bye bye, talk soon.'

'That would be *too* soon,' Pedro whispered to me, rolling his eyes and grinning. With his hand horizontal at neck level, as though he were measuring the height from the ground, he smiled and shook his head, saying, 'I'm up to here with their curiosity.'

> *Me tienen hasta el moño.*
> They have me up to the bowtie.
> Meaning: I'm fed up with them.

Tía put down the phone, smiled at each of us in turn, and nodded toward the table, where we sat. Pedro protested, 'I don't know why we came to visit you, Tía. You know about everything we do. Is there *anything at all* that we can tell you?'

'Yes, of course there is – tell me if you're going to move here for a few years. *That* should be an easy one for you to answer.'

Pedro and I looked at each other. He was a suddenly a little nervous.

'It's up to Catherine, really,' he said. Tía raised her eyebrows and turned to me.

I wasn't sure what to say. I'd become more familiar with our *barrio* and I could now easily use the buses and subway. I was enjoying my classes, the concerts were brilliant, and today's tour fascinating – and we'd even exchanged contact details with the two people we'd met.

Our apartment had begun to feel like a home, however cluttered and full of strangers it was at present. But I also felt cut off from old friends, and from familiar landmarks and customs.

'I like Buenos Aires more and more,' I said, 'but I miss family and friends. I've been in touch with one of my closest friends – she'll visit us before we leave.'

Tía looked at me sympathetically. 'I don't think I could move countries and leave all that's familiar. I'm sure your other friends haven't forgotten you – they'll think you're having a marvellous time, and I'm sure you are, aren't you?'

'Yes,' I said, a bit dispirited and trying to smile more. Tía was so kind and motherly. She sensed my tangled mind and let me off the hook, changing the subject as she turned to Pedro.

'I went to the local market yesterday. It's nothing compared to the old days. The chickens are all dead and plucked.'

She sighed wistfully and added, 'They used to be displayed live. I'd pick them up and feel the meat on them, choose the one I wanted, and give it to the stallholder. An hour later it was ready, headless and featherless.'

I felt queasy.

She turned to me, explaining, 'I needed a good, meaty chicken for my *pastel de choclo*. I couldn't let my standards drop.' Tía was referring to a local dish made with *choclo*, or 'sweet corn.'

Luckily we moved on from dead chickens and I relaxed into the sofa, adding the odd *sí* or *no* as the conversation continued. It was lovely to be with family, and to learn more about Pedro from his aunt.

*

In my usual half-daydreaming state, I wasn't sure whether I saw a movement out of the corner of my eye. I stopped daydreaming. Pretending to listen to the conversation and without moving my head, I shifted my gaze so that I could examine the passageway outside the screen door. An animal the size of a rat lumbered toward the street.

I turned to look directly at the 'thing' and my eyes nearly popped out of my head. Pedro and Tía followed my gaze.

Pedro shouted, 'A tortoise!' He sprang up and raced outside to grab it. He didn't look at all surprised to see a tortoise on the premises. I guessed that tortoises were a common pet in Argentina.

He brought it inside and held it close for me to see, upside down. It was the size of Pedro's hand, and its heart pounded madly, pushing up against its plastron with each beat.

'Look at that heartbeat – it's scared to death,' I said.

But Pedro wasn't worried about its heart.

'What do you feed it?' he asked Tía.

'Oh, lettuce, that's all they eat. I've tried carrots, tomatoes, everything.'

'They? There's another one?' Pedro looked around and saw a second tortoise bringing up the rear. 'No wonder they're running away from home. Lettuce? Nothing else?'

'As I said, I've tried everything.'

Pedro frowned, and grabbed a peach from the fruit bowl. Tía Diana remonstrated, 'You can't waste that peach.'

Pedro ignored her. 'Watch this, they love yellow foods.' He broke it open and offered it to the tortoise. It ate the peach immediately, or more accurately, 'It ate the peach slowly,' as tortoises do. Tía was amazed.

Pedro patted one of the tortoises on its shell, though the tortoise probably didn't notice.

'Poor things – eating lettuce for months,' he said. He looked at Tía. 'Has it been months? Weeks? However long, it's been *too* long. And all that time, yearning for tasty food. Did you try apricots? They also eat succulents – did you try cactus?'

Tía Diana laughed. 'I'm so glad you're here. There aren't any other biologists in the family. By the way, they don't have names yet – any ideas?'

'That's easy,' I declared. 'Touché and Ninja.' When she looked confused, I tried to describe the two cartoon shows 'Touché Turtle and Dum Dum' and 'Teenage Mutant Ninja Turtles.' I failed miserably in my attempt and Pedro provided the Spanish translations – *La Tortuga d'Artagnan* and *Las Tortugas Ninja*. I wasn't completely convinced that Tía knew of either show, because she wore a puzzled frown during Pedro's explanation, but happily for me, she agreed to the names and it was official.

Pedro and I took the tortoises to the courtyard behind Tía's house. Their heartbeats had normalized. They disappeared, at tortoise pace, into a hole in the wall of the courtyard.

Touché, away! I thought. *I hope they'll eat well now, and they won't run away from home again.*

The buzzer sounded. Tía picked up the edge of the curtain. 'It's Martín.'

Echá los fideos que estamos todos.
Throw the pasta (into the water) as we are all here.
Meaning: Everybody's here now. The expression is used when unexpected guests appear. It is similar to 'Let's put the kettle on.' It does not mean that a meal is to be prepared.

Pedro sighed with resignation, 'There go the tom-toms again. How did he get here so quickly?'

Más rápido que un bombero.
Faster than a fireman.

He added, 'Felicitas must have been on the phone to him as soon as she hung up.'

Martín kissed Tía and me, and gave Pedro a hug, saying, 'I hear they're about to plaster the walls. Are you ever going to finish? You must be driving Catherine crazy. Felicitas called Antonia, and Antonia told me you were here, so I asked Rodolfo to drop me off – he had to go into town but he'll come and see the renovation tomorrow.'

What it's like to have seventy cousins, I thought.

Tía offered us a coffee. When I told her I'd like to help, she asked me to find the biscuits in the dresser. I opened one of the doors at random, not knowing where the biscuits would be.

'Tía keeps everything in there,' Pedro said. 'She's even kept my cousins' old school books.'

I saw a pile of old exercise books, and other objects that Tía must have collected over the years – pottery, a stone egg, a child's doll, postcards from Spain – items that didn't fit anywhere else in the small house. But no biscuits. I closed the door.

Before opening another door, I put myself in Tía's shoes. She was shorter than I, and more likely to use the lower section of the dresser for items she used regularly. I guessed the biscuits were there, and opened one of the doors.

But instead of biscuits, I saw piles of dusty plates with matching cups, a teapot, a milk jug and a sugar bowl.

Tía must have seen my surprise. 'I'm keeping that crockery set for Susana. She lived next door, and left Argentina forty years ago to live in Canada. I put the crockery there so it would stay safe.'

Pedro was visibly annoyed. 'But Tía, Susana died in Toronto over ten years ago.'

'Never mind, it will do for her children.'

'They don't even know it exists. They live in Canada. Let me see – I can't remember the pattern.' He took out a dish and examined it, and as he turned it over we saw colourful flowers on a white background.

Tía turned to me and said, 'It's pretty, isn't it?'

At the same time, Pedro looked up and announced, 'It's hideous. No one in the family will want this. You should throw it out.'

'But Pedro, you know that nothing is thrown out in this house,' she said, placatingly. Pedro and Martín exchanged glances and Martín shrugged.

She turned to me again and said, 'I found out later that they left Argentina in fear of their lives, during the military regime. They were the lucky ones.'

She continued, 'At the end of the road, an academic and his family were taken away one morning and never came back. The day they disappeared, there were clothes hanging on the line to dry. No one dared enter that property for years. During those years the clothes turned to faded rags, blowing in the wind.'

I shivered, and my mind went blank.

I must have stood there for a few seconds without registering what was going on, because I noticed that Pedro now had a packet of biscuits in his hand. I took it from him, opened it and ate three at once. That wasn't enough to stop the feeling of faintness that had overcome me, so I grabbed a lump of sugar from a bowl on the table, as a chaser.

These references to the 'disappeared' came up every so often in conversations in Argentina, but I'd never knowingly been near a home that had been affected.

Did Tía need to get that image out of her mind? Is that why she mentioned it? Whatever the reason, it was now imprinted on my memory where it would stay forever. It was frightening to know that within the last forty years, in this very street, such terrible events had transpired.

I knew from Pedro that thousands of people had disappeared during the military regime. It was a time when merely to paint a slogan on a wall, or to take part in a demonstration against the regime, was deemed subversive. 'Subversives' were picked up in the street, or taken from their homes, and sometimes never seen again. Pedro himself had left the country during that time.

Tía shook herself, and moved on to another topic of conversation. I ate a few more biscuits, trying to stop thinking about those faded clothes on the line.

Now that Tía had more of an audience, she took out the photos of her grandfather and of all her aunts and uncles.

The photo of her grandfather was an original, and must have been over one hundred years old. In sepia tones, it revealed Pedro's great grandfather as a tall thin Spaniard wearing a beret and smoking a pipe. *Like José with his beret and pipe – but a hundred years earlier,* I marvelled.

La foto era del año del ñaupa.
The photo was from the year of the *ñaupa*. No one seemed to know what *ñaupa* meant, except 'very old.' The word may have come from *Quechua*, the indigenous language of northern Argentina, where it meant 'the past.'

Because of the hazy background, it was hard to tell whether the photograph was taken in the open air, or inside a room using a 'flash.' In those days a 'flash' meant a dangerous and startling blaze of light caused by burning powdered magnesium. Judging from great-grandfather's wide-eyed look, it probably *was* taken with a flash.

Tía's mother, Pedro's grandmother, looked stern in her photograph, as did all her brothers and sisters. They must have been told not to smile or the camera would break.

Tía resumed her reverie. '. . . I was three when our family left Spain for Argentina. My mother never saw her father again. I can't remember Spain – only the garden of our house. I have no garden here, only a concrete patio.'

Pedro turned to me, saying, 'When I was a boy, before the lot was subdivided, there was an open area behind the house. My grandfather had fruit and olive trees, grape vines, and a vegetable and herb garden. Enough for all the family and a few neighbours.'

And so the afternoon continued, a friendly, laid-back interlude during our renovation saga.

*

Soon it was time to go, 'time' being the operative word. In each room, Tía's clocks were set to slightly different times.

Only the kitchen clock was correct.

The one on the television was five minutes faster than the one in the kitchen. 'So that I don't miss my favourite television shows,' she said.

The one in the bathroom was ten minutes faster than the one on the television. 'So that I get a move on in the mornings,' she explained.

Once Pedro, the scientist, had inspected all the clocks in the house and fully appreciated the system, we were free to go. We kissed and hugged our goodbyes.

On the way we visited Esteban, yet *another* of Pedro's cousins, who lived nearby. 'So the tiles are being laid – what colour? By the way – what's this I hear about the external unit of the air conditioner? Sounds dangerous.'

We eventually extricated ourselves from Esteban's house and journeyed home.

Sitting in the bus with Pedro, I thought of the morning's tour of *Palacio San Martín* and how we'd exchanged contact details with Alastair and Matías. And I reflected on our afternoon with Tía, and the family warmth of her home, with relatives phoning up and dropping around for visits. From now on, when I saw a row of houses like the ones on her street, I imagined that I'd be searching for one similar to hers, with its lace curtains in the front window, and envisaging – even longing for – the family life inside.

Pedro interrupted my reverie. 'Did you mean what you said to Tía? That you like Buenos Aires more and more?'

'Yes of course I did. And the more I find out, the more interesting it is. Culturally, it's amazing. I love the music and theatre in Sydney, but here there's so *much* on offer, and it's so accessible.'

'I told you it was cultural.'

'Yes but it's hard to see that from a distance. And your family is friendly. And most people are very courteous.'

'And didn't a few of your friends say they'd visit?'

'Hmm, yes, but only Sarah's coming.'

I rested my head on Pedro's shoulder. To take my mind off the noise of the traffic and the many conversations going on around us, I turned my mind to our trial period.

I marvelled at how Buenos Aires had crept up on me unawares. Because, from time to time, I asked myself, *What if I did agree to stay?*

Would it be the same as London, which was exciting at first, and where my communications work was interesting, but where homesickness drew me back? Possibly. But the dynamics had now changed completely – I was no longer on my own. If Pedro and I had been in London together, and he'd wanted to stay, perhaps we would have ended up living there.

I fell asleep before we arrived home. Pedro shook me awake, and I stumbled after him to the door of the bus. He stepped down first, and turned to offer me his hand. We strolled home, arm in arm.

*

Tired, but happy from a wonderful day, I glanced at the home phone and saw that we had unheard messages. I pressed 'play,' and sat on the bed, opening my laptop.

I was amazed to hear that there were four messages. One was from José regarding the air conditioner's external unit. 'Pedro, did you hear that one?'

I waited for his response, 'Yes,' from the other room, before I deleted it.

The second one was from Nora, my Spanish teacher, saying that she couldn't make one of our classes next week.

The third was from my friend Sarah in Sydney, telling me she'd emailed me the flight details for her visit. 'Sorry I missed you. Hope you're bearing up amongst all that renovation chaos. Talk soon.'

The fourth was from Mum. 'Hello, at last I figured out the international code – and you're out! You're always beating me to it, but now I know how to call you. Let's have a lovely long chat soon.'

What a pleasant end to the day. So special after a day with Pedro's family. Sarah and Mum felt so close when I heard their voices.

And now that I had opened my inbox, I found eight emails. The first was from another friend, Debbie. It was the first email she'd sent in over three months. During those months, all my phone calls to her had gone to voicemail.

'At last I opened up the attachment to that email you sent a couple of weeks ago,' she wrote. 'I was so busy before Christmas – sorry. Loved the newsletter and tracked back to the one you sent during the silly season. Very interesting! I forwarded both of them to a whole bunch of other people – hope you don't mind. When are you sending the next one? Keep it up.'

The second was Sarah's, with the flight details.

As for the next five, perhaps Debbie had encouraged mutual friends to open the attachments to their emails, or perhaps it was a crazy coincidence, but they had all read the attachments and commented positively. Even Jo, my lawyer friend, a workaholic like me – like the *previous* me – had written.

And the last email was from a complete stranger, telling me they'd received my interesting newsletter from Debbie, and asking me which neighbourhoods in Buenos Aires were best for tourist accommodation.

It was satisfying to know that my newsletters had prompted an enquiry. Writing them at last felt worthwhile. It crossed my mind that I could write a blog, one day, should my observations elicit more interest.

I felt so inspired that I quickly sketched out a third newsletter. Topics would include the *Ateneo* bookshop that Pedro had mentioned, and free concerts at the magnificent *Teatro Colón*. Maybe closed-door restaurants that were only accessed through word of mouth, but served some of the best food. Maybe open-air artisan and organic food markets, or shopping for leather goods. Maybe something about art and architecture.

I'd include the history of the eight-hundred-acre *Reserva ecológica*. This ecological reserve was situated on the coast, beside *Puerto Madero*, a redeveloped portside neighbourhood near the centre of town. Decades ago, the reserve was a disposal site for rubble from building sites. The in-laws told me that the area had been inundated by floodwaters raging down rivers from southern Brazil and Paraguay, covering the building rubble with silt, and forming lakes. Exotic species from the north – plants, and animals such as birds and reptiles that had hung on to branches in the raging torrents for a thousand kilometres – populated the area. Park rangers now patrolled the reserve, as though it had always been a natural ecological wonder. For me the story echoed the magic realism of South American fiction.

Not to be confused with the *Reserva ecológica* was the proposed *Eco parque*, a large new park in *Palermo*. The *Eco parque* would replace the old eighteen-hectare zoo when it closed later in the year. I'd read that the Victorian-era pavilions had been declared national historic monuments and were to be restored.

I'd have to research all these subjects, and to visit the *Ateneo*. There was plenty to keep me occupied, and so much more to discover about the city.

Pastel de choclo — Sweet Corn Pie

Tía Diana was the family expert in <u>pastel de choclo</u>, a delicious pie common in Chile and northwest Argentina, and also found with variations in Bolivia and Peru. <u>Pastel de choclo</u> was similar to a shepherd's pie, but made with both chicken and beef, and with a sweet corn topping instead of mashed potato.

Pedro wanted to impress Tía with his version of the pie when we were all invited to the in-laws for dinner that Saturday. He and I spent much of Saturday afternoon at the in-laws, preparing the components of the pie, but it was well worth the time. I reminded him of a dinner in Sydney where one of our guests had enjoyed the dish so much that he'd scraped glaze off the clay bowl, where sweet corn topping had stuck to the sides.

<u>Choclo</u>, the word for 'sweet corn' in South America, was derived from <u>chuqllu</u>, meaning 'tender maize' in Quechua, a local indigenous language. Sweet corn originated in Central America and, by the time we made our <u>pastel de choclo</u> that Saturday afternoon, it had been used in South American meals for three thousand years. It had been an important part of the Inca diet.

In Chile, the meal was commonly served in individual dishes called <u>pailas de greda</u> or 'dishes of clay.'

Pedro first tasted this dish in Australia, after he'd moved there from Argentina in his late teens. He tried it at a Peruvian restaurant in Sydney, long before Peruvian cuisine appeared on the international gastronomic radar. Unfortunately, the restaurant closed due to a lack of interest in South American food at that time.

This is Pedro's version of <u>pastel de choclo</u>.

Ingredients

Mince (i.e. ground beef) mixture
3 tbsp olive oil, or more if the mince is dry

½ red capsicum, medium to finely chopped — but not quite a brunoise. See the recipe for Chicken Casserole at the end of Chapter 3 for brunoise.

4 brown onions — 2 feathered (for feathering, see Tuna Fish Pie from Galicia recipe in Chapter 8), 2 chopped

4 cloves of garlic, chopped

500g beef mince, not too lean, as you want the <u>pastel de choclo</u> to be moist

Salt and pepper

½ tbsp cumin

2 tsp paprika

1 tsp thyme

1 tbsp oregano

1 hot red chilli, sliced or chopped. The chilli is optional

Chicken
Two thighs with their drumsticks

Salt and pepper
2 tbsp olive oil

Sweet corn topping
6 cobs of corn, or 8 if using individual dishes to serve
10 leaves of basil, chopped or torn
Salt and pepper
¼ tsp nutmeg
½ cup milk
1 knob of butter, about 15-20g

Other ingredients – added when preparing the pie
12 whole black olives, pitted, and rinsed if very salty
⅓ of a cup of raisins, preferably soaked in warm water so they swell up
2 hard boiled eggs, sliced
Salt and pepper
White sugar

Method

Mince mixture
To prepare the mince mixture, add the oil to a large frying pan that can be covered with a lid.

Before the oil gets too hot, add the capsicum and cook for about 4 minutes to release the flavour.

Add the onion and garlic and sauté for a few minutes, then put the lid on and allow to sweat until the onion is translucent – about 8 minutes.

Add the mince and brown it. Make sure it separates and cooks thoroughly and not in lumps.

While the mince cooks, add salt and pepper to taste, and add the cumin, paprika, thyme, oregano and chilli.

At the end of the cooking process the meat should be juicy. If it is not, add olive oil before you stop cooking the meat.

Set aside, leaving the frying pan to be used in the next step – don't wash it.

Chicken
Cut each thigh/drumstick combination into three pieces, one of them being the drumstick, i.e. you will be left with six pieces of chicken.

Add salt and pepper to the chicken.

Use the same frying pan as you used for the mince.

Add oil to the frying pan, heat it and add the chicken.

Brown the chicken, then add the lid to the frying pan and leave to cook at a lower temperature. The chicken should be cooked through, but not dry. This could take about

15 minutes.

Remove the chicken from the frying pan and allow it to cool.

Once the chicken is cool you can use one of these two approaches for presentation: either as chunks — not thin shreds — of chicken that have been taken off the bone, or as small pieces including the bone, e.g. drumstick or the thicker part of the wing.

Set aside.

Sweet corn topping

With a sharp knife, remove the kernels from the corncobs. Corn bits and juice will fly everywhere as you do this. An alternative is to grate the kernels off the cob — use a coarse grater.

Place the kernels and the basil in a food processor and mix for a few minutes until you have a uniform but still textured consistency. You do not need to have a smooth paste, as it is more interesting to have texture on the top of the *pastel de choclo*.

Pour the mixture from the food processor into a saucepan. Add salt, pepper and nutmeg.

Add ½ of the milk and cook on a medium heat, stirring constantly — otherwise the mixture could easily stick and burn.

Add more or less milk depending on how much liquid is released by the corn. The topping should have a creamy consistency.

Cook for 7-10 minutes, stir in the butter and remove from the heat.

Presentation

This dish can be presented as a single pie or as separate individual pies. In the latter case, individual portions are presented in clay dishes, or in small bowls if clay dishes are hard to find.

For a single pie

Pedro uses a 26cm diameter pie dish that is 6cm deep.

Place chicken chunks in the base of the dish.

You do not have to cover the base of the dish completely.

Pedro is a salt addict and adds salt and pepper to the chicken before adding the mince mixture.

Cover the chicken with the mince mixture.

Spread the olives, raisins and slices of hard-boiled egg over the mince.

Cover the entire dish with 1½-2cm of the sweet corn topping.

Sprinkle white sugar on top.

Cook in the oven at 180-200°C for half an hour. Then if you have an oven grill combination, put the *pastel de choclo* on a higher tray in the oven, and turn on the grill so that the sugar turns a golden brown. Or, turn on the oven to maximum.

Serves 6 averagely hungry people, or 4 very hungry people. If you have a side dish, there will be no problem serving 6 people with the quantities outlined above.

Serving

Whether you present this as a whole pie or as individual portions, please remember that the dishes will be extremely hot. We once placed the pie dish on a wooden breadboard on top of the table and it burnt the breadboard and warmed the table top.

Warn your guests about the bones in the chicken, if you left them in.

Hints

This can be a time-consuming dish if you prepare it all on the same day. You can easily prepare the mince mixture and the chicken the day before.

You can use frozen corn.

The mince mixture is an ideal filling for <u>empanadas</u>.

10

A PICK-ME-UP

We were now in the seventh week of the eight-week renovation – the DIVIDING WALL REMOVAL WEEK. The upper half of the wall disappeared, and bags of rubble piled up along the passageway. A waist-high section of wall remained for a counter, and a wine rack would be anchored to the roof beam above.

Pedro said it was time to organize the granite bench tops. In Sydney, granite was incredibly expensive. But in Argentina, there were mountains of it, and it was much cheaper than laminate. Santiago had advised Pedro to save money by dealing directly with the granite workshop, and I accompanied him. It was the day that Nora was unable to meet me for my Spanish class.

We boarded an air-conditioned bus, enjoying the escape from forty-degree Celsius heat and eighty per cent humidity. Fifteen minutes later, Pedro nudged me. 'Look, that's *Chacarita* cemetery,' he said, pointing to a high wall that loomed up on our right. 'It's huge – one hundred hectares – it was established during the yellow fever epidemic in the 1870s. We should go one day and have a look – lots of famous Argentines are buried there.'

'Hmm,' I said. 'Maybe.' I wasn't keen on cemeteries, even though I loved history. The one cemetery that sounded interesting was in *Recoleta*, because of its opulence. That cemetery was the resting place of the famous Eva Perón or *Evita*, who in 1945 married the Argentine President Juan Perón.

'Nora mentioned a freemason tour of *Recoleta* cemetery,' I told Pedro. 'She said that many of the tombs have masonic symbols, and that freemasons played a big part in Argentina's independence movement.'

'She's right,' he said. 'José de San Martín and Manuel Belgrano – two of the leaders of Argentine independence – were freemasons. So their mausoleums aren't on consecrated ground. San Martín's is in an annex off the cathedral, and Belgrano's is outside a church in *San Telmo*.'

My eyes must have widened at this sudden disclosure of information – Pedro wasn't usually a font of historical knowledge – because he hurried to explain.

'Every Argentine school kid learns about the heroes of Argentina – their battles and their victories. As for the freemason link – that's just common knowledge.'

We got off the bus near a row of shops, not far from the cemetery. The area was certainly less tourist-friendly than *Recoleta*, and not as clean. It wasn't an area that I would have liked to visit at night.

We passed a number of shops with headstone displays before arriving at the address. As soon as we stepped inside we were greeted by a haze of granite particles.

Through the haze, we saw huge three-centimetre-thick slabs of granite leaning against the walls. Their surfaces were grey with dust, and many had protuberances that I guessed were the undersides of kitchen sinks. They seemed to be awaiting delivery to homes across the city.

As though floating through a lunar landscape, we followed an army of footprints into a huge, high-ceilinged shed. Skylights poured soft grey beams of light across the floor and the walls, over the massive shelves holding granite in various states of readiness, and over the machinery and the workers. An enormous fan whirred above us, useless in its attempts to clear the air. *This haze must be what asbestos clouds look like*, I thought. A screeching sound from the rear of the shed made me jump. A granite sheet was being polished by one of the men. He wasn't wearing a protective mask, or earmuffs.

Roberto, the owner, shook Pedro's hand and turned to me. We kissed on the cheek. I was getting used to doing this with complete strangers.

'Come into my office, it's quieter,' he said. We were directed through the haze and into a space that served as Roberto's workplace.

He closed the door behind us. There was less haze in there, but no surfaces that were free of dust. Roberto nodded toward two chairs and we sat.

Pedro worked through the measurements with Roberto. The radio played a familiar song from the 80s, Bruce Springsteen's 'Dancing in the Dark.' I smiled inwardly, thinking of the sunlight seeping into the shed.

Roberto placed dull grey samples of granite in front of us and wiped them clean to show us speckled burgundy, orange, and shining black.

'Coffee?' asked Roberto. 'I can leave you for a couple of minutes so you can choose a colour.'

We accepted his offer, and he moved to an alcove behind his desk. A sagging wooden bench held an electric kettle and four mugs. Beneath the bench was a tired looking refrigerator.

With all the granite in the workshop, it was the last place I would have expected to see a bench made of wood.

En casa de herrero, cuchillo de palo.
In a blacksmith's house, a wooden knife.

Ironically, a new song began, the oldie, 'That's Just The Way It Is, Baby,' by The Rembrandts. It could have been the industrial health and safety anthem for the business.

The easy-going approach to safety was not as surprising to me as it might have been when we'd first arrived. We'd seen men demolishing a wall as they stood on top of it, whacking the bricks below them with a pickaxe. Pedro told me that according to Santiago, the laws were strict, but there was a patchy approach to compliance, especially in smaller businesses. Not that Australia was perfect in terms of work health and safety standards – I'd recently read an Australian article lamenting the re-emergence of industrial dust diseases.

We chose the granite colour immediately, having seen many samples on our exploratory shopping afternoons. It was a mottled pink and grey, to match the beige tiles we'd chosen. Pedro continued to discuss dimensions and costs, but my mind wandered and I imagined mountains and fresh air.

Cazando palomas.
Hunting pigeons.
Meaning: Daydreaming.

At last the invoice was finalized and we escaped into the street.

*

Pedro didn't have any pressing 'building site' issues, so I suggested a visit to *Las Violetas*, a grand café in the *barrio* of *Almagro*. I'd wanted to return to the café ever since we'd met Felicitas there for a coffee, one Sunday afternoon.

Pedro jumped at the idea, and we chose a bus route that left us ten blocks from the café. Our path led us past the 'flower sellers corner' of the *barrio* of *Almagro*, and as we approached, the dull grey of the sidewalk disappeared under a brilliant cascade of colours. Dazzled, I recalled how Pedro had wooed me, often bringing bunches of flowers to my office on his way home from work, and encouraging me to leave. I'd found out since, that an ulterior motive had been to put an end to my unhealthy workaholic lifestyle, with its long working days. How our lives had changed since then.

I turned to Pedro. 'I don't know how I coped with that job in Sydney, it was crazy. I'm so glad I left that company.' I now saw how perceptive he'd been in Sydney, and later in Punta Arenas, when he mentioned my stress levels. Quitting that job – and leaving behind the numbers, the meetings, and the politics – was, in retrospect, an even better decision than it had felt at the time.

It was one o'clock, the end of the school 'morning,' and more than once, we crossed the street to avoid clusters of children and parents. In a daily ritual across the city, they gathered on sidewalks and spilled onto the road, holding up traffic. Parents often left cars double-parked outside schools, adding to the chaos.

Primary school kids dragged trollies behind them as though they were going away for the weekend. Others laboured under the weight of a bulging backpack.

'Their homework must be endless,' Pedro said. 'I can't remember ever carrying so many books.'

We turned a corner and a swarm of children with their bubbling, light-hearted conversations engulfed us. I smiled involuntarily when I saw one opening his eyes extra wide and grimacing, then laughing at his Dad.

> *¡Qué buena mandarina que sos!*
> What a good mandarin you are!
> Meaning: You're very cheeky.

All in all, the kids had a cheery effect on me and I thought, *I'm settling in at last.*

*

As we approached *Las Violetas*, I tried to imagine the surrounding farms and vacant lots in 1884, when the café opened. Even with the four storeys that were added above the café, decades later, the building was dwarfed by ten-storey apartment blocks.

Felicitas had told us that in the early days, the café was a convenient high-tea stop for wealthy citizens travelling to their 'weekender' country mansions. Escorted by men in top hats, the women in their long dresses swept down from their carriages and entered the café with a flourish.

> *Tenían la vaca atada.*
> They had the cow tied up.
> Meaning: They were very wealthy. From the practice of affluent families who took a milking cow with them on the ship to Europe, so that their children could have fresh milk daily.

The café's huge windows, soaring columns and brass fittings complemented the formal appearance of the waiters. The floors were Italian marble, the doors were curved glass, and a series of beautiful stained-glass windows completed the picture.

The waiter told us that the *Maria Cala High Tea*, named after the opera singer, was designed for two. He pointed to a massive tray of sandwiches and cakes being shared by four people at the next table. It was way too much for four, let alone for two, so we asked for *miga* sandwiches. At first I couldn't choose between the *pavita y morrón* or 'turkey and roasted capsicum' and Pedro's choice of *jamón y alcaucil* or 'ham and artichoke.' Ultimately we ordered the latter, and shared. Just as well, because the fillings were generous. Perfect for two.

*

We left the café at three in the afternoon. One or two people were walking their dogs, others rushed past us with bulging shopping bags, and yet others were out for a stroll.

> *Dar la vuelta del perro.*
> To do the dog walk.
> Meaning: To go for a walk – without the dog. Derived from the practice – in country towns – of a Sunday evening walk around the main square.

A dog-walker and his twelve charges passed by on the opposite sidewalk. It had been obvious to me on our early visits to Buenos Aires that dogs were popular pets, and I'd mentioned them in my first newsletter. I now knew that dog-walkers were common in more affluent *barrios*.

The corollary to the large dog population was that pedestrians were careful where they stepped, even though many dog owners were responsible. About three blocks from our apartment, we crossed the road behind a woman and her poodle. Upon a signal known only to the two of them, she fished out a plastic bag, opened it and placed it on the sidewalk. The dog moved to the bag, strategically stood over it, and made a direct hit. The woman picked up the bag and placed it in the nearest bin.

We were still joking about this, impressed that she'd managed to train the dog so perfectly, when we arrived at our street. Our apartment was two blocks away.

Pedro groaned.

'Oh no,' he said. 'A power cut! Look – those shops are dark inside. That one across the road has a generator going.'

'That's the last thing we need,' I said, disconcerted, and hoping that our block was spared.

I'd heard that power outages were common, but no one could explain why they happened in some blocks, and not in others. The most common answer to my search for an answer was, '¡*Me mataste!*' 'You killed me!' which meant, 'I haven't the slightest idea.'

'If there's no power, I guess the elevators won't work,' I groaned. 'We'll have to walk up five floors.'

'Or the lights, the kettle, the microwave, the music, or the cordless phone,' said Pedro, his voice becoming quieter as he listed each of those useful aspects of everyday life.

'At least we have a flashlight,' I said, but I knew I didn't sound too cheerful.

I remembered how we'd bought the flashlight on the subway, and felt ashamed that I'd been so alarmed by the salesman. Since then I'd seen many different 'subway' items being sold. The protocol was now obvious. The seller placed an item on the lap of each seated commuter. An alighting commuter removed the item from his or her lap and placed it on the seat they'd vacated. If another commuter wanted to sit on that seat, they picked up the item and placed it on their own lap, for the seller to collect. Or, of course, they bought it – as we did. I was impressed with the honesty displayed by the commuters.

That subway trip to *Café Tortoni* was so long ago now. I remembered my feeling of anticipation, looking forward to our six months in Buenos Aires. At that stage I had no idea that we'd be starting an endless and tiresome renovation. But I also had no idea that I would find Buenos Aires a fascinating city that would gradually reveal its many layers – rather than confuse me at each street corner.

I was daydreaming as usual, and Pedro interrupted my thoughts with unwelcome power-cut information. 'It gets worse,' he said. 'If there's no power, we'll run out of water within a day or two. We'll have to carry water up the stairs.'

'Oh my God,' I said, rattled by the idea. I hadn't thought of that. But of course, the water had to be pumped to a tank on the roof, and gravity-fed from there.

When we reached our block, we passed one building after another without foyer lighting. With dread, I looked into our foyer. Sure enough, the lights were out.

*

There was nothing we could do about the power cut. We had to deal with it as best we could. In the apartment, hot and bothered from climbing to the fifth floor, we filled all the saucepans with water so that we'd at least have a supply when the tank ran out. I assumed our neighbours were doing the same.

At dusk we lit our way down the steps to the foyer using the flashlight, having resolved to be as positive as possible. Part of this positive plan was to try a new dining experience. We struck out toward a *cantina* that Santiago had recommended.

A *cantina* was a plainly furnished, family-run restaurant offering simple home-style Italian fare. This one was eight blocks away – hopefully it had escaped the blackout.

Way before reaching the avenue we heard a hubbub and the clanging of many pieces of metal on metal. What we *didn't* hear was the more familiar and regular car-rally start – a roar of engines, replicated endlessly throughout the day, when red traffic lights turned to yellow and cars took off, not waiting for green, dodging vehicles that continued to cross the avenue in front of them.

Soon the smell of burnt rubber wafted around us and my throat seized up. By the time we reached the avenue, the metallic cacophony was deafening. A row of five burning tyres, each piled high with rubbish, blocked the avenue. Behind this 'barricade' a large crowd had gathered, and many in the crowd were clanging the lids of cooking pots together.

It was my first *cacerolazo*. I had heard about these demonstrations from the in-laws but I'd never seen one. The word *cacerolazo* came from *cacerola* or 'cooking pot.' The largest and best-known *cacerolazo* took place in Argentina during the 2001 crisis, when mainly middle-class people demonstrated against the freezing of bank accounts. *Cacerolazos* often took place spontaneously when citizens grew sick and tired of government action – or inaction – and wanted a resolution. A small group of people would gather, clanging their metal saucepan lids, and soon others would join them to form a crowd.

Three police cars were parked nearby, and policemen and policewomen watched the process. We approached one of the demonstrators and he stopped clanging his saucepan lids. I asked him why they were demonstrating.

He looked at me as though I were from Mars.

'Power cuts of course. Haven't you been affected?'

'Today – yes – three blocks away.'

Whereupon he became even more furious and sputtered with anger.

> *Se le volaron todos los pájaros.*
> All the birds flew away from him.
> Meaning: He became really mad.

'Damn!' he said. 'Damn all politicians. Damn them all!' He repeated a few words that I assumed were swearwords before he calmed down, though when he explained, he was shaking with frustration.

'My sister and her husband and their two kids are staying with our family and we live on the seventh floor. She isn't well and we've been carrying water up the stairs for two days. We try to make it fun for the kids, but our patience is wearing thin. I'll bet you don't have power outages in your country. I want to grab a few politicians by the scruff of the neck and keep hold of them until they see reason.'

Los agarraría de las pestañas.
I'd grab them by the eyelashes.
Meaning: I'd grab them by the scruff of the neck.

He said, 'The electricity company says – each day – that the power will be back soon, but of course they do nothing.'

Mucho ruido y pocas nueces.
Lots of noise, few nuts.
Meaning: Lots of noise but little action. Probably derived from Shakespeare's 'Much Ado About Nothing.'

I sympathized with him. He certainly had a right to be upset. Pedro and I were also upset, of course, but power outages were much worse for families with young children, for the elderly or disabled, and for pregnant women.

We skirted past the crowd and continued in the direction of the *cantina.*

*

The *cantina* was a change from the restaurant we had visited for dinner a few times, and where we had become 'regulars', always choosing the *Menú ejecutivo* or 'Executive Menu'. A *Menú ejecutivo* provided limited meal options at a reduced price, and was offered by many restaurants at lunchtime, but in that restaurant it was offered throughout the day. The waiter recognized us after the first visit, and after the second visit he guessed our order before we opened our mouths. I usually ordered their standard dish, *Arroz con pollo* or 'Rice with Chicken,' a delicious and balanced meal of rice, vegetables, and chicken. I had to make sure I didn't say *Pollo con arroz* or 'Chicken with Rice' – a quite different meal, consisting of a piece of grilled chicken accompanied by white rice. Once, when I was very tired, I chose the latter by mistake.

With relief, we saw that the *cantina's* city block functioned normally, electricity-wise. A back-up generator sat outside the restaurant, 'at the ready.' Through the windows we saw that all the tables were set for dinner. The tablecloths were a red and white check, and each table displayed an unopened bottle of red wine. The walls of the *cantina* were adorned with old photos of the one- and two-storey houses of the *barrio*. Between the photos

147

were pennants in the colours of the Italian flag – green, white and red.

Being nine o'clock and early for Argentina, we were the first to arrive. We were greeted by the owner, an elderly man with a walking stick, who handed us over to a waiter before returning to stand beside his wife. She sat by the kitchen entrance and kept an eye on the waiters and table service.

A basket of freshly baked bread and a plate of antipasto were plonked on the table before we had a chance to peruse the menu. The dishes offered were Italian or Argentine, and the wine list was Argentine. Soon a few other patrons arrived and more waiters appeared.

Reviews of the *cantina* described the portions as generous, so we ordered two entrées and one main, all Italian, and two glasses of Malbec. One of our entrées was *vitel toné*, a dish we'd last eaten at Christmas at the in-laws. Our other entrée was an excellent beef carpaccio. For the main course, we chose *chivito* or 'young goat' with a garlic and wine reduction, and a roquette and Parmesan salad.

By ten-thirty the restaurant buzzed, and a line had formed outside. Tables that were vacated were immediately filled. Three or four families had brought babies and toddlers, all wide awake and full of energy. The waiter told us that the kitchen stayed open until one-thirty in the morning.

Because the first two courses were delicious, we ordered desserts. Pedro chose *sambayón* or 'zabaglione' and I chose tiramisu. We were disappointed. The *sambayón* was passable, but way too expensive. And my tiramisu lacked flavour compared to the tiramisu that Pedro made at home. The desserts arrived with a free glass of limoncello or champagne.

For much of the evening, I managed to push the power cut and its challenges to the back of my mind and to enjoy the meal and the ambience. It felt as though we were in Buenos Aires for a normal holiday, and became lost in Pedro's descriptions of his boyhood adventures. When he was eleven or twelve, he and his friends built a raft so they could sail away down the river, like Huckleberry Finn, only for the raft to sink as soon as it was launched in the local stream. Another time, when he and his friends were fourteen or fifteen, they went camping in the hills south west of Buenos Aires and were trapped in a cave by a snowstorm.

At midnight I looked up, and saw that there was still a line outside.

'Perhaps we should finish our coffee and let someone else eat,' I said.

Pedro agreed. We paid and headed back toward reality – toward the renovation-in-progress apartment we had begun to call our home, a climb up the stairs with the flashlight, a candlelit night, and hopefully, running water.

*

Three blocks from home the street lighting stopped and the *barrio* assumed an eerie aspect. Building foyers were dim with emergency lighting. A few hurricane lamps and candles flickered in windows. Clouds reflected the light of the city, funneling it into the ravine formed by black cliffs of endless apartment blocks, and dimly illuminating the road between shadowy trees.

'Welcome to the *dark side*,' I said to Pedro. I wasn't as upset as I'd expected. And not as upset as I would have been four months ago, when we first arrived.

Even so, as we trudged up the stairs for the second time that day, perspiring in the close heat, I hoped that the electricity would return soon.

'Mum says that these blackouts always happen in summer when it's hot and humid, like now, and when the air conditioners are at full blast . . . and always when it's an effort to struggle up the stairs,' said Pedro.

He added, 'I'll tell José there's a power cut, in the morning. And I'll tell the skylight man – and the guys who'll polish the floor. At least we have a fixed phone line – though we can always charge our cell phones at Mum's.'

We lit a few candles as soon as we entered the apartment.

What a long day. Dusty granite workshop, beautiful flowers, grand café, power cut, *cacerolazo*, *cantina*. The workshop had been gloomy with its clouds of granite particles, but the afternoon had been delightful.

I hoped the power would be back soon, and that the renovation could continue. At present the work schedule was on track. And we'd managed to spend time together, mostly looking for useful building or kitchen items but occasionally, like today, stealing a few hours from renovation duties.

However, power outages were not factored into our timetable. Would the outage last for a long time, or would there be others to deal with?

These thoughts raced around in my mind for a long time, as I tried to get to sleep.

> *No podía pegar un ojo.*
> I could not glue an eye closed.

*

Hardly had I fallen asleep when a loud ringing noise woke me up. I was still trying to register where the sound was coming from, when Pedro raced into the living room with the flashlight. I realized it was the phone. The ringing stopped, and I heard Pedro speaking in English. I guessed the call was from Australia. There was concern in his voice. I stumbled toward a pool of light, where he crouched on the floor beside the telephone.

'Your sister,' he said, handing the receiver up to me, the cord stretching.

I leaned back against the wall. 'Annie?'

'Thank God I've got hold of you,' she said. 'Mum's fallen and broken her hip. She's in hospital. She's shaken but okay. I sent you a text message but you didn't answer.'

I was half asleep and couldn't comprehend what she was telling me. 'What? Say that again. What happened? Mum?'

Annie snapped back. She sounded stressed. 'As I said, she's fallen and broken her hip.'

I slowly slid down the wall and sat on the floor. I felt tears forming.

'Is she okay? Is it bad?' It seemed like only yesterday that Mum had phoned, leaving her cheery message. It went through my mind that I might never see her again.

'She's bearing up. She's been asking for you. I'll get you the ward phone number.'

My hand, holding the phone, was shaking. Tears ran down my cheeks.

'I'll fly back!' I said.

'Just call her, and call me tomorrow. I'm at the farm, to be nearby.'

'I don't have a pen.' I couldn't think straight.

Pedro shone the flashlight around the living room, and found a sheet of paper and a pen.

'What's the number?'

*

My hand trembled, and I misdialled twice before I got through to the ward.

'Mum! How are you? I wish I was there. What did you do? I'll get a flight back.'

'Hush dear, I'm fine,' she said, sounding spaced out. 'There's no need to end your lovely holiday because I fell over. Promise me you'll do no such thing.'

It was reassuring to hear her gentle voice, but so worrying to know that she was in hospital, on the other side of the world. We talked for a short while, but she sounded so tired that I made the call brief, and told her I'd phone the following day.

I didn't wait until the next day to call Annie, but rang her immediately, my hand still trembling, tears still coursing down my cheeks.

'What did the doctors say? Will she be okay? I'll see what flights there are.'

'They'll operate tomorrow – it's a standard procedure. There's no point flying over – by the time you get here she'll be on the mend. Stay there, and I'll update you tomorrow.'

'But . . .'

'For heaven's sake, Catherine, there's *nothing* you can *do*. Just stay there.'

'If you think so . . .'

'I *do*. But you should think seriously about this Argentina move – how does it feel to be so far away at a time like this? I'd hate it. I'd feel useless.'

Annie had hit a raw nerve.

I hung up and turned to Pedro. He put his arm around my shoulder.

'I could *never* live here,' I sobbed.

I gave him a hug, then trudged to the bedroom, tripping over a carton of kitchen appliances and hurting my shin. I lay on the bed, crying in great heaving sobs.

Lloré como una magdalena.
I cried like a Magdalene.
Meaning: I cried my heart out – like Mary Magdalene.

Pedro followed me. He sat beside me and held my hand. He said nothing. I cried myself to sleep.

I dreamed that I was helping Mum to cross the road in front of our apartment. She looked very old. Her face was pale, her gait unsteady, a walking stick grasped tightly in her hand. I held up my hand and the traffic screeched to a stop. A crowd of people clapped their hands and rattled saucepan lids together.

*

I woke with a start the next morning.

I should go back, I kept thinking, *Annie shouldn't have to shoulder it all on her own. But she said not to.*

Pedro sensed my confusion, asking, 'What can I do? Look for flights?'

'I don't know. I just don't know,' I said.

I went into the second bedroom and threw the drape off the sofa. I sat heavily, forgetting its fragile state. It shuddered, and I gripped one of the arms in case it collapsed, but it survived the jolt.

Pedro picked up his cell phone and followed me, staring at the screen as he punched keys, 'I'm checking one of the travel sites.'

'Are there any flights?' I asked.

'They're all full. But I'm sure we could turn up at the airport and get seats. Will we try that?'

'Yes . . . no . . . I don't know. Maybe wait a day. I'll call Annie – tonight. I suppose. Yes, I'll call her tonight.'

Then I realized that Pedro had mentioned seats for *us*, not for *me*. I was touched. I must have dozed off on the sofa, because when I woke up, I saw Pedro tiptoe past the bedroom door carrying shopping bags in one hand and a takeout coffee in the other.

'Go back to sleep,' he said. 'I'll wake you up with a tiramisu.'

I smiled in spite of my worry, placed a cushion on the sofa for my head, and dozed off again.

Tiramisú – Tiramisu

I very much welcomed the tiramisu – Italian for 'pick me up' – after hearing about Mum's fall. Pedro enjoyed it too, as he needed cheering up, now that the renovation was delayed.

For Pedro, tiramisu was an ideal dessert. Like most Argentines he had a sweet tooth. He loved coffee so much that he gave espresso machines to close friends and family as Christmas presents, increasing his chances of being offered a decent coffee when we dropped by. And he loved eating soggy biscuits after dunking them in his coffee. A tiramisu blended all these food choices.

This recipe is a traditional Italian one, with mascarpone cheese and no cream. It's a combination of recipes given to Pedro by various Italian friends.

Ingredients

5 eggs
250g caster sugar
500g mascarpone
Savoyard or 'sponge finger' biscuits as needed
1 cup strong black coffee from an espresso machine. If you don't have a coffee machine, why not go up the road and get a strong espresso takeout coffee.
Marsala or a coffee liqueur
Dark chocolate of a good quality

Method

Separate the eggs, and keep the egg whites in the fridge for whisking later.
Add the sugar to the egg yolks. Beat at high speed until pale and smooth.
Add the mascarpone and continue to whisk until smooth again.
Have the egg whites as cold as possible and add a tiny bit of salt before whisking. Whisk egg whites to soft peaks.
Fold the mascarpone/sugar/egg yolk mixture into the egg white mix.
Assemble the dessert:
To the coffee, add a generous dash of Marsala.
Dip one biscuit at a time in the mixture. Allow the biscuit to soak for a couple of seconds but not until soggy.
Place each biscuit in a separate dessert dish, or if using a large bowl make a layer of soaked biscuits.
Generously ladle the mascarpone mixture over the soaked biscuits, to more than cover each one.
Refrigerate 3-4 hours, or preferably overnight, to set. Remember to cover carefully so that other smells from the refrigerator do not seep into the tiramisu.
Grate dark chocolate over the dessert just before serving. For an interesting variation you can sprinkle freshly ground coffee on top, instead of chocolate.
Serves 6 to 8.

Hints

The egg yolk and sugar mixture should be whisked thoroughly to a pale yellow, almost white coloured cream before adding the mascarpone.

The egg whites, as for meringues, need to be beaten to soft peaks. But don't over whisk them.

Prepare the tiramisu with enough time to set in the fridge. Overnight is preferable.

Don't soak the biscuits through with the coffee, otherwise the excess liquid will settle at the bottom of the dish.

The coffee has to be cold and of high quality, not instant.

Use fresh eggs. Remember that the eggs are raw, so the tiramisu should be consumed on the date of intended consumption and not kept any longer.

11

CURRENT EVENTS

By midday, I knew I wouldn't be rushing home, at least not that day. Annie was right – by the time I arrived, the operation would be over. I sat listlessly on the sofa.

Pedro glanced at me from time to time with concern. He'd never seen me in such a state. He'd cheered me up temporarily with the 'power-cut' tiramisu. The tiramisu hadn't set, because we couldn't use the fridge, but it was delicious all the same.

Eventually he finalized his renovation-postponement phone calls, taking a break from time to time to give me a progress report.

'The tradesmen aren't fazed about the power outage,' he said, 'even though José pretended to be upset and told me he'd end up bankrupt.'

> *Me voy a quedar en Pampa y la vía.*
> I'll be left in Pampa Road by the railway.
> Meaning: I'll lose everything. Refers to the location of a railway station in the 1870s. From there, the railway led to a racecourse in the countryside. Commuters travelling to the racecourse were only sold return fares, so that if they lost all their money, at least they could get back to town.

'At first I didn't realize he was joking, and told him I'd let him know as soon as it was over. That I wouldn't leave him in the lurch.'

> *No te voy a dejar en banda.*
> I won't leave you on the sideline – probably the sideline of a soccer pitch.

'But anyhow, my calls are done. Let's go out somewhere. No point hanging around here,' he said.

'What if Annie phones?' I said.

'She won't for another few hours – she'll be fast asleep right now. We'll

154

have our phones, and there's free Wi-Fi in almost every café. You can easily talk to her if you want.'

I nodded mechanically, not able to think where to go.

'How about *San Telmo*,' he said. 'I can show you where I went to school.'

'Okay.' *Anywhere*, I thought. *As long as we're together.*

'And Mum said we could shower at her place, if we run out of water here.'

'That's nice,' I said. I felt the lack of enthusiasm in my voice.

He tried to make me smile, saying, 'She wants to know how your Mum is. I imagine she'll call every day. And once she tells the rest of the family, *they* will too.'

'*Every* day? *All* of them?'

'Many of them. But it's okay, they'll be calling *me* – only Felicitas has your number. Most of them will just send messages.'

We gathered towels and a change of clothes in backpacks to leave at the in-laws, so we could shower on the way back. It would save us going out again later, if the water tank was empty upon our return. We added our computers, so we could charge them.

I followed Pedro down the stairs, not wanting to go, but not wanting to stay.

*

'You'll see that *San Telmo* is full of elegant old European-style houses,' said Pedro when we were on the bus. 'We can have a bite to eat and a coffee – there are lots of restaurants and cafés. It's touristy with hotels and backpacker hostels, and there's a tango vibe. Lots of expats live there.'

As we entered the *barrio* of *San Telmo*, tall apartment blocks gave way to a mainly two-storey streetscape.

'We get off at the next stop,' Pedro said. I stood and followed him to the door of the bus.

We walked along a narrow, cobblestoned road flanked by houses of mixed architectural style, their decorative façades forming a continuous wall. It was clear that *San Telmo* was a very old *barrio*. The size of the nineteenth-century houses hinted at glory days – a faded glory, judging by the run-down state of many frontages. Ancient tram tracks cut through the cobblestones, a reminder of the time, a century ago, when Buenos Aires had more tram tracks than any city in the world. Many of the older buildings displayed hotel signs, some scruffy, and others elegant. Graffiti was ever present, as with many buildings in the city.

I kept glancing at my phone for messages from Annie.

On our left was a six- or seven-storey apartment block in a grand nineteenth-century European style, beautifully restored. I turned to look at it more closely, and Pedro followed my gaze, saying, 'This *barrio* was the wealthy area of town before the outbreak of yellow fever I told you about. Then the affluent families moved to *Recoleta* – on the outskirts of town.'

Beside the attractive building was an ugly two-storey house with a flat concrete façade. Its ground floor consisted of an untidy shop frontage, and the only adornments on the second floor were two plain, square windows. A man hobbled out of the shop, limping.

I gasped, thinking of Mum.

I told myself to be calm, and that the operation would go well. I tried to concentrate on our surroundings. If I kept worrying, I'd go mad.

The next house was neo-colonial, and next to it was a car park with an elegant wrought-iron, arched entrance. Across the road was a traditional café with large windows, an art nouveau curved doorway and an inviting interior. Then a house with signs of loving restoration, and after that another car park, nondescript with plain concrete posts on either side.

I walked on, fighting off negative thoughts, and noticed that Pedro was not close by. I turned around. He'd stopped in front of a house with a crumbling façade.

'A renovator's delight,' he said when I joined him. He pointed out the plaster exposed down to the bricks. The top halves of two once-beautifully-tall windows were bricked over and painted, leaving two small square windows at eye level, and the plaster decorations surrounding the balconies had fallen off, leaving ugly scars. I dragged Pedro away from the house. It was so pitiful in its faded elegance, and we moved on.

San Telmo, or at least this area of it, was charming, interesting and messy at the same time.

'That's it over there,' Pedro said, pointing to an old mansion.

'That's what?'

'My old school of course, it's what I wanted to show you.'

'Of course, yes,' I said.

The house had a double frontage, over fifteen metres wide. The arched doorway was four metres high, and the wooden door was intricately carved. The tall windows were ornamented with wrought iron Juliette balconies. Above the door and windows were lateral cornucopia reliefs. An Italian-style balustrade along the roofline hinted at the existence of a rooftop terrace.

I heard a 'ping' and snapped open my phone. But it was a message from the phone company, the same advertisement that popped up each day.

Meanwhile, Pedro caught the attention of the school's security guard and explained that he was an old student. The guard agreed to take us to the staff room, and led us across a tiled courtyard. The courtyard was longer than a tennis court and almost as wide, and open to the sky. A covered balcony ringed the mansion's second storey. I imagined that a garden and trees once surrounded the central well.

The three teachers in the staff room were pleased to meet an old student, though it was clear they were busy. I took in the high ceilings and scuffed paintwork and tried to imagine how the room might have been decorated, and how the original owners had lived, more than a century ago. Despite their wealth, they would have been a family just like Pedro's, just like mine, just like any family anywhere, with their marvellous times, their rough times, and their worrying times.

Outside again, I took another look at the frontage.

'I wish I'd gone to a school in a beautiful building,' I said. 'Mine was so dull, red brick and concrete.'

I also wished it wasn't the day after Mum fell over, because I only half-listened to Pedro as he described his childhood escapades.

We walked for a couple of blocks, and arrived at a plaza surrounded by historic houses, their lower floors given over to restaurants and antique shops. I noticed that one lovely home had been transformed into a boutique hotel without spoiling the look of the square.

'This is *Plaza Dorrego*, one of the oldest squares in Buenos Aires, and there's an antique market here on Sundays,' Pedro said, and pointed to one of the cafés. 'Let's go there. We can sit at one of the outside tables.'

I checked my phone again. No messages. That was positive, and I relaxed a bit. One day I would come back and appreciate the area in a better frame of mind.

*

The bus home took an hour, and I was impatient to call Annie. But I waited until later in the evening, so that I could speak to her when she was likely to be with Mum in the hospital. She answered the phone immediately, her voice determined and sure.

'The X-Rays show that it should be a standard operation. I can't see how it would help if you flew back.'

'But . . . we thought of going to the airport to see if there were standbys,' I said, and felt silly. I'd already decided not to go, but I couldn't admit it openly.

'Honestly Catherine, you don't need to come home. I'll call you early tomorrow your time and tell you how it went. Don't call her now because they're doing tests.'

'And if anything happens . . .' I said. I knew that hip operations were common but this was about *my Mum*.

'I'll call you straight away. It *won't*.'

We hung up and I turned to Pedro.

'What did you decide?' he asked.

'She'll call tomorrow morning to say how it went.'

Annie's calm approach had reassured me, but still, I felt helpless. It was six weeks before we were to leave. Even assuming all went well, Mum probably wouldn't be able to drive for ages. She would be an invalid in Annie's house for all that time.

*

I slept poorly, waking up several times and shining the flashlight on my watch.

Annie rang at last, at six in the morning.

'She's fine,' Annie said. 'Groggy after the operation. So you see, it's all good. Call her tomorrow when she's more alert.'

I breathed a huge sigh of relief.

'And Catherine . . .'

'Yes?'

'I don't mind being up here at the farm, and my boss is okay with it, so don't feel guilty. I'll call you again tomorrow.'

I felt as though I were floating on air as I moved around the apartment, or more accurately, around the packing boxes.

'It's the first time you've smiled in two days,' said Pedro.

'I didn't think it showed,' I said.

I started humming.

Pedro laughed. He was relieved as well. 'Let's go out again for the day. There's not much we can do without power. Why don't we go for a stroll around *Recoleta*?'

I nodded and we prepared the 'power outage' backpack to leave at his Mum's on the way. 'But let's not go to the cemetery,' I said. 'Not now – another time. I don't care how famous it is.' I shivered at the thought. I didn't want to mention my dream of Mum with a walking stick.

'I have an idea,' said Pedro, once we were on the bus. 'I found a delicatessen in *Recoleta* that sells *burrata*. They make it themselves. Let's buy some – I'll use it for our entrée tonight at Mum's. I saw a photo in a magazine of a *burrata* surrounded by ribbons of capsicum – red, green and yellow – and capers and olives, and I've thought of a few different variations. Yum.'

'What's *burrata*?' I asked.

'You're smiling again. It's mozzarella wrapped around mascarpone or a creamy cheese. It's originally from Murgia, in Puglia – Italy.'

We left the bus in *Avenida Callao*. Despite an undercurrent of concern for Mum, I felt my energy returning. And it was fun to have a mission as well as a sightseeing aim.

Unlike Sydney, where the wealthy area of town was a mansion-studded garden neighbourhood, *Avenida Callao* in *Recoleta* was lined on either side by apartment blocks, their frontages joined on either side, forming a continuous ten-storey structure along each block. I'd only been to *Recoleta* twice before, once on the saucepan quest, and once for the tour of *Palacio San Martín*. Near *Palacio San Martín,* the skyline was lower and the surrounding buildings were older and more elegant.

Pedro read my mind. 'I know it's all modern apartment blocks here, but *Avenida Callao* has imposing old buildings to the south. Some corner buildings have domes, but I don't know what style they are – you must know,' he said.

'I'd have to see them. They sound beautiful. I suppose they'd be copying a French style, mainly, though Buenos Aries architecture can be pretty eclectic. Domes can have a Russian or Spanish or Arab style, and usually Art Nouveau as well.'

We turned left into *Avenida Quintana* and I dredged up a few more facts that I'd discovered in preparing my third newsletter.

'If the owner was a freemason, the dome might be crowned by the statue of a woman holding a crown of laurel or a torch – like a mini Statue of Liberty. There's a building called *La Prensa* that has one.'

'That's the old newspaper building in *Avenida de Mayo*,' said Pedro.

'And there's one building with two corner domes side by side – the *Otto Wolf* building. It was built in 1914, in homage to the Austro Hungarian Empire. One dome has a golden Habsburg crown. The other dome has the symbol of the empire – a golden sun with rays – which is interesting, seeing as the sun would soon set on the empire.'

'How do you find out that stuff?' asked Pedro. 'Things I never knew about my own city. Where do you find all the facts?'

I shrugged, and was about to answer when he stopped at a café and held the door open for me. It was a large old-style Buenos Aires corner café with wooden-framed windows, and photos covering the walls. The waiters sported black bow ties and green vests, white long-sleeved shirts and black trousers.

We chose a table by a window. Outside, the branches of a massive tree spread dappled shade across a multitude of tables. Groups of laid-back tourists and locals enjoyed drinks. Waiters hurried between them, and back and forth into the restaurant with full trays. Beyond the tables, extensive lawns opened up the view. It was a relief to see so much sky after being hemmed in by high-rise.

Pedro said, 'We can sit outside, under that Moreton Bay fig tree, if you like – but I wanted to show you the old photos on the walls in here.'

'A Moreton Bay fig?' I asked, amazed. But he was right, it was a huge Australian fig tree, the biggest Moreton Bay fig tree I'd ever seen. Its branches, some over half a metre in diameter, were held up by concrete and steel posts, one in the shape of a man carrying a burden. The tree was a lovely reminder of home.

Pedro described the history of the café. 'It's called *La Biela*, and it sits on the site of Fangio's workshop. Fangio was that Formula One driver, and *La Biela* means "The con-rod." '

'The what?' I felt the tension in my shoulders ease, and recognized how anxious I'd been.

Now that the operation had been successful, I could think more lucidly about Mum's emergency. She had no intention of moving from her farm, and I knew for certain that I wanted to be close by, to help out, in case something like this happened again. It was clear that I could not spend a few years in Buenos Aires.

'The con-rod – the connecting rod. From an internal combustion engine. Each piston is fixed to a con-rod, and each con-rod is joined to the crankshaft. As the pistons move up and down, the con-rods act on the crankshaft – to make it spin. The crankshaft harnesses the power of the engine through a transmission system – like a clutch and gear box – making the wheels turn.'

I found it impossible to concentrate on what Pedro said. I knew I had to tell him what I thought, and I blurted it out.

'Darling, I'm sorry, but as I said the other day, I can't live in Buenos Aires.'

'And that's what a con-rod is,' said Pedro. Then he must have rewound what I'd said, in his mind, and played it back. His brow creased. 'Sorry?'

'I can't live here. I know you want me to, but I can't. Mum's fall has made me understand that.'

His look of surprise and disappointment was devastating.

I said, in a hurried voice, 'You probably thought I over-reacted that night when Annie rang, and maybe I did – *then*. But it's true. I've had more time to think – and I can't. I can't live here. I just can't do it.'

Pedro couldn't process what I was saying.

'But her operation was a success. She's fine,' he said. Then, looking uncertain, 'Isn't she? And a few days ago – on the way back from Tía Diana's – you said you were enjoying it here.'

'Yes, Mum's fine and yes, I *do* like it. Much more than I thought I would. And my Spanish is much better. But Argentina is too far away. I feel I should be near Mum. She isn't getting any younger. I don't want to be here if she has another accident.'

Pedro was nonplussed. He said, 'But I don't understand. You like it here more than you thought. You're feeling more at home with Spanish. Your Mum's well – and Annie's told you she can deal with it. What's *really* wrong?'

'I don't know. I can't describe it – at least, not any more than I have. It just doesn't feel right to stay.'

Pedro was more upset than I'd ever seen him. He was agitated, floundering, looking for explanations. He simply couldn't understand my reasoning.

'Are you *homesick*? Maybe if we go back for a month or so you'll feel better. Are you *really* sure you can't live here?'

'Yes I'm sure.'

'Why don't you think about it a bit more? Your Mum's accident was a big shock. You might think differently by the time we leave.' Pedro's voice was hopeful, but I could tell he was frustrated by my insistence.

When I didn't answer, he repeated, 'Will you think about it more – just a bit more?'

'Well . . .'

'Maybe give it a week or two, and see if you still feel the same?' he said.

His appeal resonated with me – I was good at putting off difficult decisions. 'Well, okay, if you want me to. But I can't see how a couple of weeks would change anything.'

I felt miserable. A waiter arrived to take our order. I asked for a hot chocolate and the waiter suggested a *submarino*. Pedro, seeing my look of indecision, said, 'Yes,' and ordered a coffee for himself.

Our drinks arrived. My *submarino* was a mug of hot milk on a saucer. It came with a long spoon and an object in wrapping that displayed the image of a submarine. Pedro unwrapped it, to show me a piece of dark chocolate that did, indeed, have the shape of a submarine. He launched it into the milk.

'There's your hot chocolate,' he said, his voice subdued. 'Let's finish this and we'll go and get the *burrata* for dinner.'

*

Four days later, there was still no power. Pedro was quieter than usual. He hadn't mentioned 'living in Buenos Aires' since my pronouncement at the café in *Recoleta*. He must have been trying to come to terms with my decision, and things were tense between us.

The water ran out, adding to the tension. Each day we filled bottles and buckets at street level and heaved them up the stairs. There was no other way to get water to the apartment.

> *No hay tu tía.*
> There is not your aunt.
> Meaning: There's no other solution. *Tu tía* came from *tutía*, or 'unguent,' so it originally meant, 'There is no unguent.'

I called Mum in the evenings and she was always positive, but sounded tired. Annie told me that Mum wasn't recovering as quickly as another person in the ward who'd had the same operation on the same day. Each morning, I was on the brink of buying a ticket home. But Annie kept telling me not to. 'After all, what will you do here? Sit and chat at her bedside? You can chat on the phone.'

The power outage was driving me crazy, especially carting the water. At last it got the better of me.

'Let's go and stay in a hotel,' I wailed to Pedro.

'We'd have to stay at Mum's,' he proclaimed.

'No, darling. A hotel!'

'She'll be offended – she'll expect us to stay at *her* place.'

Pedro tended to become stubborn where his family was concerned. It was both endearing and a little exasperating. I suppose I was stubborn regarding my family too, wanting to live in Australia because of my mother.

'Blame it on me,' I said.

But he was obstinate. Family was family.

'Two more nights, and we're moving out. Or *I* am,' I said, feeling defeated and tired.

That startled Pedro, and he hugged me close. 'Yes, okay, okay, we'll move to a hotel. I'll work out an excuse for Mum.'

*

That night at ten-thirty, there was a knock at the door. It was our next-door neighbour, Carla. 'I just came upstairs – we're the only building in the block without power. Do you know why?'

We had no idea. We thought that all our side of the block was 'out.' I went to the balcony, stood in a space between piles of tiles and craned my neck to either side. Sure enough, there were lights shining out of every building except ours.

We found out why the next morning. As we left the building, we bumped into two members of the owners' committee.

'It's the cable to our building from the mains,' one of them told us, pointing to short fence surrounding a deep hole in the sidewalk. The fence was threaded through with fluorescent orange tape, to warn pedestrians. 'It's melted. No wonder – it's the original forty-year-old cable with a cloth cover. The electricity company's sending a team at eight tonight – to replace it – we'll wait for them here.'

We spent the whole day with the in-laws, and returned at ten o'clock that evening. The men from the owners' committee were outside. They'd been waiting for the electricity team for two hours.

We climbed the stairs to the apartment. I was thirsty, and without thinking I grabbed a glass and turned on the tap in the bathroom.

Water sputtered, then gushed out. I stared.

Como oro en polvo.
Like gold dust.

'Water!' I shouted to Pedro, 'I'll go and see what's happening.'

Out in the corridor I saw Carla, her face illuminated by the flame from a candle. She was on her way to ask *us* why the building had water, but no power. Just then her cell phone rang and she answered. Her eyes lit up and a smile appeared and broadened.

The call over, she explained, 'That was Silvina from upstairs. We're getting water from the building next door! Their tank's higher than ours — they ran a hose between the two. They wanted to help us out.'

Nos hicieron una gauchada.
They helped us, as would a *gaucho*.
Meaning: They were generous; helpful; giving. The *gaucho* or 'Argentine cowboy' was traditionally considered to be honourable and helpful.

I felt a lump in my throat and fought back tears. How generous and friendly of our neighbours. And what a relief — I didn't really want to move out. I'd grown quite attached to our cluttered pied à terre on the fifth storey.

*

Against all my doubts, the electricity company crew *did* arrive that night to inspect the cable. The next day they dug up more of the sidewalk, and by late afternoon they'd replaced the cable and everything was back to normal.

Except, of course, for the sidewalk itself, where there was now a low pile of earth. We were told that the electricity company would replace the tiles later. Now I knew why there were occasional low piles of earth on the sidewalks of Buenos Aires, and patches of not-quite-matching tiles.

That morning we'd traipsed down five floors of stairs, but we took the elevator up when we returned. Bliss. On the way back to our building, we'd passed the electricity company's retail outlet. New glass was being installed, and a metal grid leaned against a wall nearby, probably to protect the glass. I assumed that the *cacerolazo* demonstrators, or their sympathizers, had thrown bricks through the window.

It was magic to boil the kettle and make tea, to use the coffee machine, and to know there was cold milk in the fridge. Pedro too was delighted. He took the opportunity to bring up the 'living in Argentina' subject again.

'Catherine, let's talk.'

'Okay.'

I didn't want to talk, but knew we had to. Although I worked in communications, I found it difficult to talk about myself. It was much easier to talk about 'things.'

We both sat gingerly on the decrepit sofa. He took my hands in his.

'I know you want to be in Sydney, and that's completely okay with me. I love Australia. I know I overreacted at the café, but you took me by surprise.'

He said, 'We *can* go back. I can look for a different job, away from education and the university.'

I immediately felt a sense of relief.

I thought for two seconds.

'But . . .' I said.

'But what?'

'But . . . I know you're going to give me another side of the argument,' I said. 'You always do.'

'Yes, well, you're right. Put it this way. My mother always told me to get on with my own life, and your Mum's the same – she encouraged you to go to London and now to come here. And she has Annie close by. As for my kids, I miss all three of them, but they're grown and I don't expect them to live near me. They live far away.'

'But I can't expect Annie to do everything on her own, if something like this happens again.'

'Maybe there won't be any problems for twenty years. And there are daily flights.'

Perhaps he was right. Was I seeing problems where none existed? Or was I being realistic?

And as for wanting to be near my mother in case she became sick, was I being selfish? After all, Pedro had been apart from *his* mother for over thirty years. It was all too much. I didn't know what to think.

All I could say was, 'I need time to think. Mum lives in the middle of nowhere. How can I be here with you, but worried all the time about her?'

He looked at me for a long time. 'I don't know,' he said. 'I can't make your decision for you. But if you want to live in Sydney, we'll do that. I want to be with you more than anything.'

He paused, and added with a smile, 'In any case, let's enjoy the rest of our time here.'

Then he stood and said, 'I need to make a few phone calls. By the way Mum's asked us for dinner again. I'll make us all a quick meal at her place, and we can come back early so you can talk to your sister.'

He brightened up once he was on the phone, but I could sense an undercurrent of unhappiness.

Pasta rápida – Quick Pasta

Pedro had in mind a quick pasta recipe for dinner at the in-laws. It was a terrific and yummy dish that he would often make in Sydney after we returned from an evening concert – the sauce would be ready in the time it took to cook the pasta. Pedro changed the sauce depending on the available ingredients.

Pedro's Mum needed olive oil, so we stopped on the way, at a shop where we'd tasted olive oils from the Mendoza region. His Mum wanted black-olive extra-virgin olive oil, which was a much darker green than the green-olive oil, with a strong but smooth flavour. Mendoza was the largest wine-growing region in the country and also produced most of the Argentine garlic sold in Australia.

Pedro's Mum was amazed at how quickly he prepared and served the meal. I'd already set the table, and we ate much earlier than the normal Argentine dinnertime.

Ingredients

The essential ingredients are frozen peas, capsicum and mushrooms. At the stage where you add the peas (see Method), you can also add beans or corn – frozen or pre-cooked – or cherry tomatoes cut in half.

1/4 large red capsicum, thinly sliced in 2-3cm lengths

2 cloves garlic, chopped

4 mushrooms, sliced thinly. If you can, use 2 button mushrooms and 2 Portobello mushrooms

3-4 slices of thinly sliced prosciutto. If you don't have prosciutto, use ham, pancetta, coppa or smoked bacon

Dry pasta for two people. Spaghetti works well, or a short pasta of your choice
Olive oil
Salt
Pepper
Chilli flakes or fresh chilli
1 heaped tsp oregano, or if you don't have this use thyme
1/2 cup frozen peas
A squeeze of lemon juice
A tablespoon of chopped parsley

Method

Note that if you are using smoked bacon or any meat that needs cooking, you will need to change the order below. Start by rendering the bacon, removing it from the pan, and setting it aside. You can use the fat generated from cooking the bacon, along with olive oil.

Have the julienned capsicum, chopped garlic, sliced mushroom and sliced prosciutto ready.

Put the pasta water on to boil, and when boiling, add the pasta.

While the pasta is cooking, prepare the sauce. This will take less than 10 minutes, so it will be ready when the pasta is cooked.

In a frying pan add the olive oil and once it gets to a medium heat add the capsicum, garlic and mushrooms.

Sauté 3-5 minutes until cooked.

Add salt and pepper to taste. Add the chilli flakes, oregano and the prosciutto and cook 2 more minutes.

Add the frozen peas and cook for a further 2-3 minutes.

Squeeze the wedge of lemon onto the sauce.

If the preparation is becoming too dry, add a ladleful or two of water from the pasta, and dribble a little bit of olive oil onto it as well.

When the pasta is ready, strain and top with the sauce.

Add the chopped parsley.

Serves 2.

Serving

Accompany the pasta with a Malbec from Mendoza, and crusty Italian rolls or pane di casa fresh from the bakery.

12

IN THE BALANCE

The power outage extended the renovation time by a week. The tradesmen and labourers, being used to power cuts, had switched to other jobs, and Pedro had to change his timetable to fit around their new schedules.

His first call was to a *silletero* that José had recommended, to secure the air conditioner's external unit to its frame. *Silleteros* were tradesmen who worked on the outside walls of buildings, sitting on a wooden plank suspended by a rope from the roof. It was a *silletero* who inspired my first newsletter, when I saw one painting the outside wall of a building nearby. I'd since realized that the word *silletero* came from the word *silla* or 'seat.' Seventy per cent of Buenos Aries inhabitants lived in apartments, so there was always work for *silleteros*.

Pedro hung up. 'He'll be here on Thursday – another client postponed their job. Now I've got to organize insurance for that day. At last my cousins will stop carrying on about the air conditioner. And the tiler will have finished by then.'

'Now for the skylight,' he said, dialling another number. Throughout the renovation, the corrugated sheet of polycarbonate covering the old laundry area had been held up with temporary wooden columns. Our plan was to replace the polycarbonate with glass.

Pedro brightened as he made his call. When he finished, he turned to me triumphantly. 'He can do it on Tuesday next week. And on Wednesday the parquet in the living room will be sanded and polished – we'll move the furniture into the other rooms, and stay at Mum's that night while it dries. I'll call her now.'

'That's great, darling,' I said. I unlocked the front door on my way to the café for my Spanish lesson.

Pedro was convinced the renovation would be over by the end of the next week. I could hardly believe it. In fact, I deliberately tried *not* to believe it. I knew it was psychologically healthier to believe it would be finished *one day*, than to set a time limit and be disappointed.

As I approached the café, I quickly listed all the outstanding renovation issues to myself, and found that I was thinking in Spanish for the first time. I must have been mentally preparing to update Nora.

*

With the power back on, we were using Skype for Annie's daily updates. Candles and their subsequent complications were a thing of the past – whether they'd last long enough, or fizzle out during a phone conversation, or whether the wax would spill if we moved them too quickly. Switching on the light at the wall was a novelty. It made me appreciate the advent of electricity in the late nineteenth century.

Annie said that Mum had constant visitors in hospital.

'I didn't know she had so many friends in the area. They're offering to help with the farm whilst Mum recovers,' she said. 'A couple of them live in that retirement village near the hospital – they rave about their social activities. They're trying to persuade Mum to go and live there.'

'But she told me she'd never leave the farm.'

'Yes, I know. By the way, she'll be in hospital for three of four more days. It's taking longer than they expected. I hope you're not thinking of coming home now she's better, are you?'

'Not any more. I'll be more useful when we get back in five weeks.'

'At last you're making sense!'

The days passed peacefully enough, with Pedro chasing up providers. One day, whilst I was out, the tattered and unsteady sofa and its matching armchairs mysteriously disappeared.

My Spanish conversations continued to improve. One afternoon, I visited a *dietética*, a shop selling herbs, teas, cereals and dried fruits. I took a number and waited my turn, occasionally joining in the conversation between the shopkeeper and his customers. My eye wandered to a rhyme on a board near the counter which said, '*Abrimos cuando llegamos; cerramos cuando nos vamos*' 'We open when we arrive; we close when we leave,' and I grinned – I had already found that formal opening times for small local businesses were merely a rough guide.

When my turn came I asked for red peppercorns. The shopkeeper told me they were expensive, and said, 'Don't you want green or white ones instead?'

I replied, 'My husband, being the cook, always has the last word, and he's ordered red ones.'

The shopkeeper said, 'Yes, I can understand that. I always have the last word at home, or should I say, the last *words*. Every time, my last words are

168

"Yes, dear." '

I laughed, and thought to myself that five months ago, I would have heard, 'Yes, I . . . that. I always . . . or . . . yes . . .' And five months ago I would have smiled for the sake of politeness. I would have feigned comprehension, knowing that to ask for an explanation would have led to hopeless confusion. At last my spoken Spanish was synchronizing with my broader knowledge of written Spanish. I felt confident that I would soon be able to sustain longer conversations.

*

On the SKYLIGHT DAY I returned from yoga to find a new person in the kitchen. He and Pedro were staring at a frosted glass pane in the ceiling. It was the new skylight, which had replaced the original corrugated polycarbonate.

Pedro introduced me to Horacio, a neighbourhood glazier.

As soon as Horacio and I were acquainted, Horacio reverted to his upward gazing activity. Pedro leaned against the wall and also looked upward.

'Oh well,' I thought, and did the same. Something interesting was bound to happen. I had become more involved in the renovation lately, probably because Mum was okay.

A breeze wafted in through the window beneath the skylight and all was calm.

A shout in my ear startled me.

'Begin at the corner, not in the middle!' Horacio yelled through the window, apparently at the sky.

'Don't you provide safety harnesses?' asked Pedro.

Horacio shrugged, 'I do. But they won't wear them. I can't force them to.'

> Dios le da pan al que no tiene dientes.
> God gives bread to those who have no teeth.
> Meaning: To give something to someone who does not appreciate it or cannot use it.

An up-side-down face appeared at the top of the window, followed by shoulders. It smiled. Its owner boasted, 'We don't need harnesses. You should have seen me at the top of a twelve-storey building on the avenue. There was a strong wind. It was exciting!'

My stomach churned. He looked all of twenty-two years old. I couldn't bear to watch.

I told Pedro that I was stepping out for a coffee.

169

Outside, trying to take my mind off the lack-of-harness issue, I observed the shops more closely than usual. I passed Mr Higgins' hardware shop. Pedro had told me that Mr Higgins, who looked as Irish as his name, with his fair skin, ginger hair, blue eyes and freckles, spoke no English. But he clearly represented one of the ingredients in the melting pot of Argentina's history of immigration. Next to his shop was the dry-cleaner. By now I knew that families of Japanese descent owned many dry-cleaning businesses in Buenos Aries, and this one was no exception.

As I walked, I mentally listed other local shops. Our greengrocer was Bolivian. Our closest mini-supermarket was owned by a Chinese family, and two others nearby had Taiwanese owners. Our butcher was of Italian descent. Nearby restaurants offered Armenian, Uruguayan, Colombian and Peruvian cuisines. A Polish-Ukrainian family owned the Jewish bakery. And our very own real estate agent Clara was the daughter of Spanish immigrants.

By the time I reached the café, I'd traversed a rich cultural landscape in my imagination. Those demographic reflections had crowded out the skylight safety concerns. I greeted the waiter, his mainland Spanish pronunciation calling to mind the more recent post-2008-crisis immigrants. Buenos Aires had been a destination for young and highly educated people from Spain – technologists, engineers, and computer programmers. One of them told me that many Spanish professionals found jobs in their chosen careers – impossible back home.

Pedro had also told me that, following the wave of Spaniards, there had been an increase in Colombian immigrants, and, since we'd arrived, he'd heard many Venezuelan accents in the street and on public transport.

The waiter delivered my *café con leche y una medialuna* or 'white coffee with a croissant.' In line with normal Buenos Aires practice, he would not clear the table, or present the bill, until I asked him to. I liked to sit there, quietly reading, when Pedro was renovation-busy after my classes.

When at last I asked for the bill, the waiter placed a slice of *budín de pan* or 'bread and butter pudding' in front of me. *Budín de pan* was a standard Argentine dessert, a left-over – so to speak – from the times when the British held sway in Argentine trade and industry, and many British families lived in the country.

I shook my head, 'Sorry, but I didn't order it.'

'Yes I know. The manager said you can have the last piece – seeing as you're a regular – compliments of the house.'

I accepted graciously. I was now part of the *barrio*.

When I returned, the skylight was in place and everyone was safe. I sighed with relief.

*

The skylight seal would dry within two days, and we were told that fine weather would speed the process. We woke the next morning to bright sunshine and a clear sky, and all boded well.

At midday I arrived back from a painting class to see cupboards installed in the kitchen. They looked smart, though forlorn, without the bench tops. I thought of Tía Diana's headless chickens.

'Santiago and the carpenters arrived at ten exactly,' said Pedro. 'He's like clockwork.' It was intriguing that Santiago could be prompt, as well as both friendly and existentialist, with his clients.

And he added, 'The floor polishers are due soon. Mum has houseguests tonight so we'll have to find a hotel. There must be one or two nearby.'

I had barely enough time to register that we'd be staying in a hotel, rather than his Mum's, when the buzzer sounded and the floor polishers announced their arrival, *'Ricardo y Javier.'*

'I found the floor-polishing company through Santiago,' Pedro said, before he went downstairs to let them in. 'He told me that he contracted them for something three years ago, and their work was first class.'

The sanding commenced. I watched in dismay as a sawdust storm blew into the kitchen from the living room, revealing one of the drawbacks of 'open plan.' I quickly covered a few appliances with tea towels.

Next, Ricardo and Javier put on paper masks, opened a tin of polish, and began to cover the floor with large brushstrokes. The smell of polish was overwhelming. Ricardo saw us contemplating the masks and said, 'Yes, they're hopeless, but that's all they give us. We can smell the stuff through the paper.'

The smell was too much for me, and the thin masks looked hopeless. I did my usual disappearing-to-the-café act. Surely Santiago would not recommend a business that treated its workers in such a cavalier fashion. *The owner must have let his business practices slide*, I thought, *and things have gone downhill.*

> *Hazte la fama y échate a dormir.*
> Make yourself famous and throw yourself down to sleep.
> Meaning: Rest on your laurels.

The café was calm, with few patrons. I asked for a *cortado* or 'cut' – so called, because the coffee flavour was 'cut' with a dash of milk. A *cortado* was the equivalent of the Italian *macchiato* or 'stained.'

Soon Pedro appeared in the café to tell me that the first layer of polish was finished, and that Ricardo and Javier were taking a quick break for lunch.

We ate a sandwich and returned to the dustbowl. The men were finishing the second layer, painting themselves toward us. Pedro and I grabbed our backpacks, and the men their sanding and polishing paraphernalia, and we all left via the service entrance.

The floor would dry overnight and we'd come back in the morning, to clean up. Then the bench tops would arrive, and assuming all went smoothly, the renovation would be over. Pedro and I would have four weeks together, enjoying outings, being tourists, and attending more concerts. After that it would be back to Sydney, helping Mum, and looking for a job.

*

In line with our accommodation approach in Patagonia, we didn't book a hotel, but simply went searching for the most convenient one. As he closed the foyer door behind us, Pedro said, 'Left or right?'

I chose 'right' and we set off. It soon became clear that it wouldn't be easy. After five blocks we found a hotel but there were no vacancies. Four blocks later we came upon a student hostel and guessed that a quiet and tranquil sleep was unlikely. We couldn't immediately find another place to stay in our residential *barrio*.

We walked a few more blocks, nearing the shop where we'd bought our antique furniture. 'Perhaps the shop manager will remember us, and can recommend a hotel,' I said to Pedro.

Once inside the shop, the manager told us that he lived on the other side of town, and couldn't help. His assistant leapt to the rescue, naming a pay-by-the-hour hotel. 'But if you get there at midnight, they'll let you stay the rest of the night for free,' he said.

I wondered how he knew about this hotel, and we exchanged bemused looks with the manager. The assistant saw the interchange and said, 'No, it's not what you think . . .'

> *Le salió el tiro por la culata.*
> His bullet left via the stock – it backfired.
> Meaning: His words backfired.

Telos, or hourly rate hotels, were common in Buenos Aires, a city where many young people lived with their parents until their late twenties, making it difficult to find time alone with their partner. I guessed that other people also found them useful. The word *Telo* was derived from the Spanish word *hotel*, with the syllables swapped. This swapping was typical of a local slang called *lunfardo* that originated amongst jail inmates in the nineteenth century, to confuse prison guards.

We rejected the *Telo* idea, and trudged onward through the dusk. Clouds gathered overhead. Occasionally the southwest sky lit up, and because there was no thunder, it took us a while to recognize the flashes as sheet lightning.

I was miserable.

'We're going to *San Telmo*,' I announced. 'There were lots of hotel signs there. And I remember a hotel in that square where we had coffee – let's try that one.'

'*Plaza Dorrego?* Great idea.'

We hailed a taxi.

Bursts of lightning surrounded the car as we neared the hotel. Heavy drops of rain spattered the windscreen. We ran inside before the deluge started.

From the lobby, we watched the storm light up the plaza. Thunder roared around us and water gushed from an angry black sky. Rivulets formed in the street and deepened by the minute.

Happily there was a room available, and we settled in. Protected from the tempest raging outside, we ordered room service and loitered over dinner. The floor of the apartment was drying all by itself, so there would be no need to rush home in the morning.

¡No por mucho madrugar verás vacas en camisón!
However early you rise, you won't see cows dressed in nightshirts.
Meaning: However early you rise, it won't make a difference.

I called Annie's home number on Skype and surprisingly, Mum answered the phone.

She was out of hospital.

'I'm right beside the phone so I thought I'd answer it,' she said. 'How's your holiday going?'

We talked for a long time, and after we hung up, I fell asleep immediately.

*

Next day we enjoyed a late breakfast in the hotel. I luxuriated in the simple fare – coffee and *medialunas* with orange juice. How normal it felt to have a meal in a clean and ordered dining area. How exciting to be surrounded by tourists who were discovering the city as we had been – sporadically – over the last few months.

Pedro brought up the living-in-Sydney issue again, saying, 'I'm glad your Mum's out of hospital. I know you want to live in Sydney to be near her. I'd love it if you wanted to spend more time in Argentina – but being with you is much more important.'

I was moved, hearing those tender words, though I *did* wonder whether he was leading up to another persuasive argument to stay.

'We both know that we don't *have to* be here,' I said.

'No we don't *have* to.'

'But?' I said, waiting.

As I expected, Pedro had a new angle on the subject.

'But you didn't *have* to go to London either, you *wanted* to. You went back home because you missed your family.'

'Yes . . .'

'If we'd been together in London, and I'd wanted to stay, perhaps you'd have stayed, or stayed longer.'

'Perhaps, yes,' I said. I didn't admit to Pedro that I'd already come to that exact conclusion myself, on the day we visited Tía Diana and I'd been musing about life in Argentina.

'And your mother isn't exactly doddery,' he said.

That was true. She was active, drove, and I now knew that she had a strong circle of friends.

Pedro didn't push the point.

Of course Mum could take care of herself – but only while she was able to drive. The shops were a long way from her farm. Her friends, as far as I knew, were even further away.

And then my mind switched to the dreary job that awaited us – cleaning the kitchen. It shouldn't take too long – and soon, hopefully, we'd have the apartment to ourselves and could get on with 'normal' life.

*

At the entrance to our building, we crossed paths with the upstairs neighbours, Silvina and Darío, and we stopped to chat. Darío proudly pushed their triplet pram. The three babies slept soundly.

Silvina and Darío smiled at us, each revealing a perfect set of teeth, and my mind clicked. Many months ago, Pedro had talked of finding a dentist in Buenos Aires, where the cost was lower than in Australia. But the idea of a dental visit had become secondary to rubble, kitchen tiles, taps and ovens.

I nudged Pedro and whispered, 'Dentist.'

Silvina and Darío looked at us questioningly. Pedro said, 'Catherine has reminded me about something. Tell me, who keeps your smiles so bright?'

They laughed and Darío examined his phone. As I looked over his shoulder I saw the name pop up on speed dial. Silvina described the dentist as an *eminencia* or an 'eminence.'

That sounded promising. I jotted down the number and we undertook to phone for an appointment as soon as the kitchen was clear of dust.

*

174

When we arrived at the apartment, Pedro unlocked the service entrance door that opened into the kitchen. He looked in. He usually gave way to me, but this time he stood still.

'Oh my God,' he murmured.

With foreboding I looked past him. I couldn't believe my eyes.

There was mud everywhere. Mud on the cupboard shelves, mud on the floor, and mud on the dishcloths that now hugged, rather than covered, the kitchen appliances.

I looked up. The sun mocked us. Sparkling like diamonds, water drops fell from the inside edge of the skylight. During the storm, the wind must have blown through the seams of the skylight, spreading the droplets so that they mixed with the sawdust and other dust on the kitchen surfaces to form thin layers of mud.

This was too much.

Sobre llovido, mojado.
Not only rained on, but made wetter.
Meaning: It never rains but it pours.

I was tired from the nine weeks of rubble and strangers and noise and eating out and the power cut.

It looked like a big cleaning job, not a dreary little dusting job. It was also a renovation-related fixing-the-skylight job. Another delay.

It was the last renovating straw.

La última gota – de 'La última gota que rebalsó el vaso.'
The last drop – from 'The drop that caused the glass to overflow.'

I sank down until I was sitting on the floor in the passageway. I'd had enough.

Hasta aquí llegó mi amor.
This is as far as my love went.
Meaning: 'Enough is enough.' This could refer to almost any situation.

I was on the edge of a breakdown. I was so tired of it. I wished that we'd rented a place instead of buying one.

I tried to calm down by visualizing familiar and beautiful scenes, and wiping out images of mud and floor polish. Visions of Sydney harbour flashed through my mind – eucalypts nodding in the breeze by the shore, a dinghy race across the blue water, ferries plying their way to Manly from Circular Quay.

Pedro looked at me in dismay. He squatted beside me, whispering encouragement.

'Once more, dear friends,' he said, kissing my forehead.

He knew that Shakespeare would stop me from spiralling further into despondency. It wasn't only that it was Shakespeare, either – the quote was also the name of a well-known yacht that, many years previously, had taken part in Sydney to Hobart races. How did he know that I would smile, however briefly? How did he know that I was dreaming of the harbour?

'Just once more,' he repeated. 'It's nothing, I can do it in an hour while you have a rest, or while you go and have a coffee . . . *really*. And all Horacio has to do is add silicone to stop the leak. The window isn't broken.'

I looked through the door and up at the window, and saw that it was indeed intact, and that the drops were only dripping from one corner.

He was right. The mud clearance wasn't such a big job after all. But I couldn't let him do it all on his own. Slowly my energy returned. I struggled to my feet and moved toward the door, forcing myself to put one foot in front of the other.

> *Caminar muy lento como si una pierna le pidiera permiso a la otra.*
> To walk very slowly as though each foot asked the other for permission.

We took off our shoes. We cleaned the kitchen and Pedro phoned Horacio to fix the skylight.

> *Al mal tiempo, buena cara.*
> In bad weather, a smiling face.
> Meaning: To show a brave face.

Luckily the floor polish had been dry enough to repel the water, and so our living room floor was safe.

*

Late that afternoon, the kitchen was clean. The parquet floor in the living room shone. I sat back exhausted. But as always, Pedro had an endless reserve of energy.

> *Tenía cuerda para rato.*
> He had string/cord for some time yet.
> Meaning: He had plenty of energy left. This referred to toys that were wound up by pulling on a piece of string. As the toy moved the string shortened until the toy stopped moving.

He reminded me of the owners' meeting at eight o'clock that evening. 'It'll be in the foyer. The owners need to agree a budget for the year – for any work on the building. Would you like to go?' he said.

It sounded interesting, so despite my tiredness I said, 'Why not? I'll stand at the back and watch.'

*

We arrived in the foyer at fifteen minutes before eight.

At five minutes past eight, I asked Pedro, 'Wasn't the meeting scheduled for eight o'clock?' Pedro reminded me that we were in Argentina, where being late was common. We waited.

> *No por mucho madrugar se amanece más temprano.*
> No matter how early you get up, sunrise won't come any sooner.
> Meaning: However much you hurry it won't make any difference. This had an added meaning – *Amanecer* also referred to a brain lighting up – however much a person thought about something, they would never understand it.

The external administrator arrived at ten minutes past eight, and we exchanged greetings. He explained that the meeting would commence with a quorum, or after half an hour, whichever happened earlier. A slow trickle of owners gradually filled the foyer. They murmured amongst themselves.

Soon the meeting was in full swing, Pedro in the thick of it. I leaned against the wall at the back, watching the show. At times, five people spoke at once and the noise was so intense that I couldn't tell what was going on. I need hardly have been concerned about my Spanish – had they been speaking in English I wouldn't have understood a word.

'So, what were you all signing at the end?' I asked Pedro later, in the apartment. 'And did you agree the budget?'

His eyes widened in surprise. He clearly thought I'd understood everything at the meeting. 'Yes, of course. It all ended up as expected. It was just a few formalities. But some of those owners should take it easy.'

'They sounded volatile,' I said.

'One of the owners was against every single proposal, so he drove the rest of us nuts,' said Pedro.

> *Nos estaba sacando canas verdes.*
> He was making our hair go green.
> Meaning: He was driving us crazy.

'He managed to find a problem with each one,' he added.

> *Le buscaba la quinta pata al gato.*
> He looked for a fifth leg on the cat.
> Meaning: He looked for something that wasn't there.

177

I glanced at my cell phone and was surprised to see that it was already ten o'clock, and a good time to phone Annie and Mum. The owners' meeting had lasted for nearly two hours.

It was only a day since Mum had left hospital, but she sounded much better. She admitted that she didn't exercise enough. Annie was exhausted when she came home from the office, with no energy to encourage Mum.

Estaba fusilada.
She was shot.
Meaning: She was exhausted.

Annie said, 'Mum's missing her friends. I told her you'd help her move back home.'

'We'll be there before you know it,' I answered. 'It's less than five weeks away – we've already been here five months.'

I could be there now, I thought, *to help her get up and walking properly.*

After hanging up, I checked the weather report. Logic told my brain that the skylight was fixed and that the kitchen was safe, but emotion had taken the upper hand. Once I knew that there would be no rain that night, I slept soundly.

*

It was Friday morning, and the granite bench tops were to be delivered in the afternoon.

We decided to visit the antique shop, in the hope of buying the antique Rembrandt floor lamps we'd seen when we bought the sofa and its matching armchairs. I'd noticed they were still there two days previously, when we'd dropped in to ask the shop manager about a hotel.

We took the lift down, and crossed the foyer toward the glass door. Pedro opened the door for me, but I stood back to let an elderly neighbour come in from the street. I towered over her, the crown of her head lining up with my shoulder.

She tilted her head back, her eyes searched my face, and she asked, 'Do you have a cough?'

I was so surprised that I didn't know what to say. I hadn't had a cough for two years. Pedro was similarly lost for words.

She saw my hesitation and tried to explain, 'A cough, sore throat?' and pointed to her throat.

'Er, no,' I said. Pedro looked on, eyebrows raised.

She explained, 'Ah, I thought you must have a sore throat, because you didn't say anything yesterday at the meeting of owners.'

I had to think on my feet, and said, 'No, it was because I'm not an owner.' I hoped this would be an acceptable explanation.

She looked at me with her head to one side and said, *'Buen día.'* Then she shuffled off to the lift.

In Argentina, I realized, each individual had to give an opinion, and everyone wanted to know what the others thought. Not that I would have had a clue what to say in such a situation. I certainly wasn't ready to jump into a *technical* conversation whilst it was in progress – it would be like leaping into a turbulent river on a flimsy raft.

Guiso de lentejas – Lentil Stew

Pedro made lentil stew many times in Sydney. A Spanish dish with a strong Arab influence, it was a homely and tasty stew, especially on those days when it rained and thundered outside, and all was cosy and warm inside. The night that we stayed in the hotel in <u>San Telmo</u>, protected from the wild weather, was such a night, though being summer, the stew wasn't on the menu. I included the dish as a reminder of that night.

Lentil stew was part of Pedro's family tradition. He particularly remembered one childhood evening after a family dinner of lentil stew, when his Spanish grandfather related stories of his life in Mexico and in the sugar-cane fields in Cuba. In the early 1930s his grandfather moved the family to Argentina, intending to stay for a few years. He stayed a lifetime.

Ingredients
300g dried lentils
2 medium-sized potatoes
Frying oil – sunflower or canola – for the potatoes
1 brown onion
1 large carrot
½ red capsicum
5 spring onions
200g smoked bacon with rind removed
Olive oil, if required for rendering the bacon
1 red Spanish chorizo, peeled and cut into ½cm thick slices
100g tomato paste
1 cup red wine
1 tin crushed or diced tomato
2 tbsp dried oregano
2 tsp of dried thyme
3 cloves
½ dozen roughly torn fresh basil leaves
2 tsp smoked paprika
Salt and crushed black pepper
1 litre of vegetable stock
Handful of fresh chopped parsley
Grated cheese to serve
A loaf of your favourite 'mopping up' crusty bread

Method
Rinse the lentils in a sieve and place in a pot of cold water. As a rough guide to the volume of water, estimate the volume of the lentils and double it. Bring it to a boil and let it simmer for 10-15 minutes. Remove it from the heat, drain the water and set aside. Pedro says that this part-boiling is as effective as a long cold soak.

Peel the potato, cut into 1-2cm dice and fry in oil till just golden, i.e. just before the 'cooking point.' This is easiest in a big shallow fry pan with a generous amount of oil. Take the potato dice out of the hot oil, and rest them in a suspended strainer so the oil can drain freely – or place them on absorbent kitchen paper – and set aside. This frying approach is to make sure that the potatoes don't fall apart as they cook.

Chop the onion finely and set aside.

Peel and cut the carrot in small 1-2cm cubes and set aside in a bowl.

Cut the capsicum into 1-2cm squares and add to the carrot cubes.

Thinly slice the white bulbous part of the spring onion and set aside.

Cut the green leaves of the spring onion into 2-3cm lengths and add to the carrot and capsicum.

Cut the bacon, including the fat, into thin strips. Place the strips in a cold casserole dish and use a low heat to render the fat, i.e. until the fat turns to liquid. If the bacon is too lean, add olive oil so the meat does not burn.

Add the finely chopped onion and sauté for 3-5 minutes. You may need to add more olive oil here.

Add the finely sliced white bulbous part of the spring onion, regularly stirring with a wooden spoon for 2-3 minutes.

Add the chorizo slices and cook for 1 minute or so.

Add the tomato paste and continue stirring for 2-3 minutes.

Add the carrot cubes and capsicum squares and the rest of the spring onion – the green leafy part – and mix in for 2-3 minutes.

Add the cup of red wine, mix in thoroughly and allow to simmer gently for 2-3 minutes whilst the alcohol evaporates.

Add the tin of tomato.

Cook, stirring occasionally, for 5 minutes.

Add the herbs – oregano, thyme, cloves, basil and paprika – and the salt and pepper. Add less, rather than more, salt here because the bacon and chorizo and stock all have salt. Use say 2 pinches of salt only.

Add the lentils and cover with stock. You may not use all the stock, say 800ml to a litre.

Bring to the boil, turn heat down and simmer for 20-30 minutes, checking and stirring every few minutes. If it reduces too much, add more stock, remembering it is a stew, not a soup.

Add the cooked diced potato and more stock if needed. The potatoes and lentils will draw the salt out. Check here and add more salt if required.

Serve with a sprinkling of parsley and grated cheese, and slices of crusty bread.

Serves 6.

Variations

For a variation, you could try the stew with chickpeas instead of lentils. Also why not try adding vegetables such as green beans, broad beans or mushrooms to give the stew different flavours and textures.

If you want to use a brunoise (see Chicken Casserole in Chapter 3) to give a stronger flavour to the base, make it with carrot and capsicum. Add it with the spring onion before you add the chorizo slices and tomato paste.

13

A HIGH NOTE

Our shopping expedition for the lamps was successful, and early that afternoon, I wandered off to a yoga class whilst Pedro waited in the apartment for the bench tops to arrive.

After five months of living in Buenos Aires, I felt 'at home' as I moved through our *barrio*. Besides, things were going well. The renovation was almost over, Sarah would be here soon, I'd be helping Mum – who was stronger every day – to settle in to her home in just over a month, and Pedro and I could enjoy Buenos Aires together.

When I returned from my class, the granite men had not yet arrived. Pedro assured me that they would arrive at any minute. I crossed my fingers.

At four o'clock the buzzer sounded and he raced out. A while later I heard a commotion in the passageway. I heard Pedro shout out, *'¡Cuidado!'* 'Careful!'

I opened the door to the apartment, and leapt back as a huge slab of granite was wheeled into the kitchen. Then two more, each on its own trolley. Three men organized themselves around the cupboard near the window, an awkward space, and prepared to lever the first slab from its trolley and into place. But the space was too small for three, and one of them offered to hold it on his back to guide it in.

'It's over eighty kilos,' Pedro whispered to me.

I couldn't comprehend how anyone could carry that weight.

I wasn't sure what happened then, because I'd moved into the bedroom to get out of the way. *Out of sight, out of mind,* I thought.

There was a loud scrunch, and a crack, and I ran out.

'Is everyone all right?' I asked Pedro in English, forgetting that it was rude to do so in front of the others.

'It's fine,' he answered in Spanish. 'We've had a setback. The granite slipped off the trolley. It destroyed one of the cupboard doors and cracked a tile. But it'll be fine.'

Hizo bosta una de las puertas.
It turned one of the doors into cow manure.
Meaning: It destroyed one of the doors.

'Thank God no one's hurt,' I said, then I groaned inwardly. There *was* going to be another delay.

I looked at the tradesmen looking at me, and tried to smile. I turned around, went into the bedroom and sat on the bed. I didn't know that Pedro had followed me until he stood in front of me, looking concerned.

'You might think I'm overreacting,' I said, 'but some of the things I've seen – or avoided seeing – make me so nervous. I'm sure there are good and bad work practices in most countries. I just haven't seen a renovation "up close" before. I can't bear to watch.'

'Safety laws aren't always observed. Unfortunately. Renovations can be like that, everywhere. I know from experience,' Pedro said.

'And the renovation goes on and on, as though it will never end,' I added.

I tried to be calm.

'But it's only a slight delay,' said Pedro, unease in his voice.

'That's exactly the problem. Every time, it's only a slight delay. Then there's another slight delay. Or a power outage.'

'It'll be fine. They'll fix it in a couple of days. I'll organize it all. The rest of the kitchen is practically finished,' said Pedro.

'I hope so,' I said.

*

The next day, a Saturday, I woke up early and couldn't get back to sleep. I made myself a cup of tea in the almost-finished kitchen. As my drowsiness receded, I inspected my surroundings.

I was amazed at the transformation from yesterday. Now that the granite bench tops were in place and cleaned, the colours all blended beautifully together. The kitchen and living areas flowed into each other and the feeling of space was impressive. Light streamed in through the skylight, adding a golden touch. I tried to remember the ramshackle laundry area, but it seemed a dream, or forgotten nightmare.

I couldn't understand why it had all been so overwhelming yesterday, during the PULVERIZED CUPBOARD DOOR EVENT. The door was still pulverized, but other damage was minimal.

From where I stood, I observed the living room floor. The boxes and furniture that we'd crammed into other rooms during the floor-polishing episode were back, but it was easy to see that the parquet had been beautifully sanded and polished.

We had a perfect holiday home.

The phone rang. It was Annie. It was an odd time for her to call.

'I hope it's not too early there, I always forget the time difference. It's late here. How's the renovation going?' she asked.

'Nearly over. I can't quite believe it.'

I waited with trepidation to hear why she'd called. Maybe Mum had had a setback.

But Annie had excellent news, 'I'm glad to hear it. And you didn't get divorced – even better. I called to say Mum's improved a lot, she's exercising much more without needing encouragement. She can't wait to get home, but can't drive yet. A few of her friends from up north have visited.'

'Fantastic,' I said. 'That's wonderful.'

*

After my uncharacteristic outburst regarding the renovation, Pedro seemed to register my feeling of isolation during those first weeks he'd been so absent, swept up in the renovation. He sped up the work so that we could spend more time together, and finalized all the outstanding jobs in the first two days of the next week.

On Monday the tiler replaced the broken tile, Santiago's carpenter replaced the cupboard door, and the plastering was completed.

On Tuesday the painting was finalized, and just like that, no fanfare, no big event, merely a splash of paint, at last, AT LAST, the renovation was over, along with all its hassles and heartache.

> *Muerto el perro, se acabó la rabia.*
> Once the dog died, the rabies stopped.
> Meaning: The problem disappeared when its source no longer existed.

That afternoon, the sofa and armchairs came back looking fabulous. A finishing touch.

> *El broche de oro.*
> The golden brooch.
> Meaning: The icing on the cake.

Even the upholsterer, who had tried to persuade us to use traditional dark green velvet on the antique furniture, was impressed with the warmth and attractiveness of the orange-red patterned fabric that we'd chosen long ago. I sat on it gingerly and the sofa held. I bounced on it – just to check – and it was fine.

It was two days short of a month before we were to return to Sydney.

On the Wednesday, for the very first time, we woke up to a completely finished kitchen. It sparkled. It was dry. And intact. It looked fantastic. The beige tiles, that did *not* reach to the ceiling as in a butcher's shop, the light streaming in from the watertight skylight, and the large functional space were amazing. The kitchen felt bigger than the living area.

'¡Tomá mate!'
'Drink *mate!*'
Meaning: 'Will you look at that!'

Best of all, there were the two of us – no builders, no painters, and no plasterers. We could sleep in every morning.

Pedro took the last of a series of photos. Should any friends or family in Australia be foolish enough to show the slightest interest, we would have enough to keep them occupied for hours. There was no need to show photos to the Argentine family – *their* thousands of photos had circled around the family for weeks.

I felt the stress of the last few weeks continue to evaporate as we remembered the funnier episodes of the renovation.

They were all so much funnier now that they were over.

'Are you still convinced that you want to live in Sydney?' Pedro asked.

'I can't see any way out of it,' I answered sheepishly.

I had a sense that he was going to give me another reason to stay in Argentina, and I wasn't wrong.

He said, 'We're often away from Sydney for weeks at a time, and in isolated places. In Patagonia we were out of phone contact for days.'

I nodded, not speaking.

'And as I said before, there are daily flights to Sydney. If we were here and your Mum had an accident, we could easily fly back. It would be like breaking a holiday and flying home early, and coming back when she was better.'

He was right, in relation to short-term issues.

'But it's not as easy as that. What if she needs months of help because she can't drive?' I said. 'I'll feel guilty knowing Annie's doing all the work, while I follow my heart and live here with you.'

Pedro looked miserable, but I didn't know what to do. I couldn't think of any way out of the 'I need to live in Sydney' responses to his persuading tactics.

'Let me think about it,' I said. 'What you say makes sense. But I feel torn.'

I needed to change the subject, and tried to think of a topic that was related to food or cooking.

I had a brainwave.

'Let's have a new-kitchen dinner,' I said.

This galvanized him immediately. 'Yes! Why not? We can thank everyone for their contribution and their forbearance – including yours,' he said.

But then I stopped myself in my tracks. How stupid of me to think we could have a dinner party if we didn't have any friends here – at least, not friends we'd made together.

'Who would we ask?' I said.

'Well, José and Santiago and their wives.'

'Oh, of course.'

I applied myself more. 'How about Felicitas?'

'Why not – she likes you. And Tía told me there's a new man in her life, but nobody's met him.' By 'nobody,' I knew that Pedro meant 'the family.'

'This could be a low-key way to introduce him to the family,' I said. 'Seeing as we're "fringe family" in a way, and only half Argentine.'

'And even though nobody's met him, they all know his family has a big country house,' said Pedro. He winked at me, smiling. 'So if we're friendly maybe he'll invite us.'

> *Hacer buenas migas.*
> To make good (bread) crumbs.
> Meaning: To work to become good friends with someone. Possibly refers to a tradition in Andalusia, where shepherds each brought an ingredient to make *migas*: dampened, chopped bread was mixed with oil and salt, and fried in oil with garlic, paprika and sometimes bacon.

Not waiting to see my reaction, he said, 'And remember those guys we met on the tour of the *Palacio San Martín*?'

'Oh, yes, Alastair and Matías.'

'Didn't you have a whole lot of questions for Alastair about living in Argentina?'

'Hmm, yes. And we could ask Nora, my Spanish teacher. I don't know if she has a partner. So including us, that would be eleven or twelve. And you have sixty-nine other cousins . . .'

'No more cousins!' he said. 'Only Felicitas and her man. We can have another dinner party for the cousins – some of them. Or they might overwhelm our friends with family issues.'

'What about Tía?'

'I'd love her to be a part of it, but she's refused all my invitations to see the apartment. She said she'd come over with Mum one day, for a coffee. She'd prefer that to a group of strangers. So would Mum.'

It took me a short while to register the gist of our conversation – I now realized we *did* know enough people to have a dinner party. Our decision to renovate, and my need to take myself, and when possible, Pedro, away from that very renovation, had led us directly to our new friends.

We determined a suitable date, and searched for phone numbers on our phones, or in my notebook, or on scraps of paper or business cards. And after calling or leaving messages for the anticipated dinner guests, our first dinner party in Buenos Aires was organized. Just like that.

*

I leaned back, stunned at how easy it had been, and flicked through my notebook again. Pedro moved around the kitchen, checking off the items he needed for the dinner party.

I came across the dentist's number scrawled inside the back cover of my notebook, and memories of the dripping skylight came flooding back. It was on the SKYLIGHT DAY that we had asked Silvina and Darío about their dentist.

I blotted the muddy kitchen images from my mind and said to Pedro, 'What about that appointment with the dentist? If you find you need lots of dental work, we should get started now.'

'Of course. Now's perfect.'

He phoned the dentist, and after a short conversation I heard him say, '*Darío.*' I guessed he'd been asked about the referring patient.

Pedro repeated the next question, '*¿Apellido?*' 'Last name?' He looked at me questioningly, no doubt hoping that I knew.

'Umm,' he said, and I racked my brain. How on earth would we know his last name? We only knew the first names of the people in the building.

I had a bright idea and dashed into the second bedroom where we kept our documents. I remembered seeing a printed record of the owners' meeting. Papers flew, but I found the list of owners, and Pedro's voice was calm as he read out the name I pointed to. '*Núñez.*'

He listened and made notes, then hung up. 'There's been a cancellation. They've granted me an audience at midday. Here's the address, it's on level four.'

'Excellent,' I said. 'But it's interesting that the dentist only sees patients through a personal referral. Hopefully he *is* an *eminencia.*'

We raced out, Pedro to the dentist, I to see Nora for my Spanish class. I'd rearranged the class to start later in the day.

Pedro later told me that there was no sign outside the building to indicate the presence of a dental surgery – he pressed the buzzer for level four, and was relieved when a receptionist answered. This privacy contrasted with many surgeries in our *barrio* and their huge signs,

188

'*Odontología.*' When he arrived at level four, he had to press another buzzer to get in. Once in the seat, he was admonished by the dentist who said, 'I can see you haven't been near a dentist for a *very* long time.'

> *Fuiste al dentista cada muerte de obispo.*
> You went to see the dentist as often as a bishop dies.
> Meaning: You hardly ever went to the dentist.

Pedro agreed to have a clean, implant and crown, and to leave other, minor work for future visits.

*

It was mid-afternoon when we both arrived home. Pedro had a recipe in mind for the big dinner party and wanted to test it out.

'We've still got some chilli,' he said, 'And I can make the meal mild enough. But we need a few more ingredients. Let's go to *barrio chino.*'

On the way to the bus stop, we bumped into José, a camera slung around his neck. He had the afternoon to himself, and told us he was helping his children with their homework. Seeing me looking at his camera, he explained, 'There's a wall around the corner that's full of street art. The kids want pictures for a school project and I said I'd take photos for them. Did you know that Buenos Aires is a global centre for street art?'

'You mean, graffiti?' I asked, naively. I'd seen many walls and metal shutters scrawled with large initials and tags.

'Street art's different. It's often commissioned,' he said. 'An internationally famous artist has a studio in the next block. Last Sunday, a group of artists re-painted the wall.'

We followed him around a corner to a street we had not explored, and he pointed to a wall covered with colourful paintings. A huge green and blue face of a woman with large eyes and cat's whiskers, her flowing hair pink. Bart Simpson smoking a joint, his yellow face outlined in red, with three green eyes. A yellow elephant edged with red patchwork stitching. A grey robot with red eyes, whose torso was the electricity meter for the building. A lime-green ghost covered with black thorns, with rubbery pink lips. A stencil of Charlie Chaplin. A smiling pink octopus sitting Buddha-like on a white cloud. The stencil of a motorcyclist in mid-air whirling a *boleadora* – the weapon used by *gauchos* to capture cattle. One stencilled animal was part squirrel, part dog.

> *Ni chicha ni limonada.*
> Neither chicha nor lemonade.
> Meaning: Neither one thing nor another. Chicha was a drink made from fermented corn.

José knew all the artists, and he pointed out the different styles. I loved the wild colours and the imagination of the artists, and knew I'd be investigating street art in depth on future trips.

'See you for dinner on Friday week,' I said, as we left him taking photos.

What a great Dad, I thought, remembering back to the time when we'd first met him and he'd bought a carnivorous plant to 'show his kids.'

*

Barrio chino was a short walk from the bus stop, on the other side of a railroad crossing. As we approached the crossing, lights flashed and the barrier descended, blocking the traffic. A bell rang, warning pedestrians to stay back. A few reckless people ran across the rails as the train drew near, and luckily reached the far side alive.

We crossed over when the train had passed, and were welcomed to the food shops, supermarkets and restaurants of *barrio chino* by an ornate rectangular arch guarded by the foo dogs.

Shop windows breathed colour and flavour. In one, golden roasted ducks hung side by side, in another, red dragon masks hurled fire, and in another, woks, chopsticks and teapots were crammed together.

We browsed menus, inspected herbs, breathed in the spices, bought smoky tea for me, and admired the mushroom displays, described in a mix of languages – *shitake, baby shitake, Portobello, agaricus, rosa, blanca, gírgola rosa,* and even more for readers of Mandarin.

Inside a general store, the fresh chillies caught my eye. Arranged in green, orange and red, they sat between the star anise and the dried seaweed. Wontons, dim sums and pork buns rested in bamboo steamers. Spring rolls looked inviting on their trays, and packets of rice crackers, bowls of fortune cookies, and cans of lychees were lined up on the shelves. We meandered past familiar items – dried fish, plum sauce, glutinous rice, rice flour and black beans.

The mix of aromas took me back to those days in Sydney when we wandered through Chinatown and stopped for a meal of noodles, soup or a hot pot.

Pedro found a shopping trolley and picked out a few items for the dish he planned – fresh coriander, limes, oyster sauce, coconut cream and fresh ginger. I added spring rolls to the trolley, and we ate them as we wandered down the street.

Pedro was unwinding. Today he cracked jokes more often than he had for many weeks, and he struck up more conversations than usual with shopkeepers and fellow customers.

I was admiring red paper lanterns in a shop window when I noticed Pedro was no longer by my side. I tracked back two shops and murmured,

'Oh no!' as I stepped into a hardware shop. Yep, there he was, chatting to the shopkeeper.

'I've been thinking,' he said, smiling as I approached. 'Now that we've done the kitchen, haven't you noticed that the bathroom looks rather tired?'

I grabbed his arm and dragged him out of the shop. 'No more renovations. We're on holidays.' I didn't let go until we'd left all the shops behind us.

> *Y a otra cosa, mariposa.*
> And on to something else, butterfly.
> Meaning: And that's the end of it. On to something new. Rhyming slang.

*

We found that we were walking away from the subway station, not toward it, but decided to explore more of the neighbourhood before turning back.

We crossed a narrow, cobblestone road and I paused. I thought I heard music. My head turning to catch the sound, I asked, 'Can you hear it? Is it a cello?'

We took a few steps along the road, and Pedro whispered, 'Bach.' Hand in hand, we followed the sound. The traffic noise receded, and the mellow tones wafted across the cobblestones. We determined that the music originated from behind a graffiti-covered wall, and we moved closer. When the music paused, we both clapped.

There was a murmur of voices. A door in the wall opened and a middle-aged man beckoned us inside. He had intense brown eyes and curly grey hair reaching to his shoulders. He was dressed in baggy jeans and a sloppy red t-shirt.

A group of seven young musicians were seated in a semicircle in a courtyard, in the shade of a tree. They were in their late teens or early twenties, and dressed casually. Four of them held violins or violas, another was playing notes on a cello, one sat quietly beside her harp, and one steadied a double bass. At the end of the semicircle a second cello leaned against an empty seat. A couple of the musicians greeted us, one murmured to another, and another checked his cell phone.

Our host pointed to a bench beside the wall where we could sit, and levered up the leaning cello to take his place in the semicircle. The musicians shuffled the scores on their music stands before resuming their practice.

I whispered to Pedro, 'Flight of the . . .' He nodded. Of course he knew the 'Flight of the Bumblebee.' The musicians played beautifully.

Era para alquilar balcones.
It was (good enough) to rent balconies, i.e. to get the best view.
Meaning: It was a great show.

Behind the group was a two-storey, blank grey wall running the width of the property, with three upstairs windows, and two downstairs, either side of a double glass door. Behind the glass a number of music stands partly obscured a notice board, suggesting it was a school of music.

There had been no sign on the street door, probably for security reasons, and I was reminded of Pedro's description of the dentist's surgery.

Perhaps our host had invited us in because only kindred music lovers would stand in front of a graffiti-covered wall clapping their hands, or perhaps because when he opened the door, he thought we looked friendly or benign. In any case, we felt honoured to be included.

The concert ended all too soon, and we thanked our hosts and left as the sun was setting.

*

By the time we arrived home, it was early in Argentine dinner terms, but I was already very hungry.

A esa hora ya me picaba el bagre.
At that stage the catfish was already biting me.
Meaning: I was already hungry then.

Like a magician, Pedro whipped a fillet of pink Chilean salmon from the fridge and sorted through the ingredients we'd bought at *barrio chino*.

He produced a fantastic Asian-style dish, similar to one he'd made in Sydney a few times, that would be perfect for the celebration dinner – with his delicious flan for dessert. We wanted to make our dinner memorable.

Tirar la casa por la ventana.
Throw the house out the window.
Meaning: 'Spend up big' to celebrate.

'By the way,' I said to Pedro, 'Nora asked if she could bring her daughter to dinner and I said, "Of course." We'll hardly notice one more helping, or another plate to wash.'

¿Qué le hace una mancha más al tigre?
What would another spot do to the tiger?
Meaning: One more or one less won't make a difference.

Over the next week, we explored the city. Pedro took me to places he remembered, such as the *Primera Junta* area, where tourists could travel on an old Buenos Aires tram. And to the Botanic Gardens in *Palermo*. And to a shallow artificial lake in one of the *Recoleta* parks, where model-yacht enthusiasts raced their boats. A couple of times I accompanied him to the dentist, who impressed us with his expertise and professionalism.

Other times, Pedro patiently followed me around as I tracked down famous buildings that I'd seen on the Internet. One morning we found the *Otto Wolf* building with its twin corner domes. I was intrigued to see four huge gargoyle-like condors carved out of granite at the roofline. I would have expected any large birds to be the eagles of the Austro-Hungarian Empire.

Five blocks later, we stopped for a coffee break at *Café Tortoni*, where all those months ago, Pedro had drawn the *Serviette Plan* for the kitchen renovation. And three blocks further on, I pointed out the *Bank of Boston* building, completed in 1924.

'We need to see the dome,' I told Pedro. 'Let's cross the road to get a better view.'

When we looked up again we saw a much bigger dome than most, in the shape of a bullring. Incredible. The building's architects never visited Argentina but were told that Argentines spoke Spanish, hence the design. Interestingly, bull fighting in Argentina had been outlawed more than a century earlier, in 1819.

On another day we set out for *Casa Calise*, a fabulous Art Nouveau apartment building in the *barrio* of *Balvanera*. The façade was decorated with raw granite carvings – of cherubs supporting the balconies, of half-nude females – sculpted on site in 1911. Also in Art-Nouveau style with signs of Belle Epoque, we stopped at the *Confitería del Molino*, closed and run-down, but being restored. Its name literally meant 'Windmill Tea Room,' and the vanes of a windmill could be seen above the fifth storey, at the base of an impressively tall dome. Opened in 1916, all its doors, windows, bronze handles, the marble for its stairways, and more than one hundred and fifty square metres of stained glass were brought from Italy.

Our outing ended with the *Barolo*, whose European architect designed an almost identical building – the *Palacio Salvo* – in Montevideo, the capital of Uruguay. The architect was told that these two cities were located on either side of the *River Plate*, so he placed lighthouses on the domes of each building, expecting that they would illuminate each other. But because he had never visited Argentina or Uruguay, he did not know that the cities were over two hundred kilometres apart, and that the curvature of the earth would never allow one building to be seen by the other.

It was a long day. When we arrived home, I presented Pedro with a painting I'd finished in my art class, framed and ready to hang. It was of a canal in Venice near the hotel where we'd stayed on our honeymoon.

Every evening, Pedro cooked delicious dinners, testing out the new kitchen – mouth-watering risottos, Arab-style chicken, or salmon on puff pastry with delicious toppings. One night he even made chocolate mousse.

At last we were seeing the city and enjoying it together.

*

On the Wednesday evening, I called Annie.

'Mum's thrown out the walking stick,' she said.

'That's fantastic,' I replied, even though I didn't know she'd been using one. The mention of a walking stick brought back memories of my sorrowful dream where Mum looked old and frail.

'And by the way, you're off the hook, she says she doesn't want us to rush around helping her out. She wants to live near her friends in that retirement village.'

'But she loves that farm!'

'She's changed her mind.'

'And it's no trouble to help her,' I said.

Annie said, 'And on Monday two of her friends took her up to Newcastle and they went to the retirement village to check it out. They dropped her back yesterday.'

'She went all the way up there? Is she *that* much better? But she's too young to lock herself away. I'll persuade her not to leave home.'

'Good luck,' Annie said. 'Here she is.'

'Hello dear.' It was Mum, sounding her normal cheerful self.

'Didn't you say you were never leaving the farm?' I said.

'Yes – but I can't cause an international furore whenever I'm unwell. You're phoning all the time from South America – and Annie told me that you're coming back because of me. Even Anthony's been calling from France. Anyway, I *do* live a long way from civilization. It's better to move now.'

'But you love the farm!'

'Yes,' she said. 'But if I have another setback and can't drive, I'm stuck. There's a bus into town from the retirement village if I need it. And I have friends there.'

'Don't move, Mum. We can easily help out if you need us. You can rely on Annie and me. Pedro and I don't have to stay here. This is a *trial*. It's just a *holiday*.'

'Well if you insist, I'll think about it. But . . .'

'But what?'

'I reserved a villa – a small one with a garage, so I can have my car with me. There's a garden and I can take a pet.'

'Cancel it, you don't need to move,' I insisted.

'If you think so, dear.'

I put the phone down, confused. Did Mum *really* want to leave the farm? Was I trying to stop her from doing what she truly wanted? Surely not. What I *knew* she wanted – what she had *always* wanted – was to stay on the farm. And for us to be nearby.

*

On the morning of the dinner party, we shopped for last-minute ingredients before settling in to prepare the meal. During the day, I thought of Mum and how crazy she was to even think of moving. She'd been on that farm for over twenty years.

We picked up a bunch of asparagus at the greengrocer's, having ordered it the day before. The greengrocer had bought it especially for us from the *Mercado Central* or 'Central Market.' The limes were over-ripe, so we passed on them. Pedro teased the greengrocer, questioning their quality.

> *A las limas no se las ve muy católicas.*
> The limes don't look very Catholic.
> Meaning: The limes don't look too good.

The greengrocer's wife appeared at the back of the shop and we greeted her as she gathered cabbage, zucchini, onion, butternut pumpkin, corn, spinach and carrots. She was preparing *verduritas* or 'little vegetables,' a soup mix of chopped vegetables for busy customers.

Behind the counter I spotted a baby in a pram and a young girl leaning over it. She held a sheet of butcher paper with a bright coloured drawing, to entertain the baby with the colours. Butcher paper was used to wrap eggs, six at a time. The packed eggs were piled high in every greengrocer and butcher shop we'd visited. Eggs in cartons were also stacked high in supermarkets. I wondered how many millions were trucked into the city every day. The butcher paper reminded me to ask for a dozen eggs.

To make conversation, I asked the greengrocer, 'Where do all the eggs that you buy come from?'

I expected an answer such as, *'Bahía Blanca en la provincia'* 'The town of *Bahía Blanca* in the Province of Buenos Aires.'

'El huevero' 'The egg man,' said the greengrocer, as he handed me two lots of six eggs.

Oh, well, I thought, *I suppose I should have worded the question more clearly.*

After buying limes in a different shop, we struggled back through the hot soup that was summer in Buenos Aires, perspiration dripping down our backs, looking forward to an evening of celebration with our new friends. I thought of the tiny swimming pools on many building terraces, and imagined the water temperature reaching boiling point.

> *Estaba para pelar gallinas.*
> It was hot enough to pluck chickens.

'We should have called for delivery,' I said to Pedro, 'instead of cooking. It's so unbearably hot. Sometimes it even feels hot with the air conditioner at full blast.' Would the guests notice if we ordered dinner from a restaurant and presented it to them? Probably not.

But it would defeat the purpose. Pedro had it all planned, and we had a fantastic new kitchen. 'Just kidding,' I said, before he had a chance to answer.

By now I'd learned that any food item could be delivered in Buenos Aires – fruit and vegetables, restaurant fare, coffee served in a crockery cup with saucer on a tray, pizza of course, sandwiches, barbecued chicken and meat, ice cream . . . The list was endless. But despite the huge array of delivered items, Pedro's Mum assumed that it was nothing compared to what must happen in Australia. She found it hard to believe me when I disagreed – that getting a kilo of chocolate ice cream delivered was not the way things were done.

Pedro's mother always had her supermarket shopping delivered, and one day we met one of the delivery men as he wheeled a stack of crates right into her kitchen, opened up the plastic bags that contained her shopping, and placed all the items on her counter. The milk and dairy products were cold, having been wrapped in an insulating material. After that, I understood why all those 'crates on wheels' were being pushed around the city.

*

We had hardly arrived home with our shopping, when a deafening noise almost made me jump out of my skin. It was as though someone were drilling into our kitchen ceiling.

Pedro was calm. He looked out the window.

'It's upstairs – they're putting in a new air conditioner,' he shouted at me. 'Must be for the triplets. They probably swelter in that room.'

That's all we need, I thought. The triplets were one year old and shared the second bedroom. Luckily, we never heard them crying at night, as our room was below the parent's room. Hallelujah.

It was clear why they were installing an air conditioner, but the timing could have been better – for us. If only we'd known, we could have changed the date of the dinner party, or at least started our preparations earlier.

Con el diario del lunes siempre es más fácil.
With Monday's paper it's always easier.
Meaning: It's easier to make a decision if you can be certain of the outcome. The results of weekend horse races were listed in Monday's newspaper. If you'd known the results on the race day, you would have won all the bets.

Still, there was nothing we could do about it. I tried to remember the music we'd heard at recent concerts, to take my mind off the racket. But it was hopeless, I couldn't think straight.

During a lull in the noise, Pedro said that they'd have to stop drilling at lunchtime for an hour, and at six o'clock for the rest of the day, because of the building by-laws. But that didn't help us right now. I appreciated what a commotion we must have made during the early part of the renovation, and how patient and polite the neighbours had been. Even our downstairs neighbour, Adriana, had reverted to polite greetings after her initial outburst regarding her sick father. I also knew that all the residents showed great forbearance when parties in the common room upstairs continued until three in the morning – the by-law cut-off time. Luckily the common room was a long way from our apartment.

Right now, my only option to deal with the drilling noise – at least while cooking – was to use the earplugs we'd bought before our flight over.

'Sorry, I won't be able to hear you for a while,' I shouted at Pedro, choosing two of the four earplugs. 'I don't want to have a headache during the dinner party.'

I smiled when Pedro did the same with the other two.

We carried on with the preparation, making hand signals to each other when necessary.

It was fun doing ordinary things together like shopping for food – not tiles or paint – and goofy stuff like wearing earplugs while working side-by-side. I no longer minded that we hadn't seen a whole lot of Buenos Aires – we could explore it more thoroughly on future trips. For now, we could concentrate on celebrating with our new friends.

Salmón al estilo asiático con polenta cremosa y espárragos salteados
– Asian-Style Salmon with Creamy Polenta and Sautéed Asparagus

The Asian-style salmon that Pedro cooked after our trip to <u>barrio chino</u> was delicious. Having fresh and nutritious ingredients nearby, coupled with access to Asian ingredients in <u>barrio chino</u>, meant that we could take advantage of Asian-style recipes that Pedro had developed in Australia.

As an aside, this was a pretty hardy dish to cook and could take a hammering. Pedro cooked it at a friend's place in Sydney one evening and found that the oven door didn't close properly. Being the practical person that he was, he went into the tool shed, got a sledgehammer, and used it to wedge the oven door closed. A lovely aroma escaped into the kitchen as the dish was cooking, and the salmon was delicious.

Salmón al estilo asiático
Asian-Style Salmon

Ingredients
2 medium-large red chillies, medium hot
2 big cloves garlic
1 lime
1 teaspoon freshly grated ginger
Handful of fresh coriander leaves
1 tablespoon of oyster sauce
200ml coconut cream, or coconut milk if you can't find coconut cream
A 1-kilo fillet of salmon

Method

Marinade
Cut the chillies along their lengths, and scrape out the seeds and dispose of them.
Coarsely chop the garlic and the chilli and place in a mortar.
Add the zest and the juice of one lime.
Pound with the pestle. If you don't have a mortar and pestle, use a hand blender, or a food processor, or try to squash it in a bowl with the end of a spoon.
Add the grated ginger and roughly chopped coriander leaves
Pound again to homogenize whilst visibly retaining some of the chilli and the coriander leaves.
Pour into a bowl, add the oyster sauce and the coconut cream and set aside.

Salmon
Debone the salmon and pat dry. Leave the skin on it.
On the fleshy side, cut some slits diagonally across the thicker part of the fillet. This will help the marinade to penetrate and the fish to cook evenly.

Place the fish on an ovenproof dish capable of being covered with a lid. This doesn't have to be sophisticated and could be a flattish round Pyrex dish that you can cover with a metal saucepan lid.

Make sure it is skin side down.

Pour the marinade over the salmon, ensuring it gets into the cuts.

Put the lid on the dish and place the dish in the middle of the oven for 20-30 minutes at 150-180°C. If you use a cast iron dish, you will find it cooks faster, in 15 minutes. You will need to time the cooking in relation to the thickness of the fillet.

Serve with some of the marinade.

Hints

To ensure that the salmon doesn't stick to the base of the pan, line the dish with baking paper or waxed paper.

For a more authentic feel, you can wrap the whole fish and marinade in banana leaves and bake it in the leaves.

Serves 4.

Polenta cremosa
Creamy Polenta

Ingredients

2 cups water

1 cup milk

30g butter

1 cup polenta. A quality Italian polenta that is very fine – not granular – is the best choice.

1 clove garlic

Salt and pepper

¼ teaspoon nutmeg

2 drops Tabasco

3 tablespoons of grated Parmesan

Parsley

Method

Note that polenta thickens quickly, so prepare it as you are ready to serve.

Combine water and milk in a small saucepan.

Bring to just before boiling.

Add the butter.

Turn down heat.

Slowly add polenta to the liquid whilst stirring constantly. Using a whisk is best.

Crush the garlic into the polenta.

Add salt and pepper.

Grate the fresh nutmeg to taste.

Stir 3-5 minutes. It becomes smooth and creamy.

Turn the heat off. Add the Parmesan. Check for seasoning and adjust.

Add 2 drops of Tabasco, but only if the meat dish you are preparing has no chilli in it. The Tabasco gives it a tangy punch.

Add fresh chopped parsley for colour.

Serves 4.

Espárragos salteados
Sautéed Asparagus

Pedro often accompanied dishes similar to this one with a simple side salad, such as roquette, pear, walnut and shaved Parmesan with a dressing of caramelized balsamic vinegar, olive oil and seasoning. Or with a simple Thai salad. But that night Pedro decided, instead, to prepare pan-sautéed asparagus.

Ingredients

Two bunches of fresh young asparagus spears of uniform thickness, say half a kilo

2 large cloves garlic, chopped but not too finely

¼-⅓ red capsicum, thinly sliced and cut into to 2-3cm lengths

1 whole red chilli, seeds removed and chopped coarsely. Of course the amount of chilli depends on how hot you like your food

Half a lemon

Olive oil

Seasoning

Method

Cut the blunt end off the asparagus to make all spears a uniform length, rinse them and place them in a microwave-safe dish with a lid.

Cook the asparagus on 'high' in the microwave for 1½-2 minutes. The spears should be cooked lightly and remain crisp.

Take the asparagus spears and place them in cold water to stop the cooking process and retain the green colour, then immediately drain and set aside so they continue to dry.

In a frying pan big enough to accommodate the lengths of the asparagus spears, put 3 tbsp olive oil. Before the oil overheats, add the garlic, chilli and capsicum, sauté for 1-2 minutes, and add the asparagus.

Cook the asparagus spears until they are slightly charred in a few areas, and soft enough to spear with a skewer. Just at the point where the crunchiness begins to disappear but they retain their structure, take them out to serve. At this point they should be cooked, a little crunchy and not soggy.

Squeeze the juice from the half lemon on to the asparagus and season to taste.

Serves 4.

14

A DINNER IN SPANISH

The big moment had arrived. I'd never given a dinner party in Spanish before, and hoped I'd understand everything, or at least enough to avoid any blunders. It was nerve wracking, but I took deep breaths and told myself it would be fine.

Pedro prepared a jug of *Pisco Sour*, an alcoholic drink made with *Pisco*, a grape-based colourless spirit claimed by both the Chileans and the Peruvians as their own. To the *Pisco*, he added lemon juice and sugar, and egg white for frothiness. *Pisco Sours* were excellent for generating a lively conversation in any language.

I took olives and cheese from the fridge, and arranged them on one side of a plate. I found the ham, and placed two slices on the plate, but stopped short.

'Isn't Santiago Jewish?' I asked Pedro. Buenos Aires had the world's largest Jewish population after New York, and our *barrio* was originally settled by Jewish immigrants. I was conscious of the Jewish food issue since being invited in for a cup of tea by Carla and Domingo who shared our floor. When I'd asked for milk to add to my tea, they'd swapped my non-dairy crockery for dairy crockery, and poured me a new cup of tea. An embarrassing gaffe.

'He's not strict – but let's keep the ham separate so as not to offend,' said Pedro.

Santiago and his wife were the first to arrive. 'Yum, prosciutto,' he said. 'Delicious.' I smiled at Pedro, acknowledging that Santiago was not a strict adherent. Santiago examined the living room. It no longer contained the refrigerator, the unused washing machine, the building equipment or the ever-present thin film of dust. 'Love the sofa and armchairs,' he said. 'But shouldn't they be covered in dark green velvet? Or at least grey-green?'

Before we could respond, Felicitas arrived downstairs with her new beau, Paco. Pedro went to greet them.

Pedro had once explained to me that in Argentina, most names came with standard nicknames. Usually Francisco was *Paco* or *Pancho*, Patricio was *Pato*, José was *Pepe*, from Giuseppe, Enrique was *Quique*, and Carlos was *Cacho*. But sometimes, a physical characteristic became the nickname, and the result was shocking for a politically correct Australian. People with dark skin often called themselves, or were called, *el negro*, or *la negra*. *El colorado* was 'The redhead.' Felicitas had a friend who signed her texts *la colo*, short for *la colorada*. Pedro had a friend called *el gordo López* or 'Fat López' – *el gordo* for short – another called *el flaco* or 'The skinny one,' and yet another called *el cabezón* or 'Big head.' These names were normal for Argentines, and were used in an affectionate way. Pedro's family and friends became confused when I said that the names could cause offence in Australia. 'But that's how they are!' 'That's what they call themselves.' 'Why would that be offensive?'

Nicknames were also linked to nationality. Spanish people were called *gallegos* or 'Galicians' because so many Spanish immigrants came from Galicia. Similarly, Italians were mainly from Naples and were called *tanos*, short for *napolitano*s. Of course Americans were *gringo*s. At school Pedro, with his blue eyes and reddish hair, was called *el polaco* or 'The Polish one'.

Felicitas and Paco entered with Pedro. Paco smiled, his dimples creasing. He was clean-shaven, unusual for most Argentines we'd met, his eyes a dark brown and his hair black with streaks of grey. His checked shirt was casually untucked over a pair of chinos.

The introductions began. All the men shook hands with each other in greeting, but everyone else kissed on the cheek – women-with-women and women-with-men. I assumed that the men-with-men kissing that I'd witnessed, including policemen when changing shift, was not applicable here, though I wasn't sure why.

Felicitas turned to Paco and said, 'I told you so. You see? Catherine's just like an Argentine.'

'I'm glad to be one of you,' I said, nonplussed, 'but what did I do?'

Paco stepped in to explain. 'I was concerned when Felicitas told me you were Australian. I work with foreigners, and it's awkward meeting women from England or Germany – or other northern European countries. They're so formal and distant.'

Felicitas said, 'Paco kept asking me on the way here, "How do Australian women greet? Are they like English women? Should I shake her hand, or do nothing? I assume she won't kiss me on the cheek?" '

I made a mental note to tell Sarah about kissing strangers when she arrived on Sunday.

I introduced Felicitas and Paco to Santiago and his wife. Santiago noticed a striped ribbon falling out of Felicitas' handbag.

He asked, '*River* supporters?'

As she nodded, I chimed in, saying, 'I'd love to go to one of those classic *River-Boca* matches. The atmosphere must be electric.'

'You have to choose a team first – what's Pedro's team?'

Pedro was opening a bottle of wine. '*Independiente*,' he called out, and turned to me to explain. 'It's the red team. But the stadium is now *less* red.'

'How can it be *less* red? Did the paint fade?'

'No, *Racing* fans put sandpaper on their shoes to rub out the paint.'

I laughed – it was very funny, though crazy.

Pedro said, 'But what can you expect from a team that exorcises its own stadium?'

'Exorcises?' I asked. 'What?' This was even crazier than sandpapered shoes.

Pedro smiled. 'They say – I don't believe it – that *Independiente* fans buried seven black cats in the *Racing* stadium, decades ago.'

'Cats? Whatever for?'

Pedro explained, 'For bad luck. *Racing* fans blamed the buried cats for years of poor performance.'

I had to laugh again.

'But what's that got to do with exorcising?' I asked.

'They dug up six of the cats but couldn't find the last one,' said Pedro. 'It meant they were still cursed. So a priest exorcised the stadium. Tens of thousands of fans turned up. *Racing* fans – of course.'

Wow, another world of weirdness, I thought, making a mental note to read the sports news more regularly. All I knew about soccer teams was that they had interesting nicknames. The *River* team was called *gallinas* or 'Hens,' because a chicken painted with the team colours was thrown into a soccer field after a championship loss in the 1960s. They were also called *millonarios*, because they were based in the wealthy *barrio* of *Belgrano*.

The conversation moved on, and after a while I went over to Pedro and whispered to him, 'I think Felicitas wants a glass of wine. I heard her say *"seca como lengua de loro."* Does that mean, "As dry as a parrot's tongue"?'

'Yes it does and you're right. I'm on it.'

The buzzer sounded and I took the elevator down to meet Alastair and Matías, whom we'd met on the *Palacio San Martín* tour.

*

I opened the foyer door to greet them. They were both dressed casually but fashionably in t-shirts and long shorts, with designer runners.

I kissed each of them on the cheek and said, 'They're talking football upstairs, do you follow a team?'

'Never watch it,' said Alastair, 'and Matías hates it. We surf – but we won't bore you with our stories. Have you ever been surfing?'

Matías spoke to him gently, 'She was probably *born* on a surf board, if she's Australian.' He asked me, 'So, how do you find Buenos Aires?'

'I love it. And Argentina, what I've seen of it. Patagonia is amazing.'

'Amazingly empty,' countered Alastair. 'We went surfing in Chubut Province with the penguins and shipwrecks. It was cool.'

'Very cool. Actually it was freezing,' said Matías. 'We were there because . . .'

Matías' story was cut off by the sound of knocking on the glass foyer door. It was Nora and her daughter.

I made the introductions and we all took the lifts up to the fifth floor.

'It's fantastic!' said Nora, admiring the kitchen, as José beamed.

Alastair and Matías looked confused, so she explained. 'Pedro and Catherine just spent over two months renovating. Catherine described it to me, week by week – the rubble, the dust, the leaks, the search for materials. I didn't know the kitchen was so big.'

'Oh, now I remember,' said Alastair, turning to me. 'You mentioned it when we saw you on the tour. We've recently bought a place ourselves – unrenovated. You could give us a few ideas.'

My stomach churned. I never wanted to be near a renovation again, let alone to live through one. Never ever. 'My best idea would be to move out and get an architect to do it.'

'Oh, we were thinking of project managing the renovation ourselves.'

'If there's one thing that I remember from our meeting, it was you saying that you were completely impractical,' I said. 'I remember because it resonated with me so well. You really should get an expert to do it.'

> *El que nace para melón, nunca llega a ser sandía.*
> He who was born to be a melon (for example a cantaloupe) will never be a watermelon.
> Meaning: You will never be great at something if were not born with a natural ability.

'And stick to what you know.'

> *Zapatero a tus zapatos.*
> Shoemaker to your shoes.
> Meaning: Stick to what you know.

I realized that I was browbeating them, and stopped. 'Sorry, you must of course, do what you want. Pedro can give you ideas, but I found it very trying.'

I surveyed our brand new kitchen and heaved a sigh of relief, knowing that it was all behind us.

José arrived late. His wife took the blame – she'd been visiting neighbours in the building and he hadn't been able to find her anywhere.

Hardly had we started dinner when the doorbell rang.

'Our power's gone! We must have switched on too many appliances at once. The fuse tripped – and when we tried to switch it back on, nothing happened.' It was Carla and Domingo, who shared the floor with us.

Quick thinking was required, so I thought quickly.

'Why don't you join us for dinner? You can deal with the electricity in the morning. You'll have to bring your own chairs.'

All our twelve chairs were in use. We had six for dinner parties plus four folding ones, and the in-laws had lent us two for the night.

Carla looked sheepish, and I surmised that it wasn't because of the chairs. I remembered the changing of crockery when I'd wanted milk in my tea, and guessed that she hesitated because she kept kosher. Luckily I had a brainwave and lied, 'We were just phoning for takeout. Do you eat sushi? With salmon?' I knew salmon was kosher and assumed that they could eat from takeout containers.

Carla smiled with relief, and turned away to get chairs, but Domingo heard our guests, who were now involved in a lively discussion. They had fallen silent when the doorbell rang – perhaps puzzled, because all the chairs were already taken up.

'No, but you have people visiting,' he said.

'A couple more will be excellent,' said Pedro, who'd followed me to the door. 'Please join us.'

Carla smiled again, and they disappeared down the corridor for the chairs.

Pedro phoned for delivery, a large order in case any of our invited guests also felt like sushi. At the rate Pedro's salmon dish was being demolished, it made sense. Matías particularly, kept filling his plate to overflowing.

> *Comió como lima nueva.*
> He ate like a new (sharp metal) file.
> Meaning: He ate non-stop.

The doorbell rang. I opened it and said, 'Come on in,' without thinking. But it wasn't Carla and Domingo, it was our upstairs neighbour Silvina with her triplets in the triplet pram. Silvina had occasionally dropped in with one of her babies, but never with all three. She looked frazzled, her hair was a mess and her expression was strained.

Oh no, I thought. *This looks serious.*

Silvina wiped a tear from her cheek. 'Do you think it would be okay if we fed the kids in your apartment – the air conditioning men took so long, and left the place so dusty, that we can't use the kitchen. I'm exhausted and Darío's coming home late.'

'Of course,' I said, adding without thinking, 'And you must stay for dinner.'

As I spoke, Silvina heard the hubbub from our guests. She looked mortified, 'Oh no! I'm so sorry. I'll ask another neighbour.'

She turned and bumped into Carla and Domingo, who'd appeared behind her with two chairs.

'But you *must* come in,' I said. 'Carla and Domingo have no electricity and Federico on your floor is out, so you *need* to come in. Please, please come in. You'll have to sit on the sofa.'

Silvina looked relieved. She left me with the triplet pram and raced upstairs for their food. The babies were surprisingly docile, considering it was their dinnertime. As I wheeled the pram inside, I whispered to Pedro, 'Increase the order for sushi. Silvina and Darío are joining us – with the triplets.'

'Oh my God. Where will we put them all?' he said.

Éramos pocos y cayó la abuela.
There were a few of us, and Granny dropped in.
Meaning: As if there weren't enough of us, more people turned up.

'It's okay, Silvina can sit on the sofa. When Darío arrives, he can bring a couple of chairs.'

'The new sofa?' he asked. *Feeding babies on his lovely new sofa!*

'I'll throw a blanket over it,' I reassured him.

*

The soft background music that I'd chosen for the evening was drowned out by the cacophony of seventeen vocal individuals. I found I didn't mind at all. The baby triplets contributed to the commotion with their gurgling and occasional screeching. They were happiest on the floor, propelling themselves forward by stretching out their legs and then bending their knees, buffing the newly polished parquet with their multi-coloured jumpsuits. *Just as well we mopped the floor this morning*, I thought.

The guests took the babies in their stride, meaning that they strode *around* them. Even so it was common to hear the refrain, 'Triplet ahead. Watch out!'

From time to time, a quieter interlude allowed one person's voice to be heard above the others, but the background conversations never tapered off completely. During one such moment, Matías asked Pedro, 'So how do you know everyone here? Haven't you recently arrived in the country?'

'Actually we got here over five months ago,' said Pedro, holding one of the triplets on his knee.

There was an eruption of disbelief.

'But Catherine's been taking my Spanish lessons for two months. Before that you were in Patagonia for a month, so that leaves *three*,' said Nora, my Spanish teacher.

José said, 'No, *four*, if they spent a month in Patagonia. Because it was three months ago that Pedro asked me to do the kitchen. They can't have been here for much longer than four.'

Various other guests made their own pronouncements, and all of them, except Felicitas, were wrong. She said, 'No, Catherine's correct, I remember when they arrived.'

It didn't matter that Pedro and I knew exactly when we'd arrived – each guest was adamant that they were correct, and hands flew in all directions as each of them made their point.

'Five months,' repeated Pedro above the clamour, 'And I want to propose a toast to you all for helping us to settle in.' He held up his glass, 'As my Spanish mother would say, *"Salud, pesetas y amor."* '

Salud, pesetas y amor
Cheers, pesetas and love.

'And a toast to the cook,' said José, looking at me. 'The salmon is delicious.'

Boccato di cardinale.
A Cardinal's mouthful.
Meaning: Delicious.

'Thank Pedro, not me. He's the chef,' I said, to José's look of amazement.

We all toasted Pedro, and Matías took advantage of an unusual break in the clamour of voices to retrace the thread of the conversation.

'Okay, five months. If you say so. Is it permanent or temporary?'

Pedro turned to me, expecting an answer. I hesitated, blushing slightly. I wasn't expecting to be put on the spot. I said, 'Well, we don't know yet . . .'

Matías sensed my discomfort and gave me a reprieve. He turned to Nora.

'Spanish lessons, you said?'

Inwardly, I sighed with relief and also turned toward Nora.

Nora, like Matías, must have sensed I was uneasy because she rushed to fill the silence. Or, better said, semi-silence, because of a commotion whilst

José jumped up to block off a triplet who was heading toward an open bedroom door. José closed the door as the triplet arrived, and she changed direction. Her trajectory reminded me of a ricocheting tennis ball in slow motion, as she headed to the kitchen. But I was getting sidetracked. Nora was speaking.

'. . . they're conversations – nothing formal. During our last chat, I mentioned Argentine inventions and 'firsts' – the first radio station transmission, the first bus, the invention of the biro, the world's first animated feature film, and the *Magiclick* spark gas lighter.'

There were laughs when she listed the *Magiclick*, except from the mother of the triplets, who picked up the wayward child and eyed a second one. She looked exasperated. Pedro still held the third triplet on his knee. He calmly fed it, spooning its food out of a bowl that he'd produced from thin air. Having had three kids himself, though not all of the same age, this activity came naturally to him. I picked up the second triplet and followed suit, spooning food into her mouth. Silvina, relieved, was left with the first and most rebellious triplet.

The conversation continued, with Matías adding to Nora's list, 'Yes. It's intriguing to list all the Argentine 'firsts.' They include the first heart bypass, the method of storing blood for blood transfusions so the blood doesn't clot, the once-only use disposable syringe, and the invention of the cane and traffic lights for the blind, to mention a few.'

A wake of silence followed his speech and he scanned our faces around the table, explaining, 'I'm a science teacher and I make sure the kids know Argentine inventions.'

I wished I could have written that list in my notebook whilst I fed the baby, but I knew when to accept defeat.

José jumped in during the pause to say, 'I've been trying to get a word in for ages. You've all been talking over me. I want to know what Catherine thinks of Argentina. And she hasn't told us if they're staying.'

'I love Argentina,' I answered. 'It's a beautiful country and the people are friendly and courteous. We've enjoyed our time here, and no one can take that experience away from us.'

> *¡Quién nos quita lo bailado!*
> Who will take away the dances we've already danced!
> Meaning: We've had some good times and that won't change.

I rejected the idea of describing our renovation stress, as it was irrelevant to José's question, and said, 'There are endless cultural activities – hundreds of plays each week, lots of free concerts – and the public transport is excellent, there are outstanding restaurants, a café society . . .'

'Ah,' José cut me off. 'That's *Buenos Aires* rather than the rest of

Argentina. *Buenos Aires*, of course, has everything.'

> *Dios está en todos lados pero atiende en Buenos Aires.*
> God is everywhere but he has his headquarters in Buenos Aires.

'But living here isn't as easy as it looks to an outsider,' he said.

'I agree it *can* be unpredictable,' I said.

José asked me, 'Is there anything specific that you can say you truly love here – that you find particularly engrossing?'

Luckily the triplet in my charge had closed her mouth, refusing to eat.

'She's had enough,' said her mother, taking her from me.

This left me free to talk without being distracted by the fear of food falling on the sofa, even though I'd covered it with a blanket as promised.

'I *do* love Argentine sayings, especially when they reveal South America's culture and history,' I answered.

'Which ones?' asked Nora, relaxed, holding out her glass as Pedro poured her another glass of wine.

That answer was also easy.

'One would be, *"Andá a cantarle a Gardel."* '

> *Andá a cantarle a Gardel.*
> Go and sing it to Gardel.
> Meaning: Go and complain to someone else. Carlos Gardel was the most famous of all Argentine tango singers. He died in 1935.

Everyone laughed, and two of the triplets waved their arms up and down. They were wide awake at ten o'clock. *In readiness for a life of very many late nights*, I thought.

'Any more?' she asked.

' *"Saber más que el libro gordo de Petete."* '

> *Saber más que el libro gordo de Petete.*
> To know more than the fat book of *Petete*.
> Meaning: To be the font of all knowledge. *Petete* was a cute television character who educated young children in the seventies.

'How could you know *that* one? You must have listened to *lots* of conversations,' said Matías.

'Pedro thinks I'm obsessed with Argentine sayings,' I answered, 'as well as being obsessed with planning.'

'Well if you live here, you'll certainly be cured of that. Plans are in constant flux,' said José. 'But tell us a few *English* sayings.'

That was easy.

'So, when someone's speeding, you can say they are moving "Like a bat out of hell." '

That caused a brief silence.

Then José asked, 'A *bat*? Why does a bat want to *leave* hell?'

'I have no idea, sorry. Here's another one, "Bob's your uncle." It means, "And it's as easy as that." '

'Bob? Why *Bob*?'

'A century ago, an English Prime Minister, called Robert, appointed his nephew to an important post. "Bob's your uncle" came to mean "And it's as easy as that." '

'Call me cynical, but it sounds like Argentine politics,' said Felicitas. 'We have an equivalent phrase, not so political, it's *"Listo el pollo."* '

> *Listo el pollo.*
> The chicken's ready.
> Meaning: And that's that!

There were laughs all round.

José was intrigued and asked, 'Can you tell us an Australian one?'

I rejected 'You silly galah,' 'Fair crack of the whip,' and 'I'm cactus,' before remembering one I thought they'd appreciate. I said, 'If a person does something silly, you could say, "It seems as though they're a kangaroo short in the top paddock." It's similar to your *"No le llega el agua al tanque."* '

> *No le llega el agua al tanque.*
> Water does not reach his tank. It refers to water storage tanks on the roofs of houses/buildings, and in earlier times, to water tanks on windmills.

The kangaroo reference satisfied José and he nodded, smiling. But Matías continued on the language theme.

'It's a pity that so many English words have crept into the language,' he said. 'One of the craziest examples I've heard is the verb *picapear*, from "pick up." I've heard more than one person saying, *"¿A qué hora te picapeo?"* '

I knew that this meant, 'At what time do I pick you up?'

Felicitas joined in. 'Someone told me I was *zigzagueando* as I drove the other day.'

She looked at me directly and said, 'I can't believe you've picked up those Argentine sayings. And, if you find the language so interesting, and I assume other things too, the big question is, and you've successfully avoided it so far . . . ARE you staying or NOT?'

Matías weighed in, saying, 'You *have* to stay – like Alastair said, we need renovation ideas.'

Felicitas' partner Paco said, 'I've heard so much about you – Felicitas will be upset if you disappear. Who knows when you'll turn up again?'

'What *are* your plans?' Felicitas repeated.

I was under the spotlight, and glanced at Pedro before turning back to her.

'Well, we *do* love it. But I'm concerned about my mother, and how she'll cope as she gets older. And . . .'

'Leave them alone,' Matías ordered, sensing my difficulty in replying. He turned to me, and said, 'Forget about the renovation ideas. You need to make up your own mind. I know that Alastair had to deal with those issues, and it was never easy.'

And the conversation was cut short.

*

At three o'clock in the morning, when all the guests had left, Pedro and I stacked up the dishes to wash the next day. As we worked, I recollected the evening's events and conversations. I'd only had to ask for translations once or twice the whole time. Our guests had understood my Spanish. And I could see from Pedro's face that he'd enjoyed himself.

Apart from the language and greeting protocol, we'd hosted a dinner party just like the ones we had at home.

Well, not *exactly* like the ones at home. More chaotic, certainly, like the country itself. If I'd been told, nine months ago, that within a year I'd be hosting a dinner party in Buenos Aires planned for twelve, with an extra last-minute seven guests including triplets, I would have laughed out loud.

I could see how impatient I'd been during those weeks of the renovation. Mum was better, Pedro was upbeat after the dinner party, we were part of the social network of the building, and we had made friends on our own. We could pick up from there when we came back on future visits.

*

Annie and I talked on Skype the next evening. I wanted to describe the dinner party.

But Annie interrupted me, saying, 'It's all happening here. Anthony's coming back from France. He said he can be around if Mum needs help – he sells most of his paintings on the Internet anyway. And he misses the beach. But Mum says he should stay in Europe, that all her children should do what they want, and not feel they need to be close by to help her.'

She added, 'Mum's being stubborn. I can see where you get it from. She's put her farm on the market. Remember how she reserved a villa in the retirement home a few days ago? She didn't cancel the reservation.'

'But she said she would!'

'Nothing doing. She's unstoppable. She's hardly been here since then. One of her friends at the retirement place came to Sydney again. She took

Mum to Newcastle to stay with her for a couple of nights. Mum got the estate agent to see the farm. And when she saw the villa again, she loved it even more. She wants to live near her friends.'

'Is Mum there?'

Annie ignored my question. 'I haven't finished. So, as you can see, you're superfluous to needs. Come back if you want to be in Australia, but if it's to be near Mum in case something happens, Anthony and I can handle it. Here she is.'

Mum's face appeared on the screen. 'Hello dear.' And immediately, she pre-empted my protestations.

'Yes, I know what you said last time. But I'm too old for the farm.'

'You're not old. You do everything, chop wood, cook, clean, drive, shop, look after the alpacas.'

'Well maybe you're right. I'm not *old*. Not *old old*. Not in my *dotage*.'

'That's what Pedro said to me, except he said you weren't *doddery*.'

'He's right. I'm not *doddery*. And I'm coming to visit you when you've settled in.'

There was a short silence.

'I beg your pardon?' I said.

'I've had plenty of time to read about Argentina, sitting around here all day. Your newsletters make it sound like a lovely place for a holiday. I'm bringing two of my friends.'

'I beg your pardon?'

'Well if you're not going to live here, I'm going *there*, to visit you. I won't need to think about the farm. And don't get upset dear, but I'm ready to move, I just didn't realize it before.'

'But . . .'

'It gets lonely on the farm, and my neighbours aren't exactly close by. I won't have to cook meals if I don't want to. Or drive – there's a bus stop at the door. I'll be able to see friends without dreading the long drive home.'

She said, 'I'll be sad to leave the farm, but I thought I'd be sadder. In fact I'm excited to be moving. If you want to help out, you can settle me in to my villa – that would be brilliant. But only if you have time. Here's Annie. Bye bye dear.'

And she was gone before I could respond.

Annie was back. 'Can we talk tomorrow?' she said. 'Things are busy here.'

The call over, I turned to Pedro, taking off my headphones. 'It seems Mum doesn't need me. She's moving into town where she'll be less isolated. She's coming to visit when we settle in.'

'Here? To Buenos Aires? When we settle in? *Are* we settling in?'

'Yes . . . yes . . . yes . . . and *yes*.' I jumped up and threw my arms around him.

'Are you sure you want to live here for a few years?'

'Yes.' My answer came out without thinking.

I repeated, 'Yes,' to prove to myself that I'd really said it.

'What if your Mum has another fall or gets sick?'

'In that case, it'll be as you said. As though we're on holidays. I'll fly back and help out. I won't stay and worry from a distance.'

'But won't you miss her?'

'Of course I'll miss her, and Annie, and my friends. But we can visit them. And they can visit us. And we're making new friends here.'

'But you'll miss your Mum most of all, I think?'

'Yes. We'll chat by phone, as we did in Sydney. Though I imagine she'll be out, most of the time.'

'And . . . your career?'

'You were right. I was stressed and bored. I don't want to go back to that, after seeing how we can live here together. I could try doing personalized tours, maybe on art or history or architecture – my newsletters have been popular, and I'm always answering emails about Argentina – where to stay, what to do, what to see.'

As I spoke, I was realizing that all my opposition to the move had really just been fear.

Pedro was at a loss for words.

I said, 'I saw an advertisement to teach Business English the other day, and I'll apply for that. It would be an income while I work it all through.'

'No!' said Pedro.

I was taken aback, bewildered by the vehemence of his tone. I reverted to my 'polite response' technique. I was using it frequently today.

'I beg your pardon?'

'Once you're back in that business space, you'll never get out again. And you hate teaching. Please, please, do what you love to do. Play the piano again. And learn to play another musical instrument – you've always wanted to. We'll find a way to make it work. Keep up your painting, study architecture – do *everything* you've been telling me about, do it *all*.'

I smiled, uncertain, but ready to give it a go, moved by his enthusiasm and his kindness.

'Okay,' I said.

'So it's *definitely* yes?'

'Yes. *Definitely*.'

Firme como rulo de estatua.
Solid/firm as a curl of hair on a statue.
Meaning: There is no doubt.

Pedro picked me up and swung me around the kitchen.

213

It was clear to me now that the trial period had not been a 'wait and see' exercise, but more of a 'getting used to it' process. Until Mum had sprung her moving-to-the-city surprise on us, I hadn't been able to see the wood for the trees.

El árbol me tapó el bosque.
The tree blocked (my view of) the forest.

*

The next morning I yawned my way to the kitchen to make a cup of tea. I looked around and thought, *So this is our new home for the indefinite future*, and shook myself to let the truth of it sink in.

I switched on the coffee machine for breakfast.

The phone rang.

It was Alastair, thanking us for dinner. Then he said, 'Did you mean what you said about the renovation? That we should get an expert to do it? I don't know much about building, neither does Matías.'

Sobre eso, soy un cero a la izquierda.
In relation to that, I'm a zero to the left.
Meaning: I'm hopeless at that. A reference to mathematics, and the meaningless zeroes to the left of a whole number.

'Well, a renovation can strain a relationship,' I said.

I thought back to those dusty days, the high points and the low and *very* low points. Such as the mud in the kitchen from the skylight flood.

I said, 'But you'll love your home when it's finished. What I meant was – seeing you don't have the experience – I wouldn't throw myself into the thick of it without assistance.'

Alastair persisted. 'What does Pedro think? Is he there?'

I knew that Pedro was still half asleep.

'He says he'll call you back,' I said. 'He's the one you should talk to, not me.'

Hay que hablar con el dueño del circo y no con el payaso.
You have to talk with the circus owner and not with the clown.

Pedro appeared after a while and I dialled their number and handed over the receiver. 'May as well talk to them before we eat,' I said.

He took the phone and said, 'Yes . . . yes . . . no . . . hmm.' As he talked, Pedro looked at me with an expression between a frown and a smile. He strolled out onto the balcony and carried on the conversation as I prepared breakfast.

I was squeezing oranges when he wandered back in. Something was going on in his mind. He looked at me as he said to Alastair, 'Let me think about it.' He placed the phone on the receiver and turned to me, his face smiling.

I had already guessed before he said it, 'They want me to project manage the renovation.'

His face became serious as he looked at me. 'But we need to talk. Catherine, you need to agree to it. You've said you'll live here for a while, but could you put up with me being involved with another renovation?'

'Depends. Of course I can't say no. You're so happy when you're knee deep in rubble. But we'll be settling in here, so there'll be a lot to do. Will it take much time each day?'

He thought for a moment. 'Tell you what, we'll see if Alastair can be my second-in-command, and I can check out progress each morning and leave instructions with him.'

'Okay,' I said.

'Just "Okay?"'

I looked him straight in the eyes. 'Yes. Of course it's fine. You do what you love to do, and I'll do the same.'

He was overjoyed, and hugged me fervently.

Sambayón con nuez, y merengues con dulce de leche — Zabaglione with Walnuts, and Meringues with Caramel

Sambayón con nuez
Zabaglione with Walnuts

Pedro had been honing his skills at zabaglione. He'd wanted to perfect the dessert ever since our visit to the <u>cantina</u> during the power outage, and he was now ready to test it on unsuspecting friends.

Zabaglione was found on many dessert menus in Buenos Aires, and was also found — as a range of flavours — in every local <u>heladería</u> or 'ice cream shop.' No one in their right mind would start up an <u>heladería</u> without offering '<u>sambayón</u>.' There was usually a <u>supersambayón</u> as well, implying a higher percentage of alcohol. The <u>sambayón</u> could be mixed with any of the following: almonds, chocolate-coated almonds, cherries, strawberries, chocolate chips, rum raisins or walnuts. There could be more than one ingredient, for example both walnuts and raisins could be added, as a separate flavour.

Ingredients
Aim to have the first three ingredients — egg yolks, caster sugar and port — in equal volumes:

3 egg yolks
Caster sugar. Use the eggshell to measure the volume.
Port or Marsala
Walnuts, each broken into 4 pieces

Method
Add water to a small saucepan and place on a low heat until the water is simmering.

Find a bowl that you can use in a similar manner to a bain-marie, i.e. so that you can rest the bowl on your small saucepan of simmering water but without the base of the bowl touching the water. Pedro uses a Pyrex bowl.

In the bowl, combine the egg yolk and sugar at medium speed with an electric beater until smooth and creamy. Add the alcohol and whisk it more.

Rest the bowl on the saucepan of simmering water and continue to beat whilst the mixture heats up, until it thickens.

Place a handful of the walnuts into each dessert bowl or cup, and pour the mixture over the walnuts. You can add berries with the walnuts. If you like chocolate, sprinkle grated chocolate on top.

Serve warm.

A mixture with 3 egg yolks serves 2.

Hints
Make sure that the water is not touching the base of the bowl.
Make it just before serving.

Make sure you whisk the mixture well until it's thickened enough, otherwise it will be runny and taste of raw egg.

Merengues con dulce de leche
Meringues with Caramel

With the egg whites left over from the <u>sambayón</u>, Pedro often made meringues.

Meringues were very popular in Argentina. Practically every <u>panadería</u> or 'bakery' sold them, whether singly, with whipped cream, or with strawberries and whipped cream. One of our neighbours told us that meringues should always have a layer of <u>dulce de leche,</u> regardless of any other filling.

<u>Dulce de leche</u> was a caramel spread, translated literally as 'milk jam.' We saw it on, or found it in, nearly every cake, biscuit and dessert. There were countless brands of it in every supermarket. Argentines missed it when they travelled. An Argentinian once said to me, 'After fifteen years in Australia, I'm still not used to eating a cake without <u>dulce de leche</u>. Cakes are just not cakes without it.'

<u>Dulce de leche</u> ice cream flavours were numerous – creamy, with chocolate chips, with brownie flavour, with raisins, walnuts, cherries etc. For breakfast it was common to spread toast with <u>dulce de leche</u>, and often the toast was dipped in coffee before eating.

<u>Dulce de leche</u> was one of the many dairy products sold in Argentina – milk almost flowed down the streets of Buenos Aires – Argentina being a significant dairy producer.

Pedro told me that Uruguayans, like Argentines, had a sweet tooth, and their best-known dessert was <u>chajá</u>, made from meringues, whipped cream, sponge cake and peaches.

Ingredients and Method
Have some waxed paper and caster sugar handy.
Preheat the oven to 120°C.

Whisk the egg whites to soft peaks, add the sugar and keep whisking until the mixture is viscous and glossy, with a gel-like feel. Then pipe it into dollops on wax paper on an oven tray and place in the oven.

Immediately reduce the temperature to 80-90°C for slow drying, and leave for about 1½ hours or until the meringues sound hollow when you knock them on the bottom. Turn the oven off and leave to cool down over 3 hours or so.

Hints
Make sure the bowl is completely dry before adding the eggs. Moisture in the air, i.e. a humid day, or any contamination with egg yolks will stop the eggs from whisking properly.

Add a tiny pinch of salt to your egg whites before whisking and they will whisk better.

The temperature of 120°C at the start of the cooking process will help to harden the outside of the meringues.

15

HOME

The next day I met Sarah at the airport. After more than five months away from Sydney, I looked forward to seeing a friend who knew me so well. I felt confident I could show Sarah a side of Buenos Aires that she'd enjoy. I also looked forward to hearing an Australian accent.

Ironically, when Sarah arrived, she hardly had a chance to speak. In the taxi back to the apartment, I gabbled on about our experiences in Argentina.

Meanwhile, my phone kept beeping. I continued to talk to Sarah as I checked the messages.

'What's happening with your phone?' Sarah asked.

'Nothing.'

'Nothing?'

'Well, it's just that Pedro's relatives want to know that you arrived safely. So far his Mum, his cousin Felicitas – who I told you about – and three other cousins have been in touch. My Spanish teacher too. As soon as Pedro or I say anything about our families or our Australian friends – things like Mum's fall, or your visit – they all call or send messages. I'm slowly getting used to it.'

'That's nice . . . it's different . . . I like it, it's really nice,' she said.

She didn't say much else, and we were nearly home before I realized why – I hadn't stopped talking. At last, I asked how she was.

'I'm fine – I can't wait to see Buenos Aires. By the way, after Debbie sent your newsletters to lots of her contacts, one of them changed their holiday plans from Spain to Argentina – they loved it.'

*

After Pedro greeted Sarah, he went to spend some time with his Mum, so that Sarah and I could catch up.

It was terrific to hear her news as we visited the *MALBA* museum, home to paintings by Frida Kahlo and Diego Rivera, and the Museum of Decorative Arts, housed in one of the fabulous palaces built in the early nineteenth century. I'd been to the museum before, but only for concerts in the great hall.

We caught the bus back. At one of the stops, a girl of about three years boarded the bus with her grandparents. In a loud and clear voice she said to the bus driver, '*A la casa de la abuela por favor.*'

The driver nodded, smiling.

'What did she say?' asked Sarah, noticing my grin and the chuckles from nearby passengers.

'She said, "To Granny's house, please."'

'You really *do* understand what's happening, don't you?' said Sarah. 'You've taken to Buenos Aires like a duck to water. I would never have thought it.'

'I have to admit that I can hardly believe it either. It's as though a light went on, a month or so ago, and I was one of the crowd and not an outsider.'

*

Walking home from the bus stop, we approached a crossroad with a pedestrian crossing. Sarah stepped confidently onto the crossing. I grabbed her arm to hold her back as a taxi sped in front of her, the driver hooting his horn.

Sarah was shaken, but smiled bravely at me. We looked out for other cars before continuing, and arrived at the apartment safe and sound.

'Sorry I didn't warn you about those reckless drivers. They shouldn't be put in charge of a motor vehicle,' I said.

> *Son más peligrosos que mono con navaja.*
> They're more dangerous than a monkey with a cutthroat razor.

'They're not all like that, but it pays to look out for them.' As I spoke I imagined that many other aspects of Buenos Aires life must have become second nature to me.

'It's nothing. I should have been more careful,' she said. 'But let's talk about your plans. You're not thinking of going back to the rat race in Sydney are you?'

'Seeing you makes me want to go back. But no, I've told Pedro I'll stay. We'll go to Sydney for a couple of months, and help Mum to move to her villa – then we'll come back here. I didn't take this move seriously at first, but after all we've been through together, learning more about Buenos Aires, and now knowing Mum will be okay, I see things differently.'

> *Cambió la película.*
> The movie changed.
> Meaning: It's a different story.

I added, 'And as they say, "Home is where the heart is." The problem is, part of my heart is always in Sydney with family and friends.'

'But most of it is here, I think,' she said softly.

> *Le pegó en el poste.*
> She hit the (goal) post with it.
> Meaning: She was very close to the truth.

'Yes. As long as we never live in a renovation zone again.'

We heard the sound of the key in the lock – Pedro was home. He set about preparing dinner with his new saucepans, asking Sarah, 'By the way, you're not a vegetarian are you?'

'No, why?'

'Because I'm making a chicken casserole. But also, to tell you that here, the word for meat, *carne*, usually refers to *red* meat. If you're a vegetarian, you need to be careful in a restaurant – you shouldn't say that you don't eat *carne*.'

'Why? What happens?'

'You'll probably be served chicken. Better to say *"soy vegetariana."* '

'Well I can't understand what anyone's saying, so I'm glad I'm *not* a vegetarian,' said Sarah. 'I'd be the dummy that ended up with the chicken.'

*

Sarah's visit rushed past, and within no time we were seeing her off at the airport. I realized that there were going to be many of these 'goodbyes' in future, but was confident that we would always remain close.

Later that evening Pedro had a surprise in store. He announced that we were taking the bus to a road called *Mario Bravo*. As we alighted, he announced, 'I reserved tickets to a play – the dentist gave it rave reviews. Your Spanish is so fluent now, I thought you'd enjoy it.'

I couldn't hide a big smile and hugged him.

'It's called *"El loco y la camisa,"* ' said Pedro. I translated the name of the play in my head to 'The Madman and the Shirt.'

'The theatre is what you'd call "Off Broadway," ' he said. 'Not one of those big theatres on *Avenida Corrientes*. We need to pick up the tickets at the box office.'

The box office was on the ground floor of an elegant apartment building, at the back of an arty café. A noticeboard near the door of the café was covered with leaflets and newspaper reviews of current plays. Black and white checkerboard floor tiles lent an old-style feeling to the modern counters and fittings, whilst brightly coloured abstract paintings decorated the white walls. The aroma of baking *medialunas* was mouth-watering.

We picked up the tickets and found that the theatre itself was next door, on the ground floor of a two-storey house. The approach was along a wide passageway with burgundy walls and a high ceiling. Along one side were scattered chairs, ladders, parts of theatre sets and poster display stands. Some of the stands held posters of recent plays.

Inside the theatre, the eighty or so seats were all near the stage, cosily arranged along its three sides, and no more than three rows deep.

As soon as the play began I was mesmerized. A family of four – Mum, Dad, son, and daughter – along with the daughter's boyfriend, all appeared to have a normal life. But the son, the 'madman,' could only tell the truth – and the truths kept coming out. People in the audience were laughing, then crying, then laughing. It was very moving, very 'real.'

We had a glass of wine in the café afterwards, watching as people came and went – young, old, musicians with instruments, some conservative, some arty, cyclists leaving their bicycles attached to fixed objects outside, a few nodding to each other.

'I loved the play. I can't believe that I only missed one word,' I said to Pedro.

'Which one?' he asked.

'No idea. I can't remember the context, and anyway it wasn't pivotal. I understood everything else. Amazing.'

'Not so amazing considering that you've been immersed in Spanish for most of our time here. It feels so long ago that we arrived. Ages since Patagonia.'

'Since almost getting stuck forever in *Torres del Paine* national park, and nearly falling off the earth in Ushuaia.'

Pedro said, 'And I can't remember when we last went to the theatre in Sydney – we never had time.'

'I know,' I said, and we clinked glasses.

I realized just how much we'd 'settled in' in Buenos Aires. We had friends, we were becoming part of the *barrio*, we lived in an apartment with a fantastic kitchen where we could offer hospitality to the family and new friends, we were enjoying world-class concerts and we'd now become theatregoers.

I whispered to Pedro, 'Have you noticed that this wine is a Malbec? Remember that beautiful day on our balcony in Sydney?'

He smiled.

I said, 'But just because it's a Malbec, don't think you can spring another surprise on me. This one was quite enough.'

NOT QUITE THE END

Mousse de chocolate — Translation not required

I wanted the last recipe in the book to be a dessert, as a fitting way to finish off our story. I asked Pedro for a recipe with a name that was recognizable to both Australians and Argentines. When he proposed <u>mousse de chocolate</u>, I was delighted.

An added touch was that <u>mousse de chocolate</u> was a popular flavour in many Buenos Aires ice cream shops.

Ingredients
5 egg whites
100ml cream per egg white, i.e. 500ml
125g dark chocolate
100g icing sugar, or more or less depending on taste
1/2 orange, juiced, and zest removed for use.
1 measure of Grand Marnier
Dash of vanilla extract
(Extra cream, for serving.)

Method
First prepare the chocolate. Break it into small pieces, and warm it in a steam bath (or double boiler). This is done by placing the chocolate pieces in a metal bowl that can sit over a saucepan. The saucepan will have about 3cm of water, so that when the water boils, the water does not touch the bottom of the metal bowl. Melt the chocolate a little, then add the Grand Marnier, orange juice and zest, and vanilla. Set it aside and allow it to cool slightly.

Second, prepare the Chantilly cream. In a separate bowl, whisk the cream until the soft peak stage. Do not over-whisk it or it will separate. Add the sugar and blend in.

Third, whisk the egg whites until the points are medium hard, i.e. more soft than hard.

And lastly, put all three together. Fold the chocolate into the cream. When they are thoroughly mixed, gently fold the mixture into the egg whites. This must be done gently in order to retain the lightness of the eggs.

Place in small dessert glass bowls and refrigerate.

Remember that there are raw egg whites in the mixture, so you cannot leave it for too long — it can be made on the day it is served, or the day before. Meanwhile store it cold in the fridge.

Serve with dollops of cream and lots of love.

THE END

RECIPE INDEX

ACKNOWLEDGEMENTS

I'd like to thank the following people for their encouragement and assistance.

Susan Evans, Janet Underwood and Shirley Duke for their patience in reading various drafts, and their excellent suggestions.

Maria Iribarne for reviewing the Spanish expressions and for sharing lots of laughs along the way.

The Buenos Aires Writers Group for their helpful feedback during my stays in Buenos Aires.

Nancy Grant, Sue Franklin, Jenny Brookman and Cristiana Dolce for their help prior to publication.

Susan Evans again, for her wonderful cover design.

Rachel Engelman and Helen Coyle, my editors, for their invaluable advice.

All those friends and family members who provided moral support whenever I said, 'I'm writing a novel . . .'

And most of all, Claudio, for his endless encouragement and support. And, no, he is not Pedro, who is a figment of my imagination - as are all the characters. But yes, they are his recipes. Except for one, the *flan*. That one is my Mum's.

29367435R00139

Printed in Great Britain
by Amazon